THE IMPERIAL HORSE
THE SAGA OF THE LIPIZZANERS

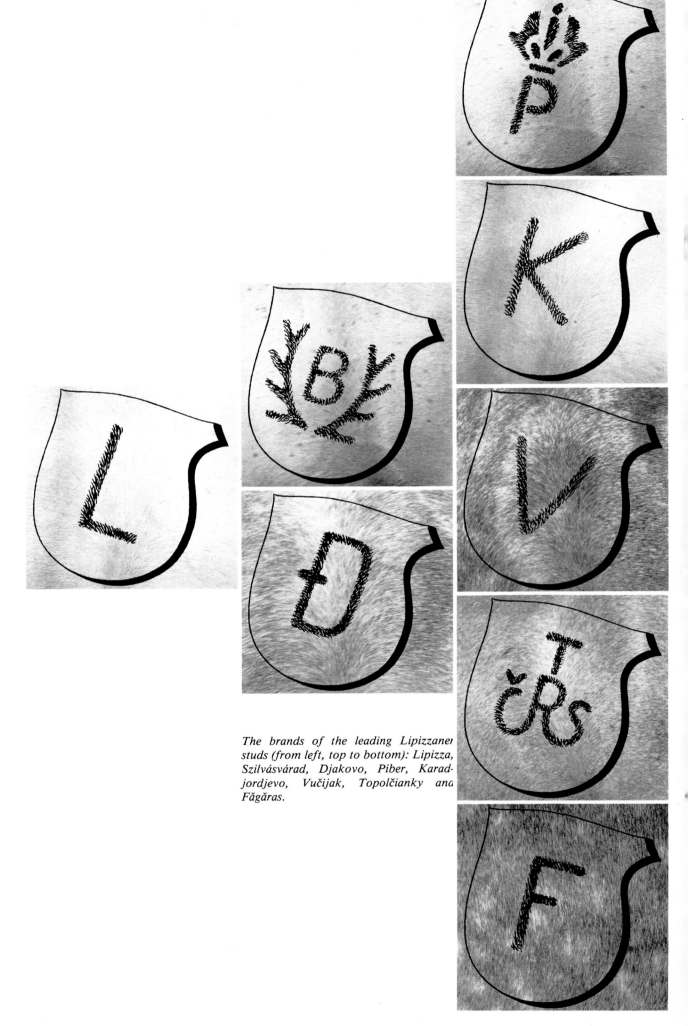

The brands of the leading Lipizzaner studs (from left, top to bottom): Lipizza, Szilvásvárad, Djakovo, Piber, Karad-jordjevo, Vučijak, Topolčianky and Făgăras.

THE IMPERIAL HORSE

THE SAGA OF THE LIPIZZANERS

HANS-HEINRICH ISENBART AND EMIL M. BÜHRER
with contributions by
KURT ALBRECHT, ANDREJ FRANETIČ
LEO MAZAKARINI, HEINZ NÜRNBERG

ALFRED A. KNOPF
New York 1986

This is a Borzoi Book published by Alfred
A. Knopf, Inc.

Copyright © 1986 by Motovun
'Switzerland' Copublishing Company Ltd.,
Lucerne
Translation copyright © 1986 by Alfred
A. Knopf, Inc.
Translated from German by H. A. Smith

*Library of Congress Cataloging-in-
Publication Data*
Isenbart, Hans-Heinrich, 1923
The imperial horse.
Translation of: Lipizzaner — Das kaiser-
liche Pferd
Includes index.
1. Lipizzaner horse. 2. Lipizzaner horse —
Pictorial works. I. Bührer, Emil M. (Emil
Martin), 1913. II. Title.
SF293.L5184 1986 636.1'3 85-23050
ISBN 0-394-54965-1

THE AUTHORS

Emil M. Bührer was born in Zurich in 1913 and after training in the graphic arts worked as an artist, editor and photographer. He was the Art Director of the journal *Camera* and of a publishing house in Lucerne for ten years. He has been head of the Lucerne copublishing office of the McGraw-Hill Book Company, New York, since 1969. Together with H.-H. Isenbart he realized the book *The Kingdom of the Horse.* He is responsible for the design and layout of this book.

Hans-Heinrich Isenbart was born in Vienna in 1923, where he studied law. He became Head of the Television Department at Radio Bremen in 1960, and has been Chief Sports Coordinator for the German TV station ARD since 1970. He is a qualified dressage and show-jumping judge, a member of the German Championship Judges Association, and, since 1957 a member of the German Olympic Riding Committee. He has published many books, including *The Kingdom of the Horse* (with Emil M. Bührer). His contributions to this volume, for which he also served as editor, are "Homage", "The Haute Ecole of Horsemanship" and "Epilogue."

Heinz Nürnberg was born in 1921 and studied veterinary medicine in Berlin from 1938 to 1941, qualifying in 1942. He has been a practicing vet in Alt Ruppin, near Potsdam, in East Germany, since 1949. Dr. Nürnberg is the compiler of the illustrated book *Lipizzaners* and has written specialist articles for equestrian journals. For this volume he wrote "The Lipizzaners," "Features of the Breed" and "Far from Lipizza."

Leo Mazakarini was born in Vienna in 1936 and has worked in publishing since 1962. He is now editor-in-chief of a Viennese house. He compiled the books *The Sacher Hotel in Vienna* and together with Susi Nicoletti *Roads to the Theater: Max Reinhardt's Pupils.* He is the author of many broadcasts for radio and television. For this volume he wrote the chapters "Highlights," "Dark Days," and "Piber."

General Kurt Albrecht was born in 1920 in St. Veit, Austria. He became Deputy Director of the Spanish Riding School in Vienna in 1965, Director in 1974, and retired last year. Albrecht's publications include *The Rules of the Art of Riding, Stories of a Dressage Judge* and *Milestones on the Road to the Haute Ecole.* His contribution to this book is "The Spanish Riding School Today — and the Challenge for Tomorrow".

Andrej Franetić was born in 1933 in a small village near Sežana in Slovenia. He studied at the Forestry School in Lubliana and at the University of Belgrade. He has been Director of the Lipizza Stud since 1971. His contributions to this book are the chapters on "Lipizza" and "The Stud and its History".

Photographs on the following pages are reproduced by special permission from photographer and film producer Kurt J. Mrkwicka, Vienna: 163, 178/179, 180/181, 182/183, 184/184, 186/187, 195, 196/197.

Other illustrations in this volume are from the following sources: Kurt Albrecht, Vienna: pages 41, 173 (center right). Animal Photography, London: S. A. Thompson: pages 8, 11, 16, 59 (center and right), 61, 72/73, 74 (right: fourth from top), 78 (top), 79 (bottom left), 108 (center left, bottom left and center right), 109 (bottom), 112 (center and center top), 113 (top left), 115 (top), 116, 120 (center top), 131 (center right), 142/143, 154 (bottom left and top right), 156, 157 (right), 158 (center and bottom), 159, 160/161, 202/203. R. Wilbie: pages 76 (top and bottom), 78 (center), 108 (center: second from top), 109 (top and center), 110/111, 112 (left, center bottom and bottom right), 154 (bottom right), 158 (top). Archiv EMB, Lucerne: row from top: pages 30 (right), 93 (top right and third drawings by Franz Coray), 94. Archivio Fotografica del Museo Correr, Venice: page 35. Archiv Lipica: pages 28 (center and bottom), 29, 31 (center and right), 53 (center: far left), 59 (left), 60, 75 (left: fourth from top), 80 (bottom), 81 (center), 110 (left), 114 (right). Artephot/Oronoz, Paris: pages 88 (left), 90. Hansruedi Beck, Lucerne: pages 88 (center and right), 89 (top). Z. Benčević, I. Brlić, *The White Horses of Lipica,* 1966, Mladost, Zagreb: pages 42/43. Bibliothèque Nationale, Paris: page 91. MVG, Lucerne: pages 45, 48 (right), 70 (bottom left), 75 (bottom right). Lisbeth Bührer, Lucerne: pages 46 (bottom), 47 (bottom left), 48 (left), 49, 74 (left, right: top and third from top), 75 (left: top and third from top), 85. Columbia Artists Festivals Corp.: Photo by Martin Reichenthal, New York: page 32. Thomas David, Vienna: pages 15, 78 (bottom left), 93 (center right), 113 (top right). Design Studio MAK, Koper: pages 6/7, 28 (top), 46/47 (top), 56/57, 58 (left), 62/63, 64/65, 66/67, 70, 71 (left), 74 (right: second from top), 75 (left: second from top and right), 76 (center), 77, 78 (bottom right), 79 (top and right), 80 (top and center), 81 (bottom), 82, 83, 108 (center: third and fourth from top), 113 (bottom right), 120 (top right), 121 (top left, center top and center left), 155. M. Dolenic: *Lipica,* 1980, Mladinska Knjiga, Lubliana: page 71 (right). Jürg Donatsch, Zollikofen: pages 18, 19. Marianne Fankhauser-Gossweiler, Hergiswil: page 31 (left). Handler, Lessing *The Spanish Riding School in Vienna,* 1972, Molden Verlag: pages 38, 52 (top and bottom left), 89 (right), 172 (top left), 173 (top). János Kalmár, Vienna: pages 5, 17, 122/123, 198/199. Juraj Kopač, Zagreb: pages 12/13. Kunsthistorisches Museum, Vienna: pages 50 (left), 54/55. Erich Lessing, Vienna: pages 105, 108 (top left), 118/119, 176/177, 189, 193 (top). Leo Mazakarini, Vienna: page 30 (left). Heinz Nürnberg, Alt-Ruppin: pages 9, 22, 23, 33, 92, 93 (center far left), 95, 98, 102/103, 106/107, 108 (center top), 112 (center right), 113 (bottom left), 114 (left, center), 115 (bottom), 117, 120 (bottom left and bottom right), 121 (bottom left and top right), 125, 128/129, 130, 131 (bottom), 132/133, 134/135, 136/137, 138/139, 140/141, 144, 145 (right), 146, 147 (bottom right), 152/153, 157 (left), 194 (left). Photographic Library of the Federal Ministry of Agriculture and Forestry, Vienna: 86/87, 104, 112 (top right), 167, 174/175, 188, 190/191, 192, 193 (bottom). H. R. Schinz, *The Natural History and Illustrations of Mammals,* 1824, Zurich: page 93 (second row from top). Tempel Steel Company: pages 148/149, 150/151. Votava, Vienna: pages 27, 164/165, 173 (center left). Werner Ernst, Ganderkesee: page 21. Yugoslav Review, Belgrade: page 47 (bottom left), 68/69, 145 (top left), 147 (left and top and center right). Austrian National Library Vienna: pages 26, 40, 51 (right), 52 (center bottom and right), 53 (top, center: fourth from left, bottom), 97, 166, 168/169, 170/171, 172 (center all portraits), 172 (top right).

TABLE OF CONTENTS

HOMAGE

See how they move — as if stepping out from the splendid gilt frame of a baroque painting, like a statue suddenly brought to life. In cadenced uplifted step they lightly raise their heavy torsos from the ground as they fly through the air in a high Capriole, returning momentarily to their decorative, monumental pose in the Levade, on outstretched hind legs.

Stirring, vibrant, dancing, lively baroque!

horse and music enchants the spectator momentarily, then, like a musical chord, slowly fades.

So we know them, symbolic of the supreme art of riding. So they are shown, fashioned in porcelain, engraved on medallions, in beauty and splendor, the stallions of the Spanish Riding School, the Lipizzaners, the imperial horses of the Austrian Empire.

The Lipizzaner has always been a horse for

That is what the Lipizzaners, the imperial white horses of the Viennese Court and their riders in their brown dress-coats and cocked hats, offer the visitor to the Winter Riding School at the Hofburg in Vienna, as they have done for centuries. In the airy ceremonial hall they seem to turn into works of art, demanding the viewer's attention as would a precious painting or sculpture. The melodious harmony of man,

show and parade. Those were the purposes for which it has been bred for more than four centuries. The white horses which today bear the name of their birthplace belong to the oldest breed of domesticated horses and still retain their original form. To be decorative and representative were their original tasks. But their many sterling qualities have ensured a wide distribution and a score of different uses for these horses. Their build, their charisma, their intelligence and docility have marked them out for dressage, for the haute école as still pursued and taught today at the Spanish Riding School according to classic tradition.

The eyes of the world are upon them, the quadruped artists in harness, the white horses with the golden tassels and the red saddle-cloths.

Here they acquire the toughness, frugality and proficiency of the breed. They lead a life which enhances the nobility of their muscular bodies and their inner characteristics, their skills and their capacity for physical exertion.

How can man in all his frailty persuade a horse of such superior strength to submit willingly to his service? He cannot control it physically without breaking its pride

with excited attention. Anyone who raises horses and wishes to train them must know their personalities and respect them. He must never lose his pleasure in horses at play. This is, and remains, the source of all the joy that may be experienced with a horse.

The visitor rarely remembers that these horses are the fruit of careful selection. The school is a center for assessing stallions and only those who pass the test may continue to be used for breeding.

The Lipizzaner stems from a functional breeding tradition which will not permit any weakening. The young stallions live for three years in the rough on the high pastures of Styria, exposed to wind and rain.

through humiliation. He must, instead, enter into its spirit, making it his friend. He will gain its confidence only when he knows it in all its moods. He must see the horse in freedom, eye-to-eye with the herd, in its natural community. He must see it as a whole, learn to understand its expression and its manner of speech. These features, the horse's personality, emerge most clearly in its youth, as it inspects everything new

Deep down all horses are the same, irrespective of their breed or of the blood they bear. Horses which over millions of years have developed from small fox-sized creatures of the jungle into the wide-roaming denizens of the steppe are designed for flight and need room. Space means security, since only here can they use their sole weapon against their enemies — their speed.

Horses, moreover, are social animals. They need the company of their fellows, a community which provides protection and an alarm system providing early warning when danger threatens. Within the community of the herd, horses feel safe only when they have found their place in the social hierarchy. Leading personalities always emerge, elites develop which the others follow and the great mass of the followers in turn consist of clearly differentiated individuals.

Today man has taken the horse under his protection. He guides the rhythm of its life, he has become the real leader. Few large herds still exist in which a naturally imposed hierarchy can develop. More often than not, they consist of small groups of mares and their foals. Since breeding is now determined by man, the stallion no longer rules the herd. Thus far has civilization changed the horse's habits from its basic nature. Nevertheless, the company of a group of fellow horses is the first requisite for the foal if it is to develop its character and its personality. It learns from its dam's example. The dam's trust in the people who take care of her is naturally transferred to her offspring. And so an interactive process is begun.

Trust in man grows in the young horse as the inborn herd instinct develops. This is not a contradiction, since over the long period of domestication and of inherited habits man has come to occupy a fixed position in the horse's life, just like the leading mare in the herd. Man is the higher power to whom even the strongest in the herd must submit. He decides on the order of things but it is also he who keeps the horses safe from danger.

As with human babies, young Lipizzaner foals belong entirely to their mothers. In fact, for the first days following birth, the dams and their foals are kept separate from the other mares. The newborn is initially aware only of its dam, and even man leaves the two entirely in peace for a while. True, the Lipizzaner's affinity to man is almost proverbial but even so, a younger mare may become aggressive towards anyone who disturbs her concentration on her offspring.

After a few days the mare and foal join the others in the foal pasture and a real play community develops. The foals quickly seek out their playmates and the breed's exuberant vitality shows almost from the start. Romping and gambolling, racing and jumping then follows, as their agility increases with every hour. Here, already, we can discern those propensities which underlie the movements which in due course are developed and cultivated by the rider in the haute école. The playful Levades and Caprioles, the vibrant, flighty Passage, each of these the spectator can observe among the young foals at play.

At first the mares try to keep close to their prancing offspring, to stay within protective reach. However this does not last long. Soon they watch relaxed from a distance as the foals run with increasing self-con-

fidence right up to the limits of the pasture. Here the Lipizzaner herd creates the most colorful picture. The sturdy dark shapes of the foals — brown, chestnut or black — flit between the snow-white bodies of the dams. Only years later will they themselves mature into the world-famous white horses. Half a year's untroubled youth passes. Then the moment comes that no young horse in human hands is spared. At the Austrian Federal Stud of Piber, the head of the stud himself traditionally rides ahead as the herd of mares and foals is brought to a large covered yard. The stable hands then lead the mares by the halter. Unmindful, the foals frolic around them. The mares are restless; they know from experience that separation from their young is impending. The yard is entered by one gate and left by another. But only the mares are taken from the yard — the foals remain, alone and abandoned. Now they are no longer foals but "yearlings." The Austrians call this process "shaving" — it is almost as if a shaving were taken from the mare's body and the bond between dam and offspring cut. At least, it's a good thing that so many playmates stay together. They can console each other for their loss. They still have a long period of — relative — freedom. In the herd, a further two-and-a-half years pass. At this stage of their lives food and movement have become the most important things. Both are equally necessary for growing up and becoming a horse, especially a riding school stallion and a breeding stallion. And to make a horse of a yearling, a gangling foal, the time spent at pasture is paramount. The meadow, the common factor still remaining from the horse's former life, is not only a source of food but also a place of movement.

The mountain landscape where Lipizzaners originated offered a dry, chalky soil. The horse still needs this today to retain its nobility, its temperament and its character. "A handful of dry grass is better than a whole wagon load of wet. ..." This is old breeders' wisdom as is, "A horse can live without oats but not without grass and roughage." The pasture on which cattle can

The herd, the meadow and the grass
are the three factors
shaping the rest of the horse's life.
The foal must have enough of each
if it is to become a real horse.

fatten is unsuitable for horses. Cattle have to grow and put on weight. Foals and yearlings, on the other hand, have to grow and form strong bones, hard sinews, and powerful lungs and heart. They have to put on muscle, not fat.

Extended grassy paddocks now become the home of the young Lipizzaner stallions, with sufficient place for the movement the temperamental youngsters require. In the summer months they move to the mountain pastures above the treeline, exposed to wind and weather. Here the body is hardened in the mountain gallop and the lungs extended in the bracing air. The unequal ground instills a sure footing when travelling at high speed.

Here in the herd the horse's character is formed, as are the social instinct, the striving for status, self-awareness and the desire for recognition. Life in the open sharpens the senses. Peers challenge each other to play, to the race, to trials of strength. Social hierarchy in the herd is formed. While the younger stallions are still a predominantly playful band, the older ones are shaping their profiles, especially the three-year-olds. Among them they decide who will lead the pack — the position of leading stallion is fought out. Among Lipizzaners this rarely happens with brute strength. Agility, nimbleness, mock fighting, and threatening displays play a greater role. There is nothing of the roughneck in the Lipizzaner, but his inborn gentleness does not stop him from being a lively, spirited horse, a proud member of the herd, vaunting his strength when it comes to gaining his station.

The fulfillment that such competition brings is the surest guarantee of a balanced character. All too frequently vices and bad habits in horses are the result of too little movement and too much boredom in their

Foals at pasture in a game of tag. In their dark juvenile dress, these two are having a race. The young creatures' sureness of balance and footing are astonishing. The pasture not only provides food but opportunity for movement as well.

youth. Among all domesticated riding horses this is seldom recognized or acted upon.

It is not surprising that young Lipizzaners are noble and self-assured, open and friendly, and trim and athletic in build with rock-hard hoofs and legs, the sinews and joints beneath the tight skin as if chiselled. They have carved a place for themselves in their world with the full, alert deployment of their natural instincts.

They are the product of four centuries of superior and consistent breeding. Docility and obedience in the service of man is inborn. Yet they will never be inferior. They are the masters.

Their silvery charm cannot be captured in words. No description, no poetry can reproduce the impression the free-ranging horse makes on the receptive observer. Hardened by long training under the saddle at the riding school, how do the Lipizzaner stallions feel on their return to the stud? Gentleness and docility are the features of this breed above all others. Yet time and again this free-living range horse is incited to movement. Full of their strength, stallions pose in an impressive male stance, as if conscious of their proud beauty. The sturdy body in light, almost fleeting move-ment − the ideal strived for in the art of riding and achieved only on those rare occasions: consumate balance at every turn, pace and jump, free of any burden. No impression is ever stronger, no aspect more revealing, than stallions at large, the royal white horses, the imperial steeds.

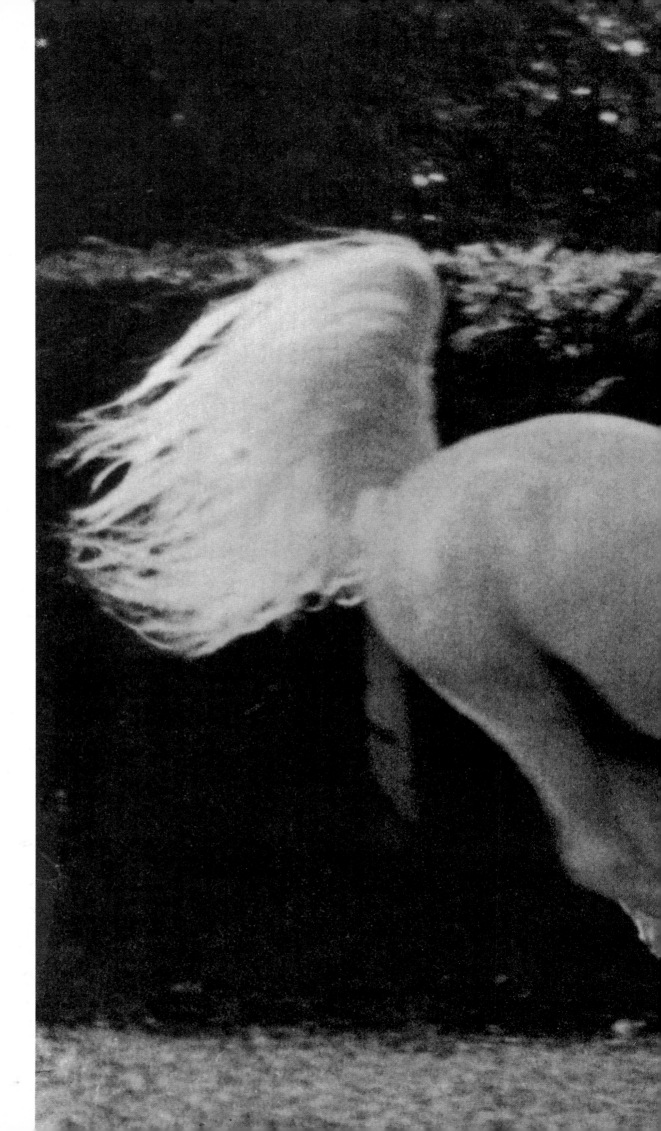

Each individual Lipizzaner bred at Lipizza in Yugoslavia, at Piber in Austria and in other countries, is a link in an endlessly long chain in which the breed's inherited characteristics are continued from the distant past into a promising, distant future. Nature's work of art in the shape of a noble horse remains as such only for the comparatively short space of its life. All that is left are pictures, drawings and descriptions. Maintaining the chain and, if still possible, perfecting it has been the work of generations of planning, consideration and instinct, though also subject to the laws of nature. There is a clear parallel here with the Lipizzaner's chief purpose, the art of riding. The perfectly trained horse beneath its rider in enhanced artistic expression, in harmony and balance, exists as a living work of art for only a brief moment. This art of training and educating the horse is only a link in the chain of tradition which is preserved and continued for the future.

Only passion and perseverance have succeeded in maintaining the Lipizzaner as the world's oldest domesticated breed of horse. While its outer appearance may have changed continually with time, adapted to the taste and the needs of each generation, nothing has really changed in the horse's outer or inner propensities. What their original ancestors gave them is still discernable today.

Their special suitability for the haute école, the classic school of riding, is world famous; their appearances at the Spanish Riding School in Vienna have brought them renown. The Lipizzaner is symbolic of the decorative baroque art of riding in the twentieth century. Yet many admirers of the Viennese exhibition horses know little about the breed's versatility.

Even its type description hints at a universally applicable horse. "For practical purposes, of medium-size, the Lipizzaner is a very tough, enduring, work-happy horse very easily satisfied with its feed, very docile, intelligent and quiet. While, like the small primitive horses, the Lipizzaner matures as late as any of the world's breeds, it reaches an advanced age in return. It is not at all unusual for them to be in harness up to age twenty-five. ..."

This description is by Hubert Rudofsky who, towards the end of the Second World War, was director of the stud at Hostau on the Elbe in Bohemia, where between 1941 and 1942 all the Lipizzaners from Yugoslavia, Lipizza (then still Italian) and Piber were united. Rudofsky played a vital role in saving the Austrian Lipizzaners see p. 00. His description indicates the many and varied purposes to which this breed can be put.

Nor will the connoisseur be surprised that these horses with their physique and character can discharge all the duties that might be expected of a horse anywhere.

Now that interest has again revived in the art of driving, the Lipizzaner has become popular as a coach horse. Nowadays, it is particularly the Hungarian whites who have gained honors and championship titles for their drivers. In doing so, they have revitalized a tradition from the times when the Lipizzaner coach horses were the most important of the imperial teams in Vienna. In many countries where Lipizzaners are now bred or where the horses from Piber and the other studs have been sold, the Lipizzaner is highly regarded for its pleasant nature and its quiet disposition beneath the rider.

Many people are unaware that in a number of countries Lipizzaners are also still bred as a steady plow and farm horse. A unique contrast is the Lipizzaner stallion in his fine gold trimmings forming a quadrille to classical music and a similar white horse in breast harness doing a heavy day in the field. But is this not, after all, a remarkable compliment to so precious a breed? "Tough, enduring, work-happy, easy to feed ...," qualities as necessary in a farm horse as in a school stallion.

The Lipizzaners are also "very docile, intelligent." How indeed could the circus have done without such decorative whites? The circus which, after all, depends on the good character, extraordinary attention, powers of concentration and good memory of its horses.

Put this way, we see the breed in a new light. They are not only parade horses or School horses with riders in brown coats and gold-edged cocked hats, they have the skills for a multitude of tasks. Even the stallions of the Spanish Riding School, specialists in "off the ground" work — the Levades, Courbettes, Piaffes and Caprioles — and artists of the haute école, are not only specialists in their own field. They are also riding horses, true to the principles of training handed down within the school through the centuries. In fact, the basis of their training under the saddle is to work as everyday horses.

The unique written instructions handed down regarding their training, the "Directives for implementing the methodical Procedure for Training Rider and Horse at the Royal and Imperial Spanish Court Riding School" prove it. Written by First Riding Master Johann Meixner in 1898 on instructions from Field Marshall Francis Holbein von Holbeinsberg, they state the following:

"The higher art of riding must never be thought of as haute école alone as it comprehends three levels of riding, namely: First, riding with the most natural posture possible for the horse ... Second, riding with the horses together ... campaign riding ... Third, riding with artistically maintained posture ... In principle, the fully trained school horse ... must therefore be usable at the faster paces and be an entirely serviceable campaign horse at all times. ..."

"Campaign horse" is the expression used by the Austrian riding masters for an everyday horse, a serviceable riding horse for all purposes under the saddle. And how pleasant it is to ride a horse of this kind, on the track or in the rough.

Thus the haute école, the imperial horses' real metier, emerges from two indispensible preliminary stages without which it could never be achieved, growing out of the natural propensities and skills of the horse. While the haute école may be regarded as an art, it is achieved, like all arts, only through nature.

in modern equestrian sports a recklessness amounting almost to destructiveness has become commonplace, there are still a few places in the world where traditional values do not die. True, vanity and pomp played a role at the princely courts in the creation of fine breeds of horses, but the exploitation of horses for the purposes only of social recognition, sporting fame or financial speculation was still far from people's minds. In those times, people were closer to nature and did not violate it, as is now all too often the case. Lipizzaners, for all their antiquity, can teach us new things about care and respect for tradition.

Man has taken the horse under his protection. How he treats it is a token of his culture. He interferes with the lives of these animals, with their reproduction and upbringing. The animals have surrendered their wild state to live in his service, but in doing so they have remained true to themselves and their nature. Nowhere is man so close to nature as he is when in harmony with a being so rich in feelings and responses and at the same time so mute. If we wish to understand horses, we must forget our human classifications and reach out into a region where things are not just seen and heard, but felt and experienced.
In their many-sided existence Lipizzaners today, like those through the centuries, have only one aim in life: to give pleasure to mankind.

The foal learns to graze from its mother. The first step in weaning it from mother's milk has been taken. Imitative instinct persuades the young horse to nibble at the grass, playfully at first until it acquires the taste for it. Then grass becomes its most important food.

The Lipizzaners have unique qualities for this art, of a kind possessed by no other breed of horses, strengthened by adroit selection in breeding through countless generations. The finished work of the school horse can be seen in the horse at pasture, with all its features and abilities which man develops, shapes and trains — without thereby destroying or distorting the nature of this animal. That is the task for which Lipizzaners have been created.

Noble horses make requirements of man. We cannot deny them our respect. Though

Overleaf: Lipizzaners in harness, straight as a die, a line of four-in-hands, Hungarian version. Here they are not only parade horses but athletes.

Lipizzaner stallion of the Spanish Riding School in the Passage. The height of expressiveness, a great movement of a noble horse beneath its rider.

The circus: a magic combination of ring, light, music and horses. The eyes of the riderless horses reflect eager obedience as they parade on their hind legs before their master and friend – in this case Fredy Knie – or criss-cross the ring at the trot and gallop in the carousel. Horses are the keynote of the circus and for many old circus people the free dressage is the high point of circus art, as here in the Swiss National Circus Knie.

The circus is not a artistic stage. The circus lives with its animals. A true circus is inconceivable without predators – and without horses! Free dressage and haute école are the core of equestrian performance. One of the greatest circus people of our time, the has a gift for the ring, a fact which never fails to fascinate us circus people, too. It has remarkable perception and exceeds all other horses in beauty and elegance. It's the ideal circus horse, taking pleasure from its daily work in the ring despite all the tension physical capabilities with which nature has endowed it. I can so clearly remember how circus performances used to be attended by cavalry officers by the dozen. They aimed to enrich and extend their knowledge, since the riders and free dressage are a cor-

Swiss Fredy Knie, says this about horses: "In actual fact, any horse can become an artiste in the circus since what we try to do in the ring is merely to show natural movement in dressage form. However, halfbloods and the heavies require far more time and patience than do Lipizzaners, for example.

"The Lipizzaner horse has performed dressage work through many generations and and energy."

As an old and trusted friend of the circus family Knie, Colonel Alois Podhajsky has this to say about working with horses in the circus:

"For me as a horseman the fascination of the circus was not only its color and variety but always the psychological commitment of the animal, the painstaking process of training and the deployment of mental and nerstone of the circus. The joyful expression of the horse as it rears on its hind legs made a lasting impression on me. Only by inner contact between man and animal can this kind of performance be achieved."

These two quotations serve better than anything else to illustrate the work of the Lipizzaner in the circus.

"Each horse a unique, irretrievable creation, a genius of its species, its finest embodiment and perfection." The poet Otto Stoessel knew to whom honor was due when the "gentlemen Lipizzaners" were concerned. The inimitable Peter Hammerschlag devoted one of his finest poems to the white stallions: "they neigh but seldom, they mutter in the stable, and when darkness descends whisper from rose-quartz nostrils stories of yesteryear, of the golden age of the Baroque."

On seeing the silvery-white horses with the Andalusian forebears all kinds of things come to mind. The imperial pomp of the Spanish Court Riding School in Vienna, perhaps, or the arid mountain pastures of

400th anniversary of the Riding Spanish School in Vienna, the horse's special attraction was once again keenly felt. This was also the case in 1980 when the parent stud at Lipizza celebrated four hundred years of its own existence.

The Lipizzaners' great moments were shared by many people who have come to know these special horses and necessarily forged firm friendships with them – from the invited guests of the riding school in Vienna to those who simply visited the Lipizzaner Stud with open eyes and open heart.

Even in modern times kings have considered it a mark of distinction to be permitted

HIGHLIGHTS

"Know ye further that among all the horses of this World the Spanish are the most holy, steadfast and magnanimous."

Georg Engelhart von Löhneysen, 1588.

Opposite: Aachen 1983: György Bardoš and his Hungarian Lipizzaner team negotiate the water-splash at the In der Soers trials course during the International Driving Championships.

Lipizza, or even the chariot races of ancient Rome. Hardly, however, does the Lipizzaner remind you of an eventing or show horse. We know, of course, that Lipizzaners have made their mark in this field, too, but seldom do they take the top prizes. This undoubtedly has something to do with the breed itself and with the fact that in its long history the Lipizzaner has not really been bred for sporting use at all. It forfeits its relaxed action much sooner than other horses, according to the Lipizzaner connoisseur Heinrich Lehrner. "And then those properties come to the fore which quickly lose the Lipizzaner points in the show ring, namely a rigid back, compact bearing, its stamping, unextended gait, often resulting in disunion at the gallop, even more so at the walk. ..."

The Lipizzaners have enjoyed great moments in the course of their history. They hark back to the carousels of the Hapsburg emperors, as parade and coach horses they were physically closer to the great affairs of state than most people of the time.

When in 1972 the Festival of the Horse was held in honor of the Lipizzaner during the

to ride a Lipizzaner. Despite its modernity the Lipizzaner affords us immediate access to the age of the Baroque.

An account of January 16, 1667, tells how Leopold I, Emperor by God's Grace of Austria and the Holy Roman Empire and one of the most splendid figures ever to ascend the Hapsburg throne, turned his wedding day into the most brilliant festival of a brilliant epoch. His bride was the beautiful Margaret, the Infanta of Spain. No celebration will ever be as fine as that of the man whom fate decreed could raise his kingdom to one of the great powers of Europe. A gigantic ship set among marvellous machines on the parade ground next to the Imperial Castle formed the decoration for a gala performance of Pietro Antonio Cesti's opera "Il pomo d'oro" followed by a fascinating "equestrian ballet!"

The guests, the finest nobility from countries throughout Europe, had taken their seats in the three-tier gallery erected in the garden of the Hofburg in Vienna. Facing the Swiss Court stood the resplendent platform and rich canopy which sheltered the emperor and his bride.

The actors appeared on the scene. Thousands of people were involved, with two hundred musicians alone. Eighty horsemen on white steeds bred in Lipizza acted out the Battle of the Elements in baroque allegory.

The knights' armor and the horses' panoplies shimmered in blue and silver: the element Air.

Other knights' armor was red, as were the tassels and fringes on their gleaming tack; the flames of Fire appeared to flare up, forming a single array with the Air.

Water was represented by horsemen shining in light blue, their horses with scalloped decoration.

Finally the element Earth appeared — eight white horses drawing an artificial garden with arbors, statues, cypresses and, in the background, Venus seated on a throne.

The two sides formed up for battle then they attacked. With elegant calm, first the two leaders, then two knights and finally the whole field performed an orderly mock battle to the strains of Baroque music. Fighting, chasing and distributing blows, horse and rider weaved in and out before their Majesties and the Court. The total impression was recorded: "since the World was formed, nothing finer has been seen than this battle of pleasure." Particularly memorable however, were the four horsemen whose horses "leapt into the air, executing the most daring figures."

Courbettes, therefore, which the descendants of the descendants of the horses of that time still perform for our pleasure today. One thing is worth noting — Lipizzaners were performing to music for the first time.

Emperor Leopold's love for his Karst-bred horses, which in those times appeared in many colors, was certainly deep and genuine. Despite the dangers besetting his kingdom, despite plague and the Turkish wars, he took an active interest in his stud at all times, reorganizing the management and promulgating the twenty-three-clause set of "Instructions for Studmaster on the Karst." These wise rules of conduct of 1658

A bronze statue of a horse and horse-keeper, cast in 1900 to a design by Joseph Lax, in front of the Parliament Building in Vienna.

had the most favorable effect on breeding and led to early prosperity. That his people showed their allegiance with equal love when His Majesty visited Lipizza can well be imagined.

Charles VI, Leopold's son and the last of the baroque emperors, felt that he had settled the indivisibility of his empire and the succession of his daughter Maria Theresa when he died in 1740. However, Frederick II of Prussia ignored all agreements, occupied Austrian Silesia and through his victory incited the Bavarians and the French to aggression. The young Empress responded with all her troops, no light undertaking. The greater was the joy, therefore, when finally Austrian Prague was cleared of the occupying French.

After a solemn "Te deum" had been sung the evening before in the Cathedral of Saint Stephen, a celebration was held in the Winter Riding School on the second of January. Eight women on horseback and eight in golden phaetons provided unique equestrian entertainment. Maria Theresa herself led the first mounted quadrille at this "Ladies' Carousel" and performed the requisite exercises with lance, sword and pistol so adroitly that she herself won a prize. "A broad allusion or bitter irony of the victory of a woman over bad faith and

weakness of the men of her time," was a contemporary historian's sardonic comment.

Archduchess Marianna, sister of the then twenty-four-year-old ruler, led the first of the two carriage quadrilles. Today it is still easy to picture this festival of noble women and Lipizzaners from the oil painting by Martin Meyten. Consequently, "It pleased Her Royal Majesty, accompanied by all the same noble and high horsewomen, some riding, some driving in the said magnificent phaetons, to return to the Imperial Palace from her Royal Riding accompanied by an indescribable number of her people in the street."

Maria Theresa and her Court had a pressing need for pomp and parade horses. Accordingly, the herd of brood mares at Lipizza grew to a handsome one hundred and fifty horses. Two hundred years after the empress' death, not only was a comprehensive exhibition mounted in the Palace of Schönbrunn in her former residential city, but the "Soiree with Maria Theresa" was also organized at the Spanish Riding School. Accompanied with a musical program and displays by the Federal Stud at Piber, eight male and eight female riders from the school in historic costumes per-

Prince Eugene of Savoy (1663 – 1736), popularly known as the Noble Knight was the true founder of the Austro-Hungarian dual monarchy. His equestrian statue at the Heldenplatz in Vienna — a stone's throw from the Winter Riding School — is by Anton Fernkorn.

Overleaf: Joseph II (1741 – 1790) was a wise and enlightened monarch with no use for pomp. However, his wedding to Isabel of Bourbon-Parma on October 6, 1760 was one of the century's greatest public displays. The famous baroque portraitist Martin van Meytens, aided by several other artists, captured the Imperial procession in oils. The painting, some twelve feet high and nearly fifty feet long, shows the procession winding its way past the Augustine Church, the Imperial Winter Riding School and the Chancellery Wing of the Hofburg. The golden carriage — next to last in the parade of 94 six-horsed coaches — in which the bride's emissary Price Joseph Wenzel of Liechtenstein was seated, still exists today.

"More than any other art,
the equestrian art is linked to the wisdom of life.
Many of its principles can serve as rules
for human conduct."

Alois Podhajsky

23

formed a quadrille in the style of the eighteenth century.

The beauty and artistry of the Lipizzaners were the makings of a good show, even among the Hapsburgs. Whether it was in 1806, for the "Pleasure of the highest Court" or in 1808, when Emperor Francis' wedding was celebrated, the Lipizzaners and the fascination they radiated were used to the best effect.

In 1814, the Congress in Vienna danced

onstrated. In a mock battle depicting Napoleon's pursuit of supreme power over the Continent, memories of the recent past were aroused. The Kings of Bavaria, Prussia, Denmark and Württemberg were in attendance, together with Talleyrand, Hardenberg, Lord Castlereagh and Metternich, who was nicknamed the "Coachman of Europe." Because the twenty-third of November did not suit the Czar of Russia, the whole costly spectacle was repeated espe-

the emperor of Austria for five years when the kings of Prussia and Belgium visited him in Vienna. Naturally, they were offered a Lipizzaner carousel. Just as people today may attend an organized "feudal" feast of lobster, salmon and caviar to benefit a charity, so on March 18, 1863, noble riders on white horses demonstrated how 30,000 Christians were rescued from Muhammadan slavery — the net proceeds from their performance were distributed among

more than it met. The "High Allies" feasted themselves and Napoleon's end (the Corsican caused something of a stir a little later when he escaped from Elba), and the host, Emperor Francis, had a carousel arranged for the cream of European nobility, which did honor to the House of Hapsburg. Horse and rider displayed their agility in ring riding, dicing on horseback and in a "Turk's head tournament." As the form of a quadrille had been chosen for this tournament, their musicality was also dem-

cially for him, down to the last detail, on the first of December. Although the next Lipizzaner carousel to be held in the riding school in 1843 — to honor the archduke Charles who had defeated Napoleon's troops at Aspern — was a truly festive occasion, the pomp and splendor displayed at the Congress of Vienna could never again be repeated.

When a host receives honored guests he offers them the best he has. Francis-Joseph I was twenty-three years of age and had been

poor weavers.

Seventeen years later Maximilian I's hunting trips were re-created in the riding school. On this occasion Lipizzaners performed in favor of "the country's poor."

A quarter of a century before the Hapsburg monarchy passed from history, at the zenith of the neo-Gothic period, a magnificent carousel was presented for the last time. On April 21, 1894, the nobility and, for the first time, "ordinary" riders from the Spanish Riding School put on a historic

pageant portraying Empress Elisabeth Christine's reception by Charles VI. Two-in-hands and four-in-hands, the quadrille of heralds, a ladies' quadrille and a knightly tournament were high points of the program. One hundred and twenty-five riders, fourteen coaches and a horde of pages and minions contributed to the occasion.

Once again, as with all previous carousels, the requirement of Emperor Charles VI was met: the program was arranged to test the capabilities of the Lipizzaner stallion. The horse was still an essential part of imperial pomp and circumstance; the carriage which took Emperor Franz Josef from the Schönbrunn Palace to the Hofburg each morning was drawn by Lipizzaners. The stallion which bore the emperor in 1867 when he rode up Coronation Hill in Budapest was also of this breed. With sword raised, His Majesty sat on the Lipizzaner stallion Maestoso Cerbero in order to receive Hungary's royal crown. Not for the first time, people spoke of "the emperor's white horse. ..."

The next festivity which was to reveal the Lipizzaners' grace, beauty and elegance to all the world took place at a time when the Austro-Hungarian monarchy still lived more in people's minds than in their immediate consciousness − in fact many decades later. The occasion was when the Jubilee in Vienna, the Spanish Riding School celebrated its 400th birthday from September 12 to 17, 1972. Opening with a gala performance in the Winter Riding School before international guests, the Lipizzaners appeared before the Imperial Palace of Schönbrunn in the course of the next day's festivities. Not only was the show put on twice, but a new choreographed quadrille was performed with twelve riders. At the festival of the horse in the Vienna City Hall, not only did the Lipizzaners from the Federal Stud at Piber demonstrate their great expertise in fours and sixes, but international visitors also honored their Viennese hosts by participating. A particular example was the "Cadre Noir" from Saumur in France.

When the Spanish Riding School celebrated its 400th anniversary in September 1972, not only Austria but the entire world of riding joined in. The Festival of

the Horse reached its zenith with two exhibitions by Lipizzaner stallions from the School in front of the Imperial Palace of Schönbrunn. Above, the festive night display. Bottom, Pas de Deux.

Eight years after these Vienna festivities, Lipizza celebrated its own four hundred years of existence. The originally Austrian and subsequently Italian Stud had become a Yugoslav Lipizzaner establishment after the Second World War and had even changed its name. "Lipizza" had become "Lipica." President Josip Broz Tito stood as high patron to the occasion. In addition to interested horsemen the world over, all the European Lipizzaner studs were invited and all answered the call. At the main event on August 31, the horses sent to Yugoslavia as "special ambassadors" appeared together for the first time. It was only then, despite the emotion of the occasion, that many spectators became aware of how greatly the individual strains differ from each other.

Colonel Rudofsky, who had played an important part thirty-five years earlier in rescuing this oldest of the world's horse breeds from exile in Hostau, found that the horses at both Lipizza and Piber continued to meet the highest standards and were closest to the classic type of horse.

The festival had commerced with the achievement of a romantic idea. An old post coach had driven past the Hofburg in Vienna on June 6, 1980. Harnessed to it were four brood mares from Lipizza. Here a mail bag with greetings from the Spanish

Riding School and the Federal Stud at Piber were loaded on board — a symbolic act.

In 1980 the white stallions from Vienna paid the Yugoslavs a further compliment. They made six appearances in the Riding Hall at Lipizza and during the main event in the new Hippodrome enchanted visitors from all over the world.

Despite all this celebration, there were still tremendous breeding problems here and there, and this was brought up at the Inter-

Above: the large School Quadrille of twelve stallions from Lipizza enters the Hippodrome. The main festivities were held at Lipizza on August 31, 1980, with Lipizzaners and four-in-hands from the various European studs and from the Spanish Riding School participating under the slogan "Four Centuries of Lipizzaners".

Right: Eight four-in-hands performed the Carousel, including (left to right) teams from Hungary, Djakovo, Rumania, Piber and Lipizza.

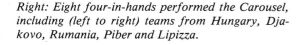

national Symposium on Lipizzaner breeding. The hundred-or-so breeders attending the Lipizza conference agreed that the way out of the crisis could be found only by a systematic exchange of breeding stallions on an international basis. "Inbreeding" was again an item on the agenda.

Increasing efforts have been made in Yugoslavia in recent years to develop the Lipizzaner as a show which could be dispatched to international shows with some prospect of success. The first laurels have already been won.

Colonel Alois Podhajsky has long been a legend as the self-assured head of the Spanish Riding School during confused times. Only older people, however, will remember him as being extremely successful in international dressage. At the 1936 Olympics in Berlin he won the bronze medal, albeit on Nero, a German full-blood. At the Olympic Games in London in 1948 he took fourth place in the main dressage event, although again not on a Lipizzaner. However, he had then taken Neapolitano Africa as his spare horse. It was on this horse that Podhajsky was seated on that memorable occasion when he asked General Patton to extend his special protection to Lipizzaners.

To celebrate the Lipizza Stud's 400th anniversary, the old post coach with the Lipizzaner brood mares Allegra XXVI, Canissa XII, Wera IV and Dubovina XIV left the Vienna Hofburg (above) and traveled via Maribor to Trieste and Lipizza, arriving on June 13.

In the Hippodrome sets had been erected representing the old post station and hostelry, in front of which Jaco, the landlord, welcomed the travelers (above). In Vienna the traditional cooperation and links between the Spanish Riding School and Lipizza were commemorated (above) by Andrej Frančetić, Lipizza's Director and Dr. Heinz Lehrner, Director of the Federal Stud at Piber, who saw the coach on its way.

Right: Lipizza riders, carrying the flags of the countries and Lipizzaner studs participating, headed the parade.

The day following Podhajsky's Olympic appearance in post-war London, the British Horse Society invited him and Neapolitano Africa to mount a personal display at the Stadium in Aldershot – tickets were quickly sold out. "Spectators from the world over followed the stallion's paces in attentive silence and when at the end of the exercise I lifted my hat in greeting, broke out in a storm of applause never previously experienced at dressage events in the Stadium," the Colonel later recalled. It was the generally accepted view that had he ridden this Lipizzaner stallion instead of Teja he would undoubtedly have won the gold medal.

Podhajsky himself had his doubts. He was all too aware of the prejudices which existed among dressage riders. The judges would "undoubtedly have compared it unfavorably as a ‹baroque horse› with the other competitors." For decades, this has been the snag with dressage, and it is still a problem today. Recently a judge was reported saying to a horsewoman, "If you come along with your Lipizzaners you can do what you want, but in no case will you get more than grade 6 from me." The lack of extension and the stallion's strong neck may not be the ideal prerequisites for dressage exercises, but they should not serve as a basis for generalization.

In 1949 the Lipizzaner Pluto Theodorosta

participated with Neapolitano Africa in a CHIO show in London and a year later in the Royal Dublin Society's Spring Show. Pluto Theodorosta's success encouraged Podhajsky to enter the stallion for international dressage events. He came second in the medium class, and first among the heavy class at a competition in Frankfurt in 1950. He was also victorious in the Olympic dressage trials in Hamburg. "It was the first time that a Lipizzaner won a Grand Prix," the colonel noted with pride.

Pluto Theodorosta thanked his rider for the trust shown in him. When he left all the victors of the Olympic dressage event trailing behind in the Stockholm Championships, he did his breed a good service – until then the Lipizzaners had been wrongly assessed by the dressage experts. The applause after Pluto's first Threefold Pirouette was tremendous.

The English rider Joan Hall, guest pupil at the Spanish Riding School, has successfully participated in many international dressage competitions and in three Olympics on the Lipizzaner stallion Conversano

Caprice, born at Piber, winning the German dressage derby three times over. Here she is shown at the 1968 Olympics in Mexico City.

During her State Visit to Austria in May 1969, Queen Elizabeth II of England visited the Piber Stud and attended an exhibition by the Spanish Riding School's famous white horses in Vienna. Her daughter Princess Anne, herself an outstanding dressage rider, was clearly at ease on the back of the Lipizzaner stallion.

Pluto's royal art was even honored by a queen; while the Vienna Riding School were guests in London in 1955, the stallion was brought to Buckingham Palace at Elizabeth II's request despite protests from the royal advisers, who were worried about the queen's safety. However, an accomplished

horsewoman, she strictly followed Podhajsky's instructions and appreciated Pluto Theodorosta's particular obedience. Could the horse have told this story about the queen to his cousins in the adjoining boxes back home in the Vienna stable, it would have been nothing new. Maestoso Flora, for example, carried Princess Beatrix of Holland for two hours through the former imperial chase in the Lainzer Tiergarten near Vienna. The Lipizzaners have good relations with Holland and not only because the country was host to the riding school. The Dutch royal sisters had ridden two Lipizzaners born in post-war exile at Wimsbach with great success in international dressage trials.

Joan Hall, a horsewoman as elegant as she is accomplished, added the finishing touches to her career as a guest pupil at the Spanish Riding School before she proceeded to make a name for herself in many international competitions on the stallion Conversano Caprice, born in the Lipiz-

zaner stud at Piber in Styria. She gave remarkable performances in Hamburg and Aachen, and at the Olympic Games, in which she participated on three occasions on Conversano Caprice – at Rome in 1960, Tokyo in 1964, and Mexico in 1968. Mrs. Hall and her Lipizzaner even won the Grand Prix in the most difficult of dressage events at Rotterdam. She was also twice victorious in the German dressage derby (1964 and 1965) and came in second on a third occasion (1967).

Pupils of the Spanish Riding School may be encountered time after time at international events. Also well worth noting were the successes of the American rider Jessica Newbery on her Lipizzaner Wallach Plutony in the mid-Sixties.

Stephan, on which the Swiss Marianne Gossweiler achieved a long row of outstanding successes, was the issue of a union between a Holsteiner mare and a Lipizzaner stallion. Stephan was repeatedly among the leaders in many dressage trials and Mrs.

*The roan Stephan which the Swiss Marianne Goss-
weiler rode to victory on many occasions was at least
half-Lipizzaner. Five times Swiss dressage champion,
Gossweiler won a silver medal on Stephan in the team
competition at the 1964 Olympics in Tokyo and the*

*team bronze in Mexico in 1968. She also gained silver
medals at the European Championships at Copen-
hagen in 1965 and Aachen in 1967, and at the 1966
World Championships in Berne. Stephan had to be
put down in 1979 at the age of 29.*

*The Yugoslav Dušan Mavec with his stallion Pluto
Canissa IV born in Lipizza, receiving the award in the
Prix Intermédiaire II at the 1985 World Cup Trials in
Lipizza. Dušan Mavec won the Yugoslav dressage
championships from 1977 to 1981 and the "Grand
Prix" in Rome in April 1985. He has been trainer at
the dressage center in Lipizza since 1982.*

*The Yugoslav Alojz Lah on his Lipizzaner stallion
Maestoso Monteaura 1983 in Rome. The pair won
the Grand Prix at the 1985 World Cup Competition
in Lipizza, narrowly beating Dušan Mavec on Pluto
Canissa IV.*

Gossweiler rode him at the Olympic Games in Tokyo (1964) and Mexico (1968), where she gained seventh and tenth places respectively, and so on each occasion secured medals for her team (silver and bronze).

While the Lipizzaner's special abilities are indisputable in both haute école and dressage, its abilities in show-jumping are very seldom seen. The best known of the exceptions was no doubt Nasello, although we do not know whether he was a pure-blooded Lipizzaner. Nasello had his successes in the Thirties under his rider Captain Filipponi. As Lehrner writes, "There can be no doubt that in particular cases Lipizzaners can also jump; doing so, however, in the manner of the Capriole, namely without using the back and generally using a great deal of nervous energy. The back is altogether a sensitive part of the Lipizzaner; were it strengthened it would certainly have a bene-ficial effect."

It is interesting to see how the Lipizzaners from Lipizza have advanced in dressage in recent years. While at the World Cham-

pionships in Lausanne in 1982 it was said that "the Lipizzaners brought life to the event, even though they could not be placed," Alojz Lah, riding Maestoso Mon-teaura, was in ninth place. The same year, the equestrian journal "St. Georg" stated, "The losers in the dressage year were the Russians — the winners the Yugoslavs, who with their Lipizzaners have made their way towards the top." They had reached the credible position of tenth in the world clas-sifications.

Riding Maestoso, Lah took first place in a Grand Prix with the CDI in Lipizza in 1982, and eighth with the CDI in Rome. Dusan Mavec came seventeenth in the World Dres-sage Championships on the stallion Pluto Canissa IV, and an excellent fourth place in the open event.

In 1983 Alojz Lah was victorious on Maes-toso Monteaura in the "Grand Prix spé-cial" and came in thirteenth in the Eu-ropean Championships at Aachen. En-couraged by all these successes, a team

from Lipizza participated in the 1984 Olympics in Los Angeles. Alojz Lah came in an honorable fifteenth, even though the judges apparently found it difficult, as Gabriele Müller-Pochhammer reported, "to familiarize themselves with these horses with quite different mechanics and a diffe-rent build from the full-bloods and their like."

We have already mentioned that Lipiz-zaners made their name in the past as coach horses. Since the discipline of driving has formed part of international events they have appeared regularly among the best in Europe and even in the world. Although the Lipizzaners at Piber are harnessed to the carriage as fillies, learning early how to work in four- and six-in-hand, no horse has been able to come close to the Hungarian Lipizzaner stud in this respect.

The first Tally-Ho World Championships were held in Münster, Germany in 1972. Eighteen drivers had registered. Two years later in Frauenfeld, Switzerland as many as

last laugh. With only ten demerits he won the last event — and is the European Champion."

The 1978 World Championships were held at Keszkemét. A hundred thousand spectators lined the eighteen miles of marathon track. Thirty-six teams from twelve nations had entered. Again, the Hungarians were clearly on top, as were the Lipizzaners.

During the World Four-in-hand Championships in the Royal Park at Windsor, however, the British team was in the lead, with Prince Philip and George Bowman. In the individual assessments, however (as might indeed be expected), the demon coachman Bardos was again victorious. "He drove his short-harnessed team of Hungarian Lipizzaners with such agility and such accuracy that the run through the eight difficult obstacles looked more like a stroll in the park."

However, in 1983 the Dutchman Tjeerd Velstra out-pointed the Hungarians György Bardos and Laszlo Juhasz (positioned third and second) in the individual assessments. Prince Philip was placed fifth, the team award going to the Hungarians.

It should also be mentioned that Lipizzaners always played an eminent role in the world of the circus, and still continue to do so. Fredy Knie, who was once called the "master of tender dressage" has a whole series of Lipizzaners among his forty-five stallions, including a Favory ridden by the star artiste Marie-José. For its part, the Althoff Circus can show twenty-three horses, most of them originating from the Yugoslav Lipizzaner Stud of Bekovo. The once famous Therese Renz of the circus dynasty of the same name also attracted much adulation in her youth on the Lipizzaner Conversano. And the Viennese School horseman Franz Ackerl, as Gerhard Eberstaller tells us, "specially in the Thirties and Forties, quite intoxicated the spectators with the beauty of the scene, with his Lipizzaners and his aesthetic approach to the art of riding, a wondrous symbiosis of discipline and relaxation, in which the horses sometimes appeared to float around the ring." There are many people, too, who re-

Wherever the Spanish Riding School's Lipizzaners appear they are given a tumultuous welcome, whether it be in the Netherlands, France, Britain or — as here — in the USA, at New York's Madison Square Garden.

Opposite: György Bardoš, the popular Hungarian four-in-hand champion, driving to a spectacular victory at Aachen in 1975. Daring, professionalism and a special talent are the qualities which gained Bardoš, an employee of the Hungarian Lipizzaner Stud, the world four-in-hand championships in 1978 and 1980.

thirty-five tally-hoes competed. The same year, the most prominent of the thirty-three teams entered at Apeldoorn was that of Prince Philip of England. The Hungarians excelled in each part of the trials. That was when the name of György Bardos began to become a legend. By 1975 he and his elegant Lipizzaner team were runners-up in the world championships — amazingly nimble, surpassing all the other participants in condition.

At the CHIO in Aachen, Bardos — an employee of the Hungarian Lipizzaner Stud of Szilvásvárad — took the lead from the start.

The European driving championships in 1977 were held at Donaueschingen in the Black Forest. Twenty thousand spectators had come to watch the thirty-two tally-hoes from ten nations compete. Imre Abonyi kept his position as the European and World Champion. In the dressage event, Bardos came in tenth, and second in the obstacle race. But "in the rough, Bardos showed that he is the king of coachmen," reported *St. Georg,* "the public laughed at the loud cries with which he calls on his horses to concentrate . . . but Bardos has the

member Fredy Knie's colorful equestrian feature with six Lipizzaners and six Arabs moving to the music of "Jesus Christ Superstar."

It was not the circus, however, which made the Lipizzaners a household name. The foreign tours mounted by the Spanish Riding School since the end of the First World War reached heights which have remained unforgotten. They began in Berlin in 1925 and continued in Aachen and London in 1927. Appearances in The Hague (1928) and Brussels (1932) followed. After the Second World War further tours were organized under Alois Podhajsky and Hans Handler. Appearances in Austria itself, especially at the Salzburg Festival, made the Lipizzaners popular in their own country. The horses went abroad in 1948 to Thun, Lucerne and Zurich in neutral Switzerland, then, in 1949, to various cities in Germany. In 1952 they travelled to Brussels and Paris and then to Spain and Portugal.

In the Forties, few people in the United States had ever heard of the "white horses of Vienna." The first trip to the U.S. was ventured in 1950, with many misgivings as to whether the stallions would stand the journey, but this trip was followed by many others. In fact, ever since Walt Disney enchanted audiences with his film *White Horses,* the Lipizzaners and their story are at least as well known as that of the Trapp Family.

The Imperial Horses have encountered the same public response wherever they go — enthusiasm and love at first sight. People respect them as the oldest breed of domesticated horses on earth, as dressage and coach horses of the noblest stature, and as the last representatives of the great classic art of riding. As Otto Stoessl once remarked, "From these elegant, thinly wrought columns which support such a mighty body, the noble line of movement gracefully flows, from the exuberant nostrils along the neck, the chest, across the shoulders, croup and leg, up and down in an incomparable harmony, a unique bodily eurhythmy."

33

When busybodies wish to do good, the opposite is usually the result. A certain Mr. Brinl headed an Imperial Commission which was dispatched to the Karst in 1785, on the orders of Emperor Joseph II, to discover where savings could be made. On his return to Vienna this official proposed that the stud at Lipizza should be closed down and the horses transferred to Holič in far-away Galicia. This could well have meant the death sentence for the entire breed. However, His Imperial Majesty, who often took a liberal view on abolishing traditional institutions, turned the suggestion down. Eight years later, when both Joseph and his successor, his brother Leopold II, were dead, the owners of the Sternberg Estate proposed to Emperor Francis II

They travelled for six weeks. During this period sixteen mares foaled. In order to spare the foals they were loaded on carts. It only goes to prove the toughness of the breed, as well as the circumspection of the personnel, that all foals survived the journey unharmed.

After arriving at Stuhlweissenburg the mares and yearling foals continued on their way to Saint George, on the banks of Lake Balaton. The other horses were divided between the towns of Tihany and Moor and delivered to safe quarters, which they occupied for six months.

The Treaty of Campoformio was signed on October 17, 1797. France and Austria seemed to be on speaking terms again. The emigrants at Stuhlweissenburg took this as

DARK DAYS

"I trust that this lovely breed, which in its long history has survived so much dramatic turmoil, will — despite the threats of history — remain in existence for the small world of horse-lovers and for the great public at large."

Heinrich Lehrner, 1984.

Opposite: France's troops under Napoleon Bonaparte spread fear and anxiety throughout Europe. This contemporary print shows the Napoleonic troops in Venice in 1797, seizing the Byzantine bronze horses of Saint Mark's for removal to Paris. Proceeding to Vienna, the French requisitioned real horses for their cavalry, and three times the Lipizzaners had to move eastward to evade capture. Hungary provided a welcome refuge for the white horses.

that the imperial horses be moved from Lipizza to their own property near Vienna. Everything would then belong to His Majesty. However the emperor refused this well-meant offer.

In the same year that the Sternberg offer was made, 1793, Austria and Prussia entered the so-called First War of Coalition. In the wars between Austria and France that followed soon after, one general stood out in the French Army, which attacked the Austrians at Rivoli in November, 1796 — Napoleon Bonaparte. A decisive battle followed in January, when the Corsicans obtained free passage eastwards. He penetrated as far as Styria and Carinthia. The heart of the Hapsburg dominions was directly threatened. When hostilities almost reached their doorstep, the management of the stud at Lipizza took fright. They decided to move the horses and contents of the leading breeding station for imperial showhorses, parade horses and coach horses to a place of safety.

On the morning of March 22, 1797 they set off. Four columns were formed to make the long march — three hundred horses, the stud's personnel and the carriages.

a good omen and decided to return home. It took them twenty-four days to get back to Lipizza. Here, they found the stables destroyed and abandoned, but being used to hardships, they believed in the future and immediately began reconstruction.

At the Lipizzaner Stud, everything was soon back to normal. The buildings were repaired, the war seemed almost forgotten. Then on January 4, 1802, an earthquake shook Lipizza for several terrible seconds. The estate lay in ruins and a new start had to be made again.

In September 1805, war broke out again between France and Austria. Napoleon and his troops advanced to the gates of Vienna and on the morning of the fourteenth of November took quarter in the Palace of Schönbrunn. In Lipizza they responded accordingly — just one day later another great trek was begun. Travelling via Fiume, they went straight across Croatia and Slavonia in the direction of Djakovo. The rain came down in sheets and the long column moved slowly along the muddy roads. Time and again they encountered the bodies of soldiers who had occupied all possible

Opposite: For two hundred years the descendants of the "Hispanic horses" developed peacefully at the Lipizzaner Stud, until Napoleon put Europe's empires in jeopardy. In 1797 flight from the Napoleonic threat took three hundred of the Stud's horses to Lake Balaton in Hungary. A two further years' exile followed

when the Emperor of the French took Vienna, the capital of the Hapsburg Empire, in 1805; once again Hungary – now Djakovo – offered asylum. And when Napoleon spread fear and terror through Europe for the last time, Lipizzaners had again to make the long trek straight through the land of the

Magyars. In 1809 they passed through Zagreb, to Pecska on the Maros and on to Karad. A return and a further hundred years' consistent development were possible with Napoleon's fall. The world wars of the twentieth century then occasioned further flight, from which many did not return.

quarters and claimed all the available space in every stable for their own horses. The Lipizzaners slept under the stars. Hunger gnawed at them, but the animals were used to meager rations. They had survived a wild flight intact, as well as a powerful earthquake. Now they were on the road again. Personnel and horses spent a whole year at Djakovar and then moved further on to Karad. After a few days disaster struck again – a conflagration levelled the stables. Exhausted, the stable hands saved what they could. To their exemplary efforts we owe the fact that Lipizzaners survive today. The Lipizzaners spent a whole year at Karad. Finally, on April 1, 1807, the emperor ordered them to be returned to their home.

Once back at Lipizza, it was hoped that breeding could be started again. After nearly two years, however, these hopes were shattered. The "Peace of Schönbrunn" separated Carniola, Trieste, a part of Carinthia and the Duchy of Gorizia from the Hapsburg Empire. If, therefore, the people of Lipizza refused to live as foreigners in their own homeland, flight was the only alternative. So yet again the long trek to Hungary was set into motion. This time they journeyed through Zagreb, to Osijek and Novi Sad in the Hungarian Pécska. For forty-six days they were on their way, with 289 horses. It was the most difficult flight so far. Of the three foals born during the march, one died; otherwise the Lipizzaners demonstrated their toughness and endurance.

However, it was the next six years in foreign fields that proved to be the hardest test. True, the horses were reasonably well-accommodated but they had exchanged the rocky Karst for vaporous bogs. Neither the feed nor the water quality came close to the conditions the Karst horses required. Of the hundred and ten brood mares, twenty-seven aborted. Signs of degeneration soon became apparent. The formerly tough horses became prone to sickness. Infectious disease became rife.

Despairingly, the stud personnel fought against these unfavourable conditions.

They might even have given up had they known what had happened at Lipizza in the meantime – Napoleon had created a Province of Illyria and appointed Marshal Marmont as Governor-General. For four years he reigned as "Duke of Ragusa" in a country which was already poor and which he made poorer. The forests which were laboriously planted in the Karst over centuries were cut down, the country's last treasures recklessly exploited.

In Pécska on the Maros, keepers and charges held out not only until Napoleon had been banished, but until he was gone for good.

During one of these forced marches, all the stud books up to 1700 were lost. While in Vienna the Lipizzaner stallions at the Spanish Riding School entertained the crowned heads of Europe with a splendid carousel – the Allies were assembled in a lively Congress – the Lipizzaners in Hungary were preparing to return home once more. Now, at last, a century of peace was ushered in. The effects of the Revolution of 1848 were barely felt here, nor were the consequences of the Austro-Prussian War of 1866, or the fatal shots at Sarajevo, the overture of the First World War.

Early in May 1915, Italy entered into secret negotiations with the Entente and, in return for territorial concessions, agreed to enter the war on the side of the Allies. Once again, the stud suffered the usual consequences. At eight o'clock in the evening on May 18, 1915, the Lipizzaners set out. Italy formally declared war on Austria-Hungary on the twenty-third of May. The horses arrived at Laxenburg near Vienna five days later, where the brood mares, the fillies and the draft horses were housed. The foals were transferred far away to the Imperial Stud at Kladrub in Bohemia.

For more than three centuries the Lipizzaner breed had proved its strength and power of survival under the worst conditions. Now, for the first time, the end seemed to be in sight. Many mares miscarried and fertility fell from the customary eighty percent to a disastrous ten percent. By November 1918 defeat in the war ended

the Hapsburg epoch which had lasted for more than five hundred years. To many, it was soon to be as distant as the royal pomp and the imperial horses. A series of minor states took over from the great power. The Revolution failed to provide for the art of classic riding in its scenario of the future. In order to fill at least a few hungry mouths, the household and campaign horses of His Apostolic Majesty, Emperor Francis Joseph I, were auctioned. The Lord Chamberlain and all his noble white horses suddenly became a small piece of folk history. However, the members of the Italian Armistice Commission demanded *their* Lipizzaners, since Lipizza now lay on Italian territory. The people living in what was left of Austria had other things to worry about. Hunger and need were pressing hard. So why not simply give the horses to the Italians who, though victorious, were not much richer?

However the question was not that simple. The Lipizzaner Stud have never been the property of the state, but entirely that of the imperial household; for centuries, the latter had paid for it from its private pocket.

The dissolution for the "Crown Properties" had been placed in the hands of Baron Eugen Beck von Managetta and it was he who retrieved the horses from the liquidated estate at Laxenburg. Finally an agreement was reached. Of the seventeen families of brood mares, Austria and Italy would each receive half. On July 16, 1919, one hundred and seven stud's horses were moved to Italy; ninety-seven remained at Laxenburg for the time being. Even so, it wasn't clear as to who owned what. Who was to be responsible for the Lipizzaners in the future, who for the stud, and who for the riding school? The Minister of War was consulted but he regretfully declined. The Minister of Education, who was thought to be next in line, also declined. The next person to become involved was Josef Stöckler, the Austrian Minister of Agriculture, who had a farming background and had only just been demobilised as a Lieutenant of Dragoons. He found a truly Austrian solution. "If nobody wants them," he said,

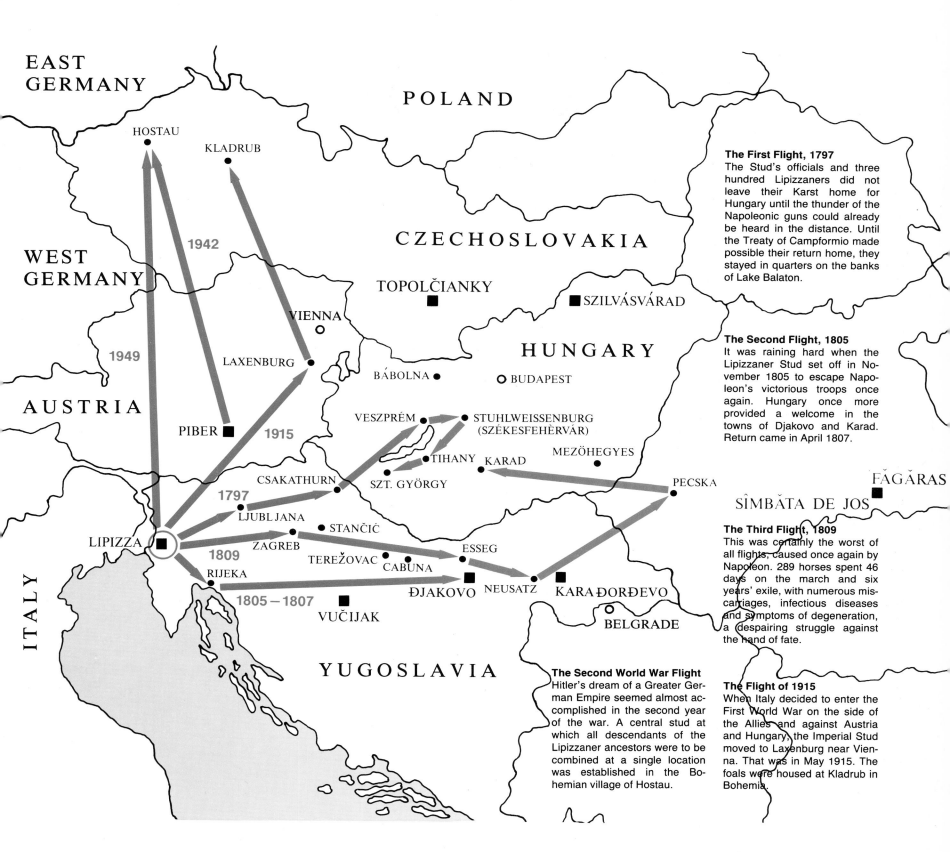

EAST
GERMANY

POLAND

HOSTAU

KLADRUB

WEST
GERMANY

1942

CZECHOSLOVAKIA

TOPOLČIANKY   ■ SZILVÁSVÁRAD

1949

VIENNA ○

LAXENBURG

HUNGARY

The First Flight, 1797
The Stud's officials and three hundred Lipizzaners did not leave their Karst home for Hungary until the thunder of the Napoleonic guns could already be heard in the distance. Until the Treaty of Campformio made possible their return home, they stayed in quarters on the banks of Lake Balaton.

AUSTRIA

PIBER ■   1915

BÁBOLNA ●   ○ BUDAPEST

The Second Flight, 1805
It was raining hard when the Lipizzaner Stud set off in November 1805 to escape Napoleon's victorious troops once again. Hungary once more provided a welcome in the towns of Djakovo and Karad. Return came in April 1807.

VESZPRÉM ● ● STUHLWEISSENBURG (SZÉKESFEHÈRVÁR)

MEZÖHEGYES ●

● TIHANY   KARAD ●

● SZT. GYÖRGY

CSAKATHURN

1797

LJUBLJANA

PECSKA ●   FĂGĂRAS

SÎMBĂTA DE JOS ■

LIPIZZA ■

1809

ZAGREB   ● STANČIĆ

TEREŽOVAC   CABUNA ●

ESSEG ●

The Third Flight, 1809
This was certainly the worst of all flights, caused once again by Napoleon. 289 horses spent 46 days on the march and six years' exile, with numerous miscarriages, infectious diseases and symptoms of degeneration, a despairing struggle against the hand of fate.

RIJEKA

1805 – 1807

VUČIJAK ■

ĐAKOVO ■   NEUSATZ ■   KARAĐORĐEVO ■

○ BELGRADE

ITALY

YUGOSLAVIA

The Second World War Flight
Hitler's dream of a Greater German Empire seemed almost accomplished in the second year of the war. A central stud at which all descendants of the Lipizzaner ancestors were to be combined at a single location was established in the Bohemian village of Hostau.

The Flight of 1915
When Italy decided to enter the First World War on the side of the Allies and against Austria and Hungary, the Imperial Stud moved to Laxenburg near Vienna. That was in May 1915. The foals were housed at Kladrub in Bohemia.

"I'll take them." And he kept his word, he and all his successors through many generations.

From November 5, 1920, the imperial horses found a new home in the burgeoning republic. They soon settled down at Piber in Styria.

The Lipizzaners which had been taken to Kladrub were kept there. No one claimed them and they formed the basic stock for Lipizzaner breeding in Czechoslovakia which, although following traditions diffe-

rent from those at Piber, proved successful. The studs had therefore been consolidated to some extent. But what future lay in store for the Spanish Riding School in Vienna? Since during the Monarchy the people had had no access to the displays, these had not become popular. Nor was there much enthusiasm at that time for institutions of this kind. Fischer von Erlach's splendid Riding Hall – the world's finest – was destined to become a swimming pool or a warehouse.

The last of the First Riding Masters in imperial times was Mauritius Herold. He remained a firm supporter of Lipizzaners, even when everyone else said that the horses had served their purpose. He believed in the magic of the white stallions, in their enchanting power – and in his own mission in life.

Herold was quick to see that for an institution so rich in tradition there was only one chance of survival – to increase its popularity and create emotional support. His

An autograph note signed by Mauritius Herold regarding his founding of the "Broom Fund" in 1921. The First Riding Master, a survivor from the Hapsburg days, he kept the Spanish Riding School from closing down after World War I.

recipe provided for charity performances open to the public which would excite sympathy and bring in a little money. Shows could also be organized abroad, and riding lessons sold to gifted and wealthy pupils.

To achieve all this, thought Herold, a medium was needed which could reach as many people as possible and influence them positively. This idea was as revolutionary as it was clever. Herold, First Riding Master at the Imperial Court Riding School turned to Friedrich Austerlitz, Editor-in-Chief of the *Arbeiter Zeitung,* the main newspaper of the Social Democratic party. Austerlitz, a man of intelligence and liberal views, immediately saw the possibilities in Herold's suggestion. He arranged for the outward-looking Social Democratic educational associations to attend the performances, where the best of the equestrian arts were put on show. Soon many of these people became popular ambassadors of the "gentlemen Lipizzaners."

The extent of Herold's ingenuity and initiative is clear from a document in which he describes the Broom Fund which he introduced in 1921. "After the Federation had taken over the Spanish Riding School, we found that there was no money left over to purchase brooms. To remedy this situation, the Writer had picture postcards printed which were sold to visitors to the Institution. Brooms were then purchased from the proceeds, and other needs were met . . ."

However, the Republic had not yet taken the institution under its wing and Herold still had to manage the Riding School as if he were steering a private business through an almost terminal crisis. However succor was at hand – Countess van der Straaten came to the rescue by organizing a sparkling display for charity. The response woke up the politicians. Herold had achieved his purpose, but at the same time had ended his career. As a young man he had failed to complete the high school studies required for a career in government service and that was more than the infant Republic could stomach.

Rudolf, Count van der Straaten, was appointed as his successor. However, this by no means spelled an end to the school's problems. When, in around 1925, at a time of mounting depression and early trouble-making by the national socialists in Vienna, the Lipizzaners and the Spanish Riding School were again on the brink of dissolution, the authorities had to give in to the clamor both at home and abroad.

Several years of relatively peaceful development gave the Lipizzaners breathing space. After Austria was linked to national-socialist Germany, the Spanish Riding School again became a "Court" institution. The riding master now wore the lieutenant's insignia of the German *Wehrmacht*. Yet this hardly touched the Lipizzaners. Things were much worse for a few months in 1940 when the stallions at the Riding School contracted pleuropneumonia, a contagious disease in which symptoms include a high fever and breathing difficulties. The School virtually stood helpless against it.

Hitler's megalomaniac power politics had led him into a war of then unknown dimensions. While the horses were not short of food at first, things were soon to change. This is where the name of the village of Hostau enters our story.

Hostau is a small provincial town in Bohemia, in the middle of what Hitler called the Sudetenland when he brought Czechoslovakia "back into the Reich." Hostau might be described as a charming, pretty village which could have been the scene for Smetana's *Bartered Bride.* It had barely a thousand inhabitants – craftsmen, rope-makers and shopkeepers. Here, however, the new masters decreed "a Lipizzaner stud of grand dimensions will be created, a center, so to speak, for all Lipizzaner strains still in existence – with extended duties and additional components." From the third year of the Second World War the Lipizzaner studs within Germany's extended dominions were brought to Hostau on the orders of the German Ministry of Food and Agriculture. First came the Yugoslav studs, then the State Stud of Stančić at Krusedol and finally the white horses from the private stud at Demir Kapija which had belonged to the kings of Macedonia. Soon after the Lipizzaners arrived from Piber – three stud stallions, forty brood mares and foals of all ages. On the day following the Italian capitulation, September 9, 1943, German troops occupied the stud at Lipizza. On the sixteenth of October the horses were taken by truck to Sežana Station and then by train to the Sudetenland. One hundred and fifty-nine horses from Lipizza left for the north, including all the male and female foals born from 1940 to 1943. They were accompanied by twenty-two of the Lipizza staff, including the stud's director, the Italian Dr. Ugo Fasani.

Hostau was very well organized. The head of the stud, who was now entrusted with some five hundred Lipizzaners (almost as many as Europe had to offer), was Lieutenant-Colonel Hubert Rudofsky. He, in turn, was answerable to the head of all studs controlled by the German Wehrmacht, the unforgettable Gustav Rau.

Together with a German vet, a U.S. colonel, an American general and a bit of luck, Rudofsky was one of the main protagonists in a tense drama, one with a happy ending, in the turbulent events immediately before the war's end.

It seems that Hostau was an ideal place for siting a stud. It encompassed the hamlets of Hassatitz, Taschlowitz and Zwirchen, and nearly fifteen hundred acres of paddock and pasture, roomy stables and all the necessary facilities. This was a dream stud; while elsewhere in Europe millions of people were being exterminated in the most inhuman of any war, here life was flourishing on an almost idyllic, enchanted isle of the blessed. Complex plans and enterprises for future breeding could be considered at leisure. "In order to ennoble and revitalize the ancient Lipizzaner blood, a number of the Lipizzaner mares were paired with particularly suitable thoroughbred stallions, as had always been done at Lipizza and in the other studs." The years at Hostau were extremely important for breeding and were beneficial to the Lipizzaner breed as a whole, with a wealth of selective potential. The short road to Hostau that so many Lipizzaners were to tread together proved a thoroughly worthwhile experience. In fact, horses and personnel fared better in these bitter war years than almost anyone anywhere else. However, the end of Hostau came in sight in April 1945. The Russians entered Budapest. Dresden was razed to the ground; Danzig was occupied; Königsberg capitulated. The Twilight of the Gods descended on Berlin.

Through the force of events, the atmosphere at Hostau on April 25, 1945 was, to say the least, uncertain. People knew from radio broadcasts that the enemy were creeping up inexorably. Lieutenant-Colonel Rudofsky was a soldier. He knew what he had to do. He telegraphed Berlin and asked whether the valuable horses should not be taken "somewhere" for greater safety. "Stay where you are!" was the abrupt reply. And perhaps that was the right answer — after all, where could they go in a world engulfed in total war? So Rudofsky had to persevere.

Despite worries, there was still something of a holiday mood at the stud. Though millions had fallen in the war, so far not a shot had been fired in Hostau. For many weeks refugees had passed through town, going westwards. Singly at first, then in droves, whole populations were on the move.

In fact, two months previously a Russian prince had arrived at Hostau and had sought asylum for himself and for several hundred Kabardin horses. Rudofsky loved horses, and there was no reason why he should not help. It was just a matter of squeezing them a bit tighter together. Here, Prince Amasov felt secure and happy, if anyone could feel secure or happy at all in those days. He learned that thirty years previously the land had belonged to the Princes of Trautmannsdorff.

Rudofsky directed the stud with circumspection. He was assisted by his staff veterinarian, Dr. Rudolf Lessing. There was one other vet here, Dr. Wolfgang Kroll, who looked after the Russian prince's horses.

Eleven days before the twenty-fifth of April, a reconnaissance team from the Twelfth U.S. Army Corps from General Patton's Third Army reached Bayreuth. General Patton's troops had a soft spot for horses. It was only three years since the cavalry had exchanged their horses for armored scout cars.

Seven days before April twenty-fifth the Americans reached Hof in Bavaria, close to the former German border with Czechoslovakia. They were not permitted to proceed further. This had been agreed with Stalin in Yalta — the area beyond the old border was to be assigned to the Soviet forces.

On the twenty-fifth, late at night, forward units of the U.S. Army and the Red Army met on the Elbe and shook hands.

Lieutenant Colonel Rudofsky was not even aware of this fact until he received an unexpected visitor, Luftwaffe Colonel Walter H., a passionate horseman and altogether a great admirer of horses. The two men quickly understood each other. The war was coming to an end, said Colonel H. to Rudofsky. That meant little to Rudofsky, who had other worries. But they appeared identical with those of his unknown visitor. "I know a way of guiding you and your horses safely through the lines," intimated the colonel. "However, we must act immediately." The colonel departed.

We, the next generation, are in a better position to access what happened than those who were directly involved as, after all, we have independent accounts from different people who experienced the same situation. We can therefore try to present an objective report.

Colonel H. was captured "after a mock battle," so he said. Members of the U.S. unit mentioned rounding up "a small German force with staff officers who had been evacuated from Berlin to a hunting lodge in the neighborhood." In any case, Colonel H. was in the hands of American soldiers who took him immediately to Captain Ferdinand Sperl. When questioned Colonel H. mentioned the Lipizzaners accommodated in the neighborhood, and Sperl immediately notified his chief, Colonel Reed, who was known throughout the Army as a horseman and an acknowledged expert on horses. Reed was fascinated by the idea of keeping the Lipizzaner Stud for the West. But how could it be done without creating an international incident?

While the first shells were falling on Hostau and several people were killed, two gentlemen from opposite sides sat down together with a common interest. Colonel H. and Colonel Reed discussed the Lipizzaners.

Rudofsky was not aware of any of this. He did not know that at this moment the future was being mapped out. Probably the "map makers" themselves had little inkling of their historic mission. Together they looked at the pictures of Lipizzaners that Colonel H. had in his briefcase. At that moment Reed hit on a promising plan. Yalta, he said, was a real obstacle. But why shouldn't the Germans themselves drive the horses across the border? "No, that can't be done," said Colonel H. Yet, some way would be found. "A little later the same day, there was a further surprise," states the American record. "The staff veterinarian Dr. Rudolf Lessing came riding through the lines from Bohemia. He was accompanied by his batman and had been ordered by his commander, Lieutenant Colonel Hubert Rudofsky, to make contact with the American troops regarding the stud." Rudofsky had received a letter from Colonel H. instructing him to send Lessing, "together with the bearer of this letter, a forester, with a bicycle and a lad." Lessing had left his lad and the horses at a lonely forcester's ledge walked on a few hundred yards over the border, where he was received by the Americans. In a farmhouse, a memorable conversation followed. Lessing stood before Colonel Charles H. Reed, Head of the U.S. Intelligence Department. "We cannot save the horses. There's the Yalta Agreement ..." Some thirty years later, Lessing reminisced about the occasion in a documentary film by Kurt Mrkwicka. "I now had to explain to the

Americans that transportation or a march on foot across the border was quite impossible. We had neither sufficient personnel nor enough gear, vehicles, saddles and so on. After a lot of to-ing and fro-ing, Colonel Reed decided to send one of his orderly officers back with me. He was told to act as go-between with Colonel Rudofsky and to try and find ways and means of perhaps evacuating the horses across the border."

Lessing was introduced to Captain Thomas M. Stuart. Together, they rode back to Hostau that night. While Lessing negotiated with the U.S. troops at Lieutenant Colonel Rudofsky's request and with his knowledge, other things had happened at Hostau. A German unit had arrived under General Schulze. The General requisitioned Rudofsky's office. A short while later he enquired as to Dr. Lessing's whereabouts. Rudofsky said he was probably somewhere outside, in the pasture or with the horses. A little later, he repeated the question, with the same answer. The general lost his temper.

When Lessing and Stuart returned to Hostau towards midnight, the vet was told he had to report to the general at seven o'clock in the morning. Clearly, the general knew about the trip across the border. At seven, Schultze gave him a rough reception. Lessing was passed on to another senior officer. He too lectured the vet harshly for his arbitrary action. Eventually, however, he ordered Lessing to bring in the U.S. spokesman. If the Americans were to plan an action at Hostau, they would encounter no resistance – anything else at this late point in the war would have been pushing credibility too far. In an adventurous manner, Stuart was guided through the German outposts. By then, the Americans too had made their decision. Reed had spoken to his superior, General George S. Patton, by radio, explained the situation to him, and had requested instructions: "What should we do about the horses?" The general, a cavalryman of the old school, was brief and to the point. "Get them. Make it fast!"

Lessing was still on his way back to Hostau after seeing the Americans when he heard that U.S. tanks were on their way. He sprang on his horse, rode quickly homewards and arrived just in time to see General Schultze hurriedly taking his leave.

White sheets were fastened to some of the houses and also to the church. Then the tanks arrived, followed by Colonel Reed in a motor car. Rudofsky met the colonel and reported. Reed said, "Lieutenant Colonel, from now on you are Stud Commandant. But for the time being you remain under my protection."

Rudofsky led his American "guests" through the stud, showed them the four Lipizzaner stallions, the eighty brood mares and the foals, the two Arab full-blood stallions, the twenty mares and thirty-five foals. Together, they also visited the horses at the outlying farms. Reed seemed satisfied for the moment. During the next few days the horses would be rounded-up and taken to the Bavarian Forest in the area around Furth. The Russians were now in Pilsen, and Hostau was becoming uncomfortable. Only the Austrian, Yugoslav and Italian horses would accompany them. The Americans had no interest in the Russian horses. Although the organizational aspect was not easy – at this point in the war, the foreign workers employed at the stud were not eager to work diligently for their masters – the departure was fixed for the fifteenth of May.

The transport of newborn foals came first, and then the horses who could not make the journey on foot. They were loaded onto trucks. The remainder followed in four groups at intervals of twenty to thirty minutes along a carefully prepared road – the intersections had been closed by Americans in scout cars in order to prevent any kind of mishap. Resting points had been allocated for the midday break for watering and feeding and were properly observed. The trek proceeded practically without resistance. Only at the Furth border crossing did a few partisans appear on the road with red arm bands and rifles. An American gun persuaded them to change their minds. Then the Americans were on German soil – secure in a country which had already capitulated.

Hostau, where years of valuable preparatory work had been done, was empty. "No neighing, no stamping, no snorting," Rudofsky noted. "It is a beautiful spring day. The thrushes are singing, the turtle-doves calling, buzzards wheeling. We are still quite unaware what bitter times have broken over us." Rudofsky, the only man to remain in the village, in his homeland, was arrested, unsung and unappreciated. The horses spent a few days in the Bavarian Forest. The Lipizzaners were then sent on to Saint Martin in Upper Austria, the other seven hundred horses to Hesse in Germany. The Lipizzaners at the Spanish Court Riding School also had their war experiences. Alois Podhajsky, the meritorious commandant of the school in those days moved some of the horses to the Lainzer Tiergarten, a park on the outskirts of Vienna; before Austria was occupied he also managed to transfer all the horses from the riding school to Saint Martin in Upper Austria. On May 7, 1945, before all the Lipizzaners had been rescued, a memorable display took place in the presence of General Patton when Colonel Podhajsky asked the general to take the school under the American Army's protection. A few days later the Lipizzaners were reunited.

The stud subsequently moved to Schloss Wimsbach in Upper Austria. The school's horses spent the next ten years at the former dragoon barracks in the city of Wels.

As it happened, the school had fallen on its feet. The American occupying powers cared for it as assiduously as had the Republican Government. The stud, for its part, had major difficulties to overcome. The Italian Lipizzaners were very soon repatriated to their original homeland, as

Overleaf: The American troops' dramatic rescue of the Lipizzaners from exile in Hostau early in May 1945 inspired Hollywood. Walt Disney's film **The White Horses,** *while wandering far into the realms of fiction, provided useful publicity world-wide for the Spanish Riding School. This is a scene from the film.*

Below: Reed entrusted Rudofsky, head of the Lipizzaner Studs centralized at Hostau during the Second World War, with the care of the horses until they were taken to the West. He continued to wear the uniform of the German Wehrmacht. In center below, U.S. Captain Ferdinand Sperl, who as liaison officer and hostage contributed greatly towards saving the Hostau Stud, astride a Lipizzaner.

were the Yugoslav horses. The horses from the Austrian Lipizzaner Stud were sent back to Piber in stages, starting with the younger animals, a process which continued right into 1952.

During the first post-war years times were hard at Piber, which was occupied by the British. There were few suitable or skilled personnel. Oddly enough, considering the British weakness for horses, relations between the stud and the occupying forces were poor. However not even the local population could have built up a good relationship with the horses at the time. There was a shortage of everything — even fodder. It took some time before things improved a little.

Despite many a difficult day, however the year had its good side, too — the geographical proximity of the Spanish Riding School to the breeding establishment proved very beneficial.

Things returned to normal only in 1955 when the Austrian Constitution was signed and the School's stallions were returned to Vienna. Everyday life at the Piber Stud finally settled down again.

The Lipizzaner breed had always comprised a very small population which inevitably introduced a series of breeding problems, as had in fact been foreseen. Keeping the breed pure had always meant that a certain amount of inbreeding was unavoidable. Not even the repeated introduction of new blood could change this.

"It cannot be denied that in a breeding population with an already relatively high degree of inter-relatedness the inner physical fitness could not but suffer," says Dr. Oulehla, present head of the Federal Stud at Piber. Degenerative symptoms such as enormous deformities of the nose and cryptorchism have occurred increasingly during the past decade. On occasion male foals are even born without any sex organs at all. "I can perhaps best explain the problems of inbreeding and the consequences resulting from this phenomenon by saying that according to our calculations, unless appropriate measures are taken within ten years or so our choice of breeding animals will be narrowed down completely and we shall have to couple closely related horses with all the consequences ..."

It is quite probable that lowered resistance resulting from inbreeding was partly responsible for the terrible disease that raged at Piber in 1983, killing twenty-two Lipizzaner foals and eight brood mares. The sickness was triggered by an equine herpes virus related to rhinopneumonitis, which has been well known since 1933 as a pathogen of viral miscarriage in horses. It causes paralysis of the central nervous system, followed by death. A serum has existed since the early Seventies but it was never injected at Piber. "It is a closed Stud," the journal *St. Georg* commented at the time, "outside horses never enter the premises and immunization with a live vaccine is not without its dangers

to horses. Inflammations can be the result." Afterwards, it was apparent that vaccination would have been the right step. The first horse fell ill on February 20, 1983. The incident was hushed up, even when other horses began to show the same symptoms. Only in mid-March did the public learn of the serious threat to Lipizzaner breeding in Austria.

At Piber they were quick to draw conclusions from the situation. A vaccination program was worked out for each individual horse. It is hoped that this will prevent the kind of catastrophe from ever happening again.

Wherever Lipizzaners live — in the studs of Hungary and Yugoslavia, in Czechoslovakia, in a small stud in the center of Germany, or at Piber in Austria — they have all not only survived these hard times but, it would seem, have overcome them. And when we see the horses pacing the meadow or undergoing training for the haute école they arouse in us what many generations of our forebears have experienced — a deep-felt joy.

The village of Lipizza lies between Trieste, Postojna and Rijeka in the heart of the so-called "Trieste Karst," a green oasis in a white limestone plain thirteen hundred feet above the Bay of Trieste. Here, the River Notranjska once ran, its dry bed now sweeping steeply down to the sea from a height of a thousand feet within less than one-and-a-half miles. The great height of the plain combined with its proximity to the sea produces a very special climate, a mixture of the mild Mediterranean and the cool Continental.

This combination of climates has of course affected the vegetation, which grows luxuriously and in great variety wherever there

and drought is not uncommon, yet lush, nutritious pasture appears wherever the soil can retain the water.

Finally, the word Karst suggests yet another meaning — the special charm of the Yugoslav landscape, particularly that of Slovenia and Croatia. Nowhere do we feel it more strongly than in the picturesque villages of the Karst, as the bright sun — or better still, the evening light — is reflected off the well-cut limestone. Everywhere are wonderful arches, walls, gables and well-heads, the product of conscientious craftsmanship.

There has long been one important difference between the landscape of Lipizza and the rest of the Karst area. While the Karst is largely bare, Lipizza is surrounded

LIPIZZA

"They are the most excellent and enduring horses that one might find, walking and pasturing on simple hard rock, where little grass grows ..."

The Archduke Charles II, Lord of Styria, Carinthia, Gorizia, Trieste and Carniola, around 1580.

Opposite: Ruined walls dating from 1580, close to the Fontana. The first buildings of the Stud are traditionally said to have been wooden sheds surrounded by a high wall. Only after 1700 were the timber buildings replaced by those of stone on the present site of the Stud.

is water and the soil is good. Warm sea breezes from the Adriatic push summer temperatures beyond 90° F, while a keen wind known as the Karst Bora can chill the blood in the winter months. However, together these extremes account for the fresh, healthy climate.

Karst is the name applied to the landscape bounded by the Bay of Trieste, the sunny plain of Gorizia, the vineyards of the Vipava Valley, the Forest of Postojna and Rijeka Bay. However the term has acquired a general geographical significance to describe a type of country not confined to the Balkans. Its characteristic feature, conditioned by the climate and terrain, is a bare, leached-out stony soil of chalk or gypsum. Rain water quickly sinks to the bowels of the earth, creating caves and potholes, great stretches of stones, and gutters and furrows in the rock, as well as a fertile, weathered soil and rich fields on the flood plain. The rain falls sparingly in summer

with dense forests of centenarian oaks, limes and maples. While the poor soil has not been conducive to agriculture, the town itself has become a favorite spot for rest, recuperation and recreation, especially in the summer months. That is why the bishops of Trieste acquired Lipizza and used it as their summer residence and also as a source for firewood.

Lipizza itself consisted originally of the old bishops' palace which, much changed, still stands today, and the huts of a small community of feudal peasants, known as the "colonists" grouped around the Fontane, the former well. There were five or six large families of peasants, whose task it was to look after the episcopal buildings and gardens; they cut wood for the bishops' requirements in Trieste and worked the small patches of arable land allowed them near the village. They were the typical "Krasovci," Slovenes who lived on the Karst, eking out a poor existence as best they could.

No one knows the exact origin of the name Lipizza. However, historians agree that it is of Slovene origin, possibly derived from *male lipa,* the "small lime." The more popular version is that it takes its name from an inn which once stood close to the village, called *Pod Lipico* ("under the small lime"). In due course, the name Lipizza (Austrian spelling) was to become world famous. When the stud was first set up, it was written "Lipitza," later the Hapsburg Court used "Lipizza," which the Italians adopted in due course when the area became Italian territory after the First World War. Today the Slovene "Lipica" is used.

When Archduke Charles, Lord of Styria, Carinthia, Carniola, Gorizia, Istria and Trieste, managed to purchase the estate

from the bishops of Trieste to set up his stud farm, Lipizza consisted of the palace now semi-derelict, and a farm in no better condition. The Turkish invasion had hit Notranjsko and the Karst in 1559, leaving Lipizza ruined and desolate. This was apparently the main reason why the Triestine bishops decided to offer the property to the archduke Charles when he visited Trieste to look for a suitable place to set up his new stud.

Today we can only guess what moved the archduke to purchase the Lipizza estate and to establish a stud farm on the impoverished, stony, parched soil, so far away from Vienna. He no doubt had his reasons. According to the archives and established tradition, even in antiquity the area was famous for breeding good horses. Because the animals were very fast, very versatile and blessed with good hooves, the ancient Romans prized them as war horses. Also popular as racing mounts in the arena, the horses were frequently harnessed four abreast for the chariot races, or used in championships. A shrine to the Thracian hero Diomedes, the patron of horses, is said to have been erected at the source of the River Timav, near Aquilea, to honor these beasts. Various ancient writers, including the local historian Baron von Valvasor, say that the smaller Karst horse was subsequently bred in this area and because of its endurance, speed and toughness, was

Aerial photo of the medieval village of Lokev, four miles from Lipizza. Here many of the Stud workers live and here the dressage rider Dušan Maveč was born. The main road from Trieste to the interior once ran through the centre of Lokev.

Right: Central feature of Lokov is the Tabor, a round building erected around 1485 as a stronghold to protect the inhabitants against attack by the Turks. The Venetians later used it as a silo for oats.

Far right: The Škratelj, a stone building at Divača.

Right: Entrance to the walled Church of St. Michael at Lokev, built in 1118 and restored after being destroyed in 1613. Behind the Church is the Chapel of Our Lady, dating to 1423, one of the many surviving examples of the vernacular architecture of the Karst area.

used as a dray horse, a pack horse and for riding.

The Spanish Riding School had been formed in Vienna in 1572. It used only Spanish horses bred in Andalusia for its displays of traditional horsemanship. Spanish horses were also used at the Viennese Court for sumptuous parades and other ceremonials. However, the continuous wars then being waged in Europe and particularly the Turkish incursions, made Spanish horses increasingly difficult to obtain; in any event, the Court was finding the large-scale acquisition of Spanish horses from Andalusia a heavy financial burden. The landscape around Lipizza is rather like that of Andalusia, with its favorable climate, its sparse but lush vitamin- and mineral-rich grass, and the hardness of its stony soil, so this may have been the deciding factor.

47

Left: The Fontana well dates back to before 1580 and is one of the few remaining relics of early Lipizza. The Fontana is the only spring in Lipizza that never quite dries up.

The contract for the purchase of the estate was signed on May 19, 1580, at which time the archduke Charles appointed Bishop Coret of Trieste as his adviser and the

the present day reveals that the three stallions he bought were "Brinco from Popo" for 127 ducats, "Brinco from Frog" for 120 ducats and "Brinco from an odd Bird" for 160 ducats. In following year, 1581, a further six stallions were purchased in Spain for a total of 3683 guilders. These stallions included an Andalusian for 815 guilders, the most expensive. It was this stallion more than any other that left its mark on the infant strain at Lipizza. He was the ancestor of all the Hermeline line, which was greatly prized at the Viennese Court.

Some accounts mention that the Triestine bishops had been breeding Karst horses somewhere near Lipizza before 1580. This stud the archduke purchased together with the Lipizza estate and transferred it to the latter soon after.

The Lipizza estate originally amounted to 770 acres, partly of woodland and partly of meadow and pasture, though this did not provide sufficient hay and grazing for the growing number of horses. So the Prestranek estate was purchased from the Sticna Monastery where the foals were subsequently put to pasture. Meanwhile at Lipizza a start was made in clearing the forest and improving the soil in order to obtain additional pasture. By 1610 the ratio of forest to meadow and pasture had already changed. However, care was also taken to create parkland and avenues of trees. Beginning in the reign of Emperor Charles VI, three new trees were planted in the avenue for every three-year-old stallion sent to the Spanish Riding School in Vienna. That was how the famous Lipizza Avenue came to be.

Today the Lipizza estate covers 784 acres, including 371 acres of meadow, 272 acres of pasture and 141 acres of forest and arable land.

Opposite: The Sežana Gate, one of the five avenues that lead to Lipizza's Riding Ground. Most of the trees along the avenues were planted in groups of three at a time and it was once the custom to plant three trees for each three-year old stallion sent from Lipizza to the Spanish Riding School in Vienna.

Above: Two roads approach Lipizza from outside, one from Sežana, the other from Lokev.

Slovene Franz Jurko as the first manager of the estate and the newly created stud.

Immediately after the contract was signed, the archduke sent Baron Khevenhüller to Spain to purchase a stallion for crossing with the tough, sturdy, hardy brood mares at the new farm. That same year, Baron Khevenhüller brought back three Brinco stallions (*brinco* means "gem", "treasure" and also "jump" in Spanish, i.e. breeding stallion). A receipt which has survived to

THE STUD AND ITS HISTORY

The archduke Charles, son, brother and father of Hapsburg emperors but never to ascend the throne himself, achieved something which for his time was truly worthy of any emperor. At Lipizza he stablished a stud which for three hundred and fifty years and more was to supply the Imperial Court, and later the Spanish Riding School, with its horses — the most remarkable horses of all time. It became an institution which today, after more than four hundred years of raising these most elegant and noble of breeds — Lipizzaners — is still the most famous Stud in the world. We have already described how the archduke happened to choose Lipizza as the site for his stud.

this that the Lipizzaners, or the "Lipizza strain of the Karst breed" as they were originally and officially called at the Viennese Court, were bred by crossing local native mares from the Karst with Spanish and Italian stallions and then, subsequently, by crossing their offspring with Spanish mares. The stock names for the mares kept at Lipizza today — Sardinia, Spadiglia and Argentina — and still registered as "original Karst mares" seem to confirm this conclusion.

That the Lipizza stud made excellent headway in the early years is clear — by 1595 thirty colts had already been taken from Lipizza to the archduke Charles's stables in

Not for many years did the episcopal estate at Lipizza become a flourishing stud. Only with difficulty was the hard Karst landscape brought under cultivation, the pasture laid down, the woods planted, and a sufficient water supply, vital to man and horse, secured beyond the possibility of failure.

Today scarcely a traveller through the region fails to make a stop at Lipizza to admire the white horses in their green oasis.

Opposite: This painting now in the portrait gallery at Ambras Castle in Innsbruck, Austria, shows the Archduke Charles II. It is the work of an unknown artist and dates from around 1579.
The print, made about 1576 by an unknown master, is of Archduke Charles at 36 years of age.

Why the began to bread horses there has still to be explained.

After the invention of gunpowder in the sixteenth century the heavy horses capable of carrying the enormous weight of a knight in full armor were no longer needed and the call now was for smaller, faster, more nimble horses for light cavalry use. This lighter breed would, however, need to retain as many of the advantages of the Spanish horse as possible.

Together with the nine legendary breeding stallions acquired by Baron Khevenhüller, twenty-four brood mares were also purchased in Spain and brought to Lipizza. As the records show, stallions continued to be bought in Spain to reinforce the Lipizza stock right into the eighteenth century. The Karst mares were covered not only by the Spanish stallions but also by others acquired in Italy — from the neighborhood of Rovigo in Polezina. We may conclude from

Graz. The stud would probably have sent all its foals to Graz each year, so even then it must have had some sixty to seventy brood mares.

With the steady rise in demand by the Court and the nobility, there was soon a pressing need to increase the number of stud horses at Lipizza. Large sums of money were spent in purchasing more land to ensure sufficient fodder for the expanding herd. The stables, too, were extended; new houses and cisterns for the stable folk were built; and the Lipizza pasture was dressed and improved. In particular, greater attention was paid to good order and breeding quality at the stud. An interesting document has survived from this period, one of great importance to the history of the stud. It is called the "First Instructions," and was intended for the Lipizza studmaster, Peter Franz Rainer.

Ferdinand I, Holy Roman Emperor from 1556 to 1564, divided his inheritance into three parts. His eldest son, Maximilian II, received Austria above and below the Enns River, the so-called

"Crownlands" and the Emperor's diadem. The younger son, Archduke Ferdinand II, was granted Tyrol and Outer Austria. His brother the Archduke Charles II received Inner Austria.

The village of Lipizza belonged to the Duchy of Carniola and was promoted to the status of a royal stud on May 19, 1580. The white stallions took the village's name.

These Instructions were really in the nature of stud rules. Dated 7 September 1658, they were drafted by the emperor himself and the name "Count Sintzendorf" also appears there. In addition to a series of directions concerning forestry, provision of forage and the like, the Instructions also contain a wealth of technical detail with particular emphasis on effective breeding and selection and methods of servicing, the special aim being the improvement of stock productivity.

The stud saw its heyday in the 1700s during the reigns of the emperor Charles VI and his daughter Maria Theresa; the number of brood mares reached one hundred and fifty. It was then that the late emperor Leopold I's long-cherished wish was fulfilled, namely the construction of a new Spanish Riding School. Until 1735, the Court's Spanish Riding School had used Spanish-Andalusian horses for demonstrating the classic art of the haute école. Only in 1735, at the dedication ceremony for the school's new building which still stands today were Lipizzaner horses also shown. Since then there have been Lipizzaners at the Spanish Riding School. The inclusion of Lipizzaners in the school's official activities in Vienna meant that the Lipizza breed was at last recognized, but new demands were also placed on the stud's breeding program.

Hitherto the stud had also supplied horses to the nobility and to the army; now, its duty was principally, and soon solely, the supply of recruits for this highest institution of equestrian art. Breeding at the stud, which had previously been guided by other more general requirements, had now to be adapted to the very special needs of the Spanish Riding School.

From then on – and until the collapse of the Hapsburg monarchy and the dissolution of the Imperial Stud – the farm sent all its suitable young three-year-old colts to the school in Vienna. Only the older stallions with riding school experience returned to Lipizza where they could no doubt be expected to produce valuable offspring.

Right: The Empress Maria Theresa (1740–1780). From left to right below: The baroque Emperor Leopold I (1658–1705); Prince Henry of Auersperg, Chief Stable Master under Maria Theresa; Duke Charles of Dietrichstein, Chief Stable Master under Emperor Joseph II (1765–1790).

Efforts towards improving quality with crosses of new, fresh blood continued at Lipizza throughout the eighteenth century. No trouble was spared in acquiring different varieties of breeding material, especially stallions. Choice stallions were obtained from Spain, Germany and even Denmark, which sired famous male lines. In 1774 a remarkable stallion, Neapolitano, came to Lipizza from Naples, he was the ancestor of the Neapolitano line. The same year also saw the arrival from Kladrub of the stallions Favory and Maestoso, ancestors of the strains named after them.

Oriental stallions were already in use at Lipizza soon after the stud was founded. The Arab stallion Vesir, the personal property of Napoleon Bonaparte, put in years of service. Other famous Arab stallions were added to the stud until 1843, but of all the oriental stallions only Siglavy was to start a line at Lipizza.

Such was the Court's satisfaction with the Lipizza breed that in 1768 twenty Kladrub mares at the Imperial Stud at Kopčany were sent to Lipizza to found a strain of heavier coach horses. These mares spent only three years at Lipizza before returning to the re-established stud at Kladrub.

Arab mares were also repeatedly used at Lipizza to revitalize the stock. Although pure thoroughbreds, the offspring of Arab stallions and mares could not compete with the sturdy Lipizzaners on the Court's strenuous travels. The breeding of the purebreds was therefore soon abandoned.

However, many crosses produced excellent results. The Austrian horse-breeders were united in their view that while Arab blood had its advantages, the best horses were those with an appreciable proportion of old Lipizzaner blood.

From time to time, English thoroughbreds and half-breds were also introduced with the intention of improving the basic stock, though this proved unsuccessful. The offspring no longer conformed with the Lipizzaner type, while the main emphasis of

the stud's work was still on improving the Lipizzaner breed. As fresh blood was crossed in, great care was taken not to damage its characteristic features.

As with breeding everywhere, the mares at Lipizza were regarded with equal importance to the stallions. Without careful selection of brood mares, breeding will make little progress. The mares of the Lipizzaner breed largely stemmed from the Lipizza Stud, though a few came from other studs.

In 1785, the emperor Joseph II dispatched a commission to Ljubljana to examine the economic state of the country and at the same time the financial viability of Lipizza and Prestranek. The commission proposed moving the stud from Lipizza to Holič in Polish Galicia where the Kopčany Stud already existed, but the emperor turned the idea down. A transfer for the Lipizza Stud again seemed imminent eight years later when, in 1793, the owner of the Steinberg

Estate near Vienna offered to accommodate the establishment. However, although the proximity of Vienna, the fertile soil and other economic grounds favored a transfer, this proposal, too, was rejected by the Court. The success in breeding was considered sure proof that Lipizza was ideally suited for producing tough, hardworking horses.

However, Lipizza was exposed to yet greater dangers. Testing times were ahead – the Napoleonic Wars, the First World War. By 1915, during the First World War, the stud had been moved four times. Although conditions in the foreign studs were as good as they could be, the Karst horses

53

were accompanied by 22 of the Lipizza people, 14 Slovenes — stable hands from Lipizza — and 8 Italians.

The Karst area, and so Lipizza as well, was awarded to Slovenia after the Second World War and thus to Yugoslavia. The latter nation thereupon demanded the return by the Allies of all horses in Western Europe which had been evacuated from Lipizza during the war. However, this did not happen. Immediately after the war ended the Allies had turned over 109 of the horses and the associated archives to Italy. Others went to the Spanish Riding School and some to the Piber Stud. After lengthy negotiations the Allies yielded only 11 horses to Yugoslavia, which were returned to the original stud, a sad remainder of the great and proud Lipizzaner herd of 179 horses evacuated in 1943.

did not take to the changed conditions. They lost their power of resistance and sickened more frequently. This and the poor quality of the hay led to miscarriages a loss of fertility, and the death of mares in foal. When the war ended in 1918, the region where Lipizza is located was awarded to Italy. The Governor of Venezia-Giulia, General Carlo Petitti, appointed a commission which travelled to Vienna to negotiate the disposal of the horses at the Stud. As the new Republic of Austria wished to continue breeding Lipizzaners itself, it eventually agreed, after lengthy discussions with the Italian delegation, that the breeding stock should be divided. At Laxenburg the Italian commission hurriedly selected the horses to continue the Lipizzaner breed in its original surroundings. It obtained representatives of six male lines and seventeen female lines, 109 horses altogether.

There were thirty Lipizzaner brood mares at the Lipizza Stud in the Thirties, increasing to fifty-two between 1940 and 1941.
In order to offset the effects of breeding failures somewhat, two stallions were purchased from the Yugoslav Stančić Stud in 1939 — 750 Neapolitano Slavonia I and 1121 Favory Slava II — which soon became Lipizza's leading *pepinniers* (breeding stallions). During the Second World War, German troops occupied the Lipizza Stud on September 9, 1943, the day after Italy capitulated. By the sixteenth of October that year, the horses had been taken by van from the stud to the railroad station at Sežana and from there by rail to the Sudetenland.
On this occasion, 179 horses left for foreign parts, including 6 breeding stallions, 56 brood mares, and all the male and female foals born between 1940 and 1943. They

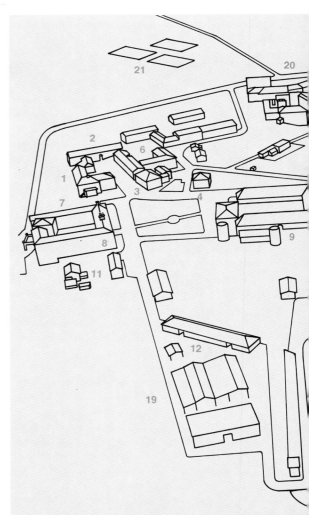

Historic stone tablets left are affixed to the "Velbanca" stallion stable. They commemorate the commencement and completion of the first stable built at Lipizza.

STABLES AND FACILITIES

We have already learned how Lipizza grew from the old bishops' palace and the small farming settlement. The palace was subsequently rebuilt and extended several times, and today only the west wing remains of the original buildings in the Renaissance style. Behind the palace, on the western side, there is a terraced garden. The archduke's quarters were on the first floor in the west wing. Here, too, the emperor stayed with his retinue when he came to Lipizza.

The chief stables, cisterns and horse ponds at Lipizza had been built and the courtyard fenced in by 1585. It was then that the administrator Franz Jurko was able to report to the archduke that a base had been laid for starting the stud.

It is interesting to note that the earliest stalls were erected not at their existing location at the center of Lipizza but on the right-hand side of the present entrance to Lipizza from Sežana, where the original foundations, surrounding walls, horse troughs and the old Fontane, which also formed the center point of the original farming settlement at Lipizza, can still be seen.

The first new building at the stud, erected in 1703, was the vaulted stable, or Velbanca, for the breeding stallions. It still stands today. The inscription on the fine stone arch above the entrance is dedicated to the Emperors Leopold I and Joseph I:

> Questa 1703 stalla FV
> Fabr: Ta soto il Gov. RE
> G: Andrea Rainer GSN.

A further inscription is cut into the crossbeam of the porch:

> Leopoldo I Plo orbl Caesare Imperante
> Josepho In Imicos Debellante

A tablet has also been hung inside the stable, stating that it was built in 1705. It reads,

> Qsta stalla FV
> FABRTA SOTO IL: GOVRE
> GIO: GASPARO NICOLETTI Q:ANT°
> G: ANDREA RAINER CSNO

The Velbanca is a long, spacious, airy vaulted hall with large windows on the southern side. It is 130 feet long and is divided into ten boxes of 16' × 13' each.

At the other side of the courtyard, opposite the palace, a long, single-story building stands on a retaining wall of north-south di-

The portal to the "Velbanca" stallion stable. The Latin inscription on the cross-beam reads, in translation, "When the Emperor Leopold I reigned and Joseph I slew his enemies, 1704."

rection. This was the site of a stable for workhorses, a coach house and the administrator's dwelling, which was later converted to a veterinary unit. The Italians altered the entire building in 1937 and installed apartments. There are two cisterns in the building's courtyard, one of which is well preserved and stands in front of the present saddlery. A small church dedicated to St. Anthony, protector of horses, stands by the road to the castle next to the former chaplaincy (now a restaurant). The church is of the traditional Gothic Karst type, with characteristic bell tower above the entrance, and it is one of the oldest buildings at Lipizza, having been mentioned in 1658.

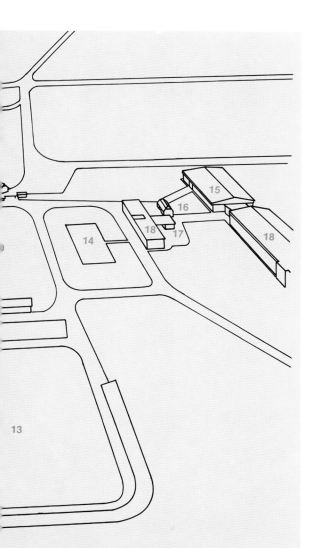

Plan of the Lipizza Stud:
1 – Palace with museum; 2 – Velbanca stallions stable; 3 – Guesthouse; 4 – Church of St. Anthony; 5 – Maestoso Hotel; 6 – Apartments; 7 – Club Hotel; 8 – Stud management offices; 9 – Brood mares stables; 10 – Paddock; 11 – Smithy and wheelwright's shop; 12 – Colts' stall; 13 – Exercise yard; 14 – Riding ground; 15 – Riding Hall; 16 – Coach house; 17 – Tack room; 18 – Stables for riding horses; 19 – Hay store; 20 – Swimming pool; 21 – Tennis courts.

Below: The Laufstala brood mares' stable, built early in the Nineteenth Century after the Napoleonic Wars. The mares are at liberty both day and night; only in the morning are they tied for feeding and grooming.

Opposite: The Velbanca, an imposing vaulted stable 130 feet long, with ten boxes for the noblest of the service-stallions, is at right.

By order of the emperor Leopold I, religious instruction was to be given and daily service held here in the Slovene language exclusively.

After the French left in 1805-6, and Lipizza entered its period of greatest prosperity, new buildings — stables, manege and residential dwellings — became necessary.

The buildings had to be solidly built but not cost too much. First, new large stables had to be built for the horses, as well as a riding school so they could be exercised in all kinds of weather. Three stables were therefore erected, in a regular square, to the southeast of the Palace and are known by the locals as the "borjač" or "brjač" or "barjač" block. The stables formed the largest single building in the entire neighborhood for its time. Today it still serves as the main stables for mares and stallions. The stables are in an open plan, 150 feet long, 30 feet wide and 15 feet high, with

The floors in all the stables were originally of compacted earth. Between the three stables is the main courtyard, the "borjač," where, during poor weather, the mares with their foals, or the foals alone, were exercised. It has been the rule in the stables since time immemorial that the first stable is reserved for young stallions, from weaning until breaking. The second stable houses mares in foal, young fillies, mares after foaling and the foals, who stay until weaned. The third stable is for fillies only.

Along the side opposite the second stable (and parallel to it) is the roofed-in manege, closing the courtyard on the southern side. It has an access to the courtyard at either end through iron gates. The manege is 100 feet long, 40 feet wide and 13 feet high. It contains only one large exercising area. A tablet appears on the northern side of the building with the inscription:

large windows. Halfway along each side wall is an enormously wide, tall door, always open. Only a wooden bar at breast height prevents the horses from escaping. Shallow stone mangers line the walls for grain; the horses are tied to them only when fed. At the southern end of the stable is a room for the groom and for tackle and fodder.

Franciscus Josephus I
Imperator Austriae
MDCCCLII [1852]

To the right on the western side of the vaulted stable, is an access to the higher level. Here lies a further set of buildings fronted by a large courtyard which the locals call the Riding School. It is about 130 feet long and 65 feet wide. On the right-

Morning gallop across the wide meadows of Lipizza.
The horses are usually put out to graze only after the
hay-making. Maintaining a humus cover is one of the
chief agricultural tasks at Lipizza.

Bottom: Brood mares on the lush Karst pasture.

hand side, to the south of the range, stands a large, old, square-shaped building, erected in 1727 in Late Baroque style. It was originally intended as a grain store and was consequently known as the Magazine. To the right of the Magazine are single-storyed dwelling houses running in a south-north direction and then at right-angles to the east. These are residential houses, numbers 14 and 15 on the plan.

Together they form the Quarters where grooms and ostlers used to live. Once these houses were probably stables as well; number 14 was the smithy and number 15 the vet's office, while the hay-barn called the Fenil used to stand next to it.

The Italians converted the former vet's office and smithy into apartments in 1938 and added another story. The fact that the court yard is called the Riding School and that the vet's office and smithy were formally located here seems to indicate that the existing houses used to be stables for the horses.

There are still two wells in the courtyard. To the east of the vet's office stood a single-story building, still a stable in the mid-1800s. The Italians converted it in 1927, increased its height and built apartments there as well.

On the left along the tree-lined avenue to Bazovica is a large open-fronted building where a smithy and carpentry shop were formerly located. The old forge can still be seen beneath the open saddle-back roof. Beneath this building is a long stable, built in 1819. On its eastern side, behind the present smithy and carpentry shop, is the walled yard, now used for exercising foals.

The last stable to be built by the Austrians was erected in 1898 for the Golden Jubilee of the emperor Franz Josef I. The stable was intended for horses while training and was therefore called the Adaptation *(Ab-richtung).* A room at each end of the building held tackle and there was also an area for preparing fodder in the middle, between the two parts of the stable. There were

stands for horses, with a few boxes in each part. An open riding ring in front of the stable was installed by the Italians; it was here that horses were trained in fine weather, and dressage and show-jumping competitions were also held.

After the Second World War, the stables and other structures at Lipizza fell into disrepair; the meadows and pasture were left untended and the forests badly thinned. Before any horses could be returned or the stud reinstated, the stables had to be repaired as best they could, to provide at least basic accommodation for the first inmates.

A large riding school was built in 1973, measuring 200' × 65' with 1,100 seats for the public. Here shows are held in the traditional manner but it is also used for training purposes and as a school for tourists.

A new stable was built in 1980 for horses during training, with sixty boxes, and a smaller shed of 130 × 65 intended chiefly for schooling horses and riders.

First overleaf: The herds spend the summer months in the cool shade of the centuries-old holm oaks. The trees are very carefully looked after in order to create stable vegetation on the formerly waste Karst soil. The trees on these wooded meadows are purposely thinned to ensure suitable undergrowth for good pasturing.

Second overleaf: Two mares tête-a-tête.

Third overleaf: The horse herd at Lipizza on its summer grazing at Odolina.

BREEDING

At the end of 1947 there were twenty-three breeding horses at Lipizza, and the reconstruction of the original herd had begun. The stud was taken over by the Federal Ministry of Agriculture together with the farms at Prestranek, Bilje, Poček and Škulje which had once belonged to it. The rebuilding work at Lipizza itself, and at Škulje, was largely completed by the end of 1949. Eleven brood mares from the Incencdvor Stud near Ilok, but originally from Demir Kapija, arrived on May 12, 1948. The Ministry allotted fifty-four horses to Lipizza in 1949, including not only Lipizzaners but also some Arabs. This breeding material proved to be very pure and of high quality, so that a good basis was soon formed for re-establishing the stud.

By 1950, Lipizza again possessed almost as many horses as during the Italian administration. It was with these horses, most of them original and pure-blooded Lipizzaners, that breeding was to be recommenced at Lipizza; no simple task, because the horses had been selected neither for appearance nor for working qualities. A great deal of work had to be done to put the stud back on its feet.

As already mentioned, the major problem was finding good, dependable breeding stallions to impart their superior genetic features to descendants. Particular attention was therefore paid to selectivity — a large numer of stallions were tried out to find which could produce good offspring.

1

The breeding stallions and brood mares used for breeding at Lipizza today. At left, the stallions Conversano Wera III (1), Maestoso Allegra XXII (2), Pluto Canissa IV (3), Siglavy Gaeta XII (4), Neapolitano Thais XXIII (5) and Neapolitano Allegra XXII (6). Below and right: The brood mares Slatka XVI (1), Thais XXIII (2), Allegra XXVI (3), Wera XI (4), Bonadea VIII (5) and Samira XIII (6).

2

2

3

4

5

4

6

6

One stallion which met the requirement was 1116 Conversano Gaeta. Subsequently the stallions were repeatedly exchanged with other Yugoslav studs, but those which became justly famous for their progeny were 650 Siglavy Savica, 188 Favory Sana I and Conversano Dubovina. The position with the brood mares was similar, if not quite so critical. To improve the herd, four brood mares were purchased from the Italian Monte Maggiore Stud in 1955.

The stud's goals in breeding was discussed deeply and at length. The decisive question concerned the type of Lipizzaner to be bred at Lipizza, bearing in mind that Lipizza was the home stud for the breed. The strong, heavily-built type of horse popular with the Italian administration between the wars was abandoned, as it had departed completely from the classic type associated with the former Imperial Stud.

On the other hand, there seemed little point in aiming for the classic type of the baroque era, as in those days the Lipizzaners were produced largely only for institutions specializing in the traditional styles of the haute école. Now only one such institution remained and that used the Piber Stud as its own source.

The breeders of the time therefore instituted a policy of differential breeding. However, this period was unfavorable for horse-breeding generally. There was increasingly less call for horses by the army and agriculture, and this hit Lipizza, with its pattern of general breeding, particularly hard. By the end of the Sixties, the stud faced a severe financial crisis. In 1959, when the stud had 10 breeding stallions, 40 brood mares and 86 colts and fillies – 136 horses altogether – a start was made in

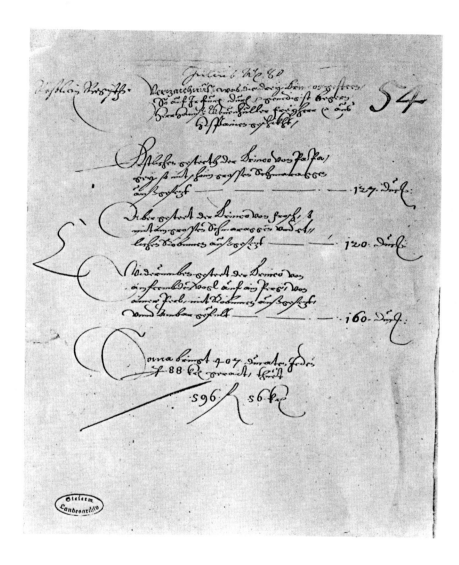

Facsimile of an account dating from 1580 for the purchase of three Spanish stallions ("Brincos").

reducing the numbers by selling them. Serious thought was given to closing the stud altogether. Questions were asked even in Parliament in Vienna, and protests appeared in the world Press. A year later, at the stud's 380th anniversary, an organised campaign was mounted to keep the stud intact. President Tito, who visited Lipizza in June that year, took an interest in the stud and was ultimately responsible for its survival. After these vicissitudes the stud revived. It now began to work towards three important objectives.

First, breeding was stabilized and extended.

A clearly defined policy was adopted of breeding and selection for an original Lipizzaner of the classic type with a slightly larger frame, a more pronounced stride, and stronger withers to cater to the needs of the sportsmen and of the traditional riding school in particular.

Secondly, greater emphasis was laid on the traditional principles of the Spanish Riding School and the Driving School, to improve the criteria for assessing the merits of breeding animals and their selection, and at the same time to foster the tradition of the classic arts of riding and driving. The sport-

ing aspects of horsemanship and dressage were also developed, as a discipline.

Finally, the stud was opened up to the outside world, which meant introducing facilities for tourists, recreational riding and driving.

To do justice to all these aims and, especially, to its new breeding objectives, the stud had to rethink its breeding policy. While tested stallions were already being used for breeding, efforts were also made to gain new blood – in particular, by purchasing the stud stallion Maestoso Bonavoja from the Piber Stud in Austria. This

The small Church of St. Anthony was built in 1650, first mentioned in 1658 and renovated in 1979. Church services there have always been held in the Slovene language.
The old post coach at Lipizza, which formerly carried the post between Trieste and Vienna, now stands in the foyer of the Club Hotel, opened in 1980.

stallion, which serviced the stud from 1973 to 1980, left many valuable offspring. The same may be said of the stallion 305 Conversano Dubovina which was used for breeding at Lipizza from 1972 to 1979. An exchange of stallions was made in 1981 between Lipizza and Piber.

The kind of attention paid to selecting stallions was now devoted to the work of selecting brood mares. Only those mares which corresponded to the desired type were used for breeding — those averaging 16 hands, with well developed withers, a head shaped according to the rule book, and an extended gait and correct movements.

Years of breeding experience at the stud, views and opinions expressed by international breeders at the stud's 400th anniversary and the success that the Lipizzaners gained in international dressage competitions formed the basis of an individual breeding program at Lipizza from which it could develop its own special objectives.

Today a modified Lipizzaner of the classic type is bred with a slightly larger frame, pronounced withers with a good saddle position, a low, spacious gait, and a noble, regularly formed head with a fine neck.

The first trials take place after one year's schooling. The features considered are temperament, character, constitution, performance, will to work, learning ability during riding, intelligence, utilization of fodder, the mechanics of movement and correct walk, trot and gallop. Stallions and mares who achieve less than sixty percent of the total points possible go to the tourist stable or are sold. Young mares achieving more than seventy percent of the total are transferred to the breeding herd.

Fillies which successfully pass the performance test and fully meet the requirements of the Lipizzaner as bred at Lipizza are selected for breeding at age five and are covered by a breeding stallion meeting the stud's standards.

Now, 405 years after the foundation of the stud and 31 years following its rebirth, we may well ask about the situation of the stud at Lipizza and its prospects for the future.

We can say in all certainty that Lipizza's wounds have healed; in fact, breeding has regained the position the stud enjoyed prior to its break-up at the end of the First World War.

Partly due to lack of suitable breeding material and partly to revitalise the stock, so much new blood has been introduced into the breed in recent years that, both at the present time and in the foreseeable future, there is not the slightest risk of excessive inbreeding or degeneration.

In assessing the performance of its breeding stallions, in continuing old-established traditions and in its approach to dressage and driving, the stud will continue to be guided by the classic rules of haute école. Only this will ensure the successful breeding of the Lipizzaner at Lipizza and the promotion of the Lipizzaner throughout the world.

Above: The fifteenth century Rectory stands between the Church of St. Anthony and the Velbanca vaulted stable. From 1960 to 1971 it was Lipizza's only guesthouse.

Above right: The façade of the only part of the Bishop's Palace remaining from the time the Stud was formed. Now it houses the Stud management offices.

Right: Tourists return from a full day's tour, tired but happy. The first concern is now for the horses, which must be returned to their stables, drenched, groomed and fed. In 1984 more than 2,000 horse-lovers spent several weeks' riding holidays in Lipizza.

Left: An old chestnut tree guards the entrance to the courtyard of the Bishop's Palace. The old Rectory, is at right in the picture, while the entrance to the Velbanca vaulted stable can be seen at the back and, at left, the façade of the remaining part of the Palace.

A MECCA FOR HORSE LOVERS

Above and right: Lipizza's first hotel, the Maestoso, built in 1971. It has 150 beds, restaurants, discotheque, nightclub and swimming pool. A Lipizzaner carriage-and-pair is available to guests for exhilarating drives around the Stud.

Left: The inner court of the new Club Hotel is roofed with glass and filled with flowers. The hotel is intended for equestrian guests exclusively.

Below and below left: Pleasures of the Karst: quiet, recuperation and conversation among friends over ham, cheese and red Teran wine in a typical Karst cellar or in the old Hostelry at Lipizza.

Steps were taken early on to implement the stud's second objective — to introduce and develop a classic riding school, dressage and the art of driving. The famous specialist on horses and horsemanships, Akarov, had already formed an equestrian group at Lipizza in 1952 which was intended to re-introduce the art of riding according to the principles of the Spanish Riding School. After only a few years' work, remarkable success was achieved, and as early as 1956 the Lipizza team was able to display the easier elements of the classic riding school. The same year Alfons Pečovnik, then a horseman at Lipizza, gained second place in the medium class with the mare Thais XI in the open event at the International Championships in Vienna.

By 1957, twenty-six stallions and mares were being trained in the riding and driving school at Lipizza. The specialist Milan Belanović, then appointed head of the Riding School, continued Akarov's work. The results showed in successful appearances at Aachen, Verona and Lipizza. However, despite its successes, the school had to suspend its work in 1960 as a result of financial difficulties. The greater number of stallions

and mares already broken in had to be sold and their riders had to seek work abroad. Only in 1973 was the school re-introduced at Lipizza, when the Czech trainer Emil Šulgan came to the stud and began working with some of the original riders, most of whom were working at Lipizza as stable hands, and with some newcomers. The stock of dressage stallions had to be built up again, starting once more with young

Morning training as a carriage-and-pair for brood mares along an avenue at Lipizza.

playing simpler elements of the traditional art. But they were soon held twice a day and included the more difficult elements of traditional horsemanship; Flying Change of Leg à Tempo, the Walk, Piaffe, and the Passage and Levade. Training of the first stallions on the long rein began in 1978.

The riders at Lipizza also began to take part in international dressage competitions. The Lipizza Stud organised its first interna-

colts. Šulgan was succeeded in 1975 as trainer by Lieutenant-Colonel Djordje Petrovič, recently retired as head of the School of Cavalry. The group with which he began to work systematically and consistently included fifteen horsemen with a range of previous skills, and more than twenty colts and five stallions able to meet the requirements of the haute école. In just a few years, Petrović was able to prove his worth.

The displays of the classic art of riding, which were soon to become an attraction for visitors to Lipizza, had been held regularly since 1970. Initially they were mounted by a small number of horses dis-

Above: Four-in-hand with brood mares from Lipizza competing at Cremona in Italy. At below, cohesion in the team, harmony in travel.

tional dressage championship in 1974, the events including a Saint George and Intermédiaire I. Twenty-one horses took part from West Germany, Austria, Rumania, Italy and Switzerland and, for the first time, riders from Lipizza.

In subsequent years, the stud continued to hold international dressage championships. In addition from 1976 on the team regularly attended the Balkan Dressage Championships with their Lipizzaner stallions, taking second or third places.

As already mentioned, Lipizza had encouraged the introduction and development of all kinds of riding for sport and pleasure, with an eye to the tourist. This of course in-

cluded making full use of the natural advantages of the area including Lipizza's abundant historical interest and beauty. However, the paramount attraction was the Lipizzaners being put through their paces.

The Great Riding Hall at Lipizza, built in 1973, is used twice daily from April to October for demonstrations of the classical riding school. The stands can seat 1,100 spectators. It is here that most of people experience for the first time thrill of the Lipizzaner display, perfectly formed, silvery-white horses beneath perfectly seated riders, greeting the guests on their smooth entry at the walk along the center line of the track (above), at a strong, extended trot along the diagonals (left), or in the Pas de Deux, a movement of the highest elegance and precision bottom left.

Bellow: Elegance and precision do not come by themselves. The price paid is intensive, unrelenting training of horse and rider, often on the track during the silent hours.

This approach was necessary for two reasons. It was clear after 1945 that the stud could not operate profitably through the breeding and possible sale of its horses alone, without substantial government subsidies. After all, a generous Imperial Court and a privileged nobility no longer existed. Furthermore, Lipizza's historic past, its splendid situation and the proximity of the much-frequented coasts of Istria were so captivating that they insisted on being put to good use. Therefore, after obtaining permission to put the famous horses and historic stabling on view, the stud was officially opened to the public in 1960. In that first year, Lipizza attracted only a few hundred visitors. Ten years later visitors numbered 30,000; by 1975 this had shot up to as many as 150,000. In addition to viewing the old stables and the magnificent imperial horses, there was a growing interest in watching short displays of the classic art of riding.

The closeness of Trieste and its popular beaches, the thousands of people from Western Europe eager for a chance to ride one of the noble Lipizzaners, and above all, the large numbers of horsemen and women wishing to spend their vacations riding in Lipizza – all this demanded the systematic promotion of riding as a sport. In 1960, the number of hours that guests spent riding was 540; by 1970 this had increased to 7,000; and by 1975 the number had doubled to 14,000 hours.

Naturally, this explosion in tourist traffic meant that more hotel beds and accompanying services were required. A new hotel was therefore built in 1971 and named after the famous Lipizzaner stallion Maestoso.

Left: The Great Quadrille is always a fascinating sight, with many complex figures briskly performed. Voltes large and small, the figure-of-eight, the change on the full and half defile (below) or from the circle, changes of tempo, walk, trot and gallop, traverses (left) and displays on the long rein (bottom) — all these are anchored in the tradition of the Haute Ecole of the Spanish Riding School.

Because the number of visitors and riders continued to increase, a large new riding school capable of holding an audience of 1,100 was built at Lipizza in 1973. During the tourist season (April to October) displays within the classical riding school range are held here twice a day. As at the Spanish Riding School, the Lipizzaner stallions are put through their paces, young horses showing their natural gait, the older horses displaying the gait and tricks of the haute école, including the long rein and the Airs above the Ground school.

The new building is also used for training young stallions in haute école and sporting dressage; and as a school for guest riders.

Nearly all buildings at the stud, especially the stables for breeding horses, were in very poor condition after, the war, as there was no money available to maintain them. The decision to renovate all the stables as the stud's 400th anniversary approached is therefore all the more understandable. The roofs, façades and interiors of all the stables from 1 to 11, several outbuildings, and also the small old church at Lipizza were renovated through and through.

As the number of riding horses and the number of young stallions participating in the dressage school continued to increase, the available space in the stables soon became cramped. To deal with this problem, a new stable with sixty boxes was built in 1979, with a 200- by 65-foot riding school attached.

It soon became apparent at the Hotel Maestoso that horse-lovers and riding enthusiasts liked to lead their own lives. What they sought was peace and quiet and, especially, contact with the horses. Consequently, another hotel, the "Hotel Club," was built in 1979, intended especially for guests coming to Lipizza to principally for the horses and to experience the magic of Lipizza's natural beauty from horseback. A racecourse measuring 140 yards by 75 yards was completed the same year. It now copes with all the major equestrian events and can hold 10,000 spectators.

The facilities were further improved in 1979 with the addition of four tennis courts, along with a building designed for an unusual purpose – a Marriage Hall where couples may take their vows in a splendid environment and with full ceremony, including coach and horses.

When we consider all the efforts and achievements of the last two decades in breeding, haute école and dressage, and in catering for the visitor, there is no denying that Lipizza was ripe for its great festival,

Below: Lipizza's riders and horses have entered for the major international dressage championships with increasing success. Here Alojz Lah rides the stallion Maestoso Monteaura in the Passage. This pair won the FEI World Cup for Dressage on May 19, 1985 at Lipizza.

the 400th anniversary of its foundation. President Tito agreed to act as its sponsor. While certain cultural and other events were held earlier as part of the 1980 anniversary, the major event was the revival of the old mail coach on the Vienna-Trieste run. Drawn by four brood mares from Lipizza, the coach picked up a bag of mail at the Hofburg in Vienna during a resounding send-off on June 6, 1980.

For Lipizza, and especially for the true heroes of the day – the Lipizzaners – the display held from August 28 to 31 and called "The Lipizzaners through Four Centuries" was the most splendid and the most important historically. For the first time in four hundred years the Lipizzaners (if only

symbolically, as six horses were loaned by each of the other studs) returned to their cradle, the place of origin. Stallions from The Spanish Riding School in Vienna, where 245 years previously the Lipizzaners from Lipizza had made themselves a name and won a place in the classic art of riding, came to Lipizza for the first time, setting the ceremonial framework which such a

The international flow of visitors to Lipizza offers workers at the stud an excellent opportunity to exchange information, ask questions and discuss the fine points of routine work. Horse care, veterinary medicine and the success of haute école and dressage riders are all subjects of debate. Health and successful breeding are of particular interest.

noble and ancient breed truly deserves.

The exhibition by the Lipizzaners, in which all of Europe's Lipizzaner studs participated, underlined the fact that breeding aims, and consequently the present-day type of Lipizzaner horse after four hundred years of breeding, differed widely from one Lipizzaner stud to another. An international commission of horse-breeders chaired by Hubert Rudofsky, the great connoisseur and doyen of the horse-riding world, confirmed that the groups displayed by the Lipizza and Piber Studs had achieved the highest level and also came closest to the traditional type of Lipizzaner. For Lipizza and its breeding methods this recognition was undoubtedly satisfying.

The Lipizza Stud has been given its own veterinary service to promote the general health of the horses, take prophylactic measures and, especially, to take care of hooves. In recent years there has been little sickness and none at all of an infectious nature.

The extraordinary resistance of the horses at Lipizza has been put to the test during the stud's repeated removals in its four hundred years of history, when losses were kept to a minimum despite demanding cross-country treks in cold conditions.

Numerous experts have reported on the toughness and resistance of the Lipizzaners, their imperviousness to diseases of the tendons, joints and hooves, and the rare occurrence of lung disease. The famous expert on horses, Count Wrangel, once wrote, "Better health than that of the horses at Lipizza could hardly be desired. Local sickness is unknown, bone defects such as spavin, for example, and others are extremely rare. Mortality is very low. The sharp *bora* wind tends rather to increase than to reduce their power of resistance. The heat and shortage of water in high summer have no detrimental effects on the horses' health, as they are used to it from birth."

Since 1979 there have been occasional outbreaks of colic and influenza, and only few cases of strangles *(adenitis quorum)*. It has been the practice since 1978 to innoculate breeding animals and young horses at the

The St. Hubert's Hunt is only one of the varied range of leisure activities at Lipizza. The "pack" below follows the "fox" (above, the stallion Favory Sana) through woods and pasture.

Opposite: Visitors to Lipizza may spend several days riding in the neighborhood of the stud, perhaps going to see the Illyrian fortress Predjamski Grad near Postojna.

Today, no doubts remain about the genetic continuity of the Lipizzaner as a pedigree. The Lipizzaner is here to stay at Lipizza.

Tourism is the element which now ranks a close second to horse-breeding as the most important activity. The huge influx of tourists could present dangers for Lipizza as a stud; however, breeding rules are carefully observed and limits placed on the requirements made of the stock. A strict and clear dividing line between breeding and tradition on one hand and services for tourists on the other has produced very good results. Nowadays the income from tourist traffic may be regarded as an essential requirement; and a stimulus for the successful development of quality breeding.

stud against colic and the brood mares against infectious miscarriage *(rhinopneumonitis)*.

As already mentioned the local Karst hay is still the basis of the feed. Hay is harvested on the stud's own 370 acres of hayfields and on 74 acres at the Odolina Estate near Materija. All other components of the feed, such as wheat, corn, straw, minerals and

vitamins mixed into the fodder must be purchased.

The extraordinarily high fertility at Lipizza during the past ten years — in some years as high as ninety-five percent — is worth noting. There has been a downward trend, however, in the last three years when pregnancies were achieved in sixty to seventy percent of cases.

There is no doubt that Lipizza will continue to safeguard its cultural and historic values and will succeed in retaining the wonder of its white horse for generations.

The breeding of these oldest of Europe's purebred horses goes back more than four hundred years. To trace the breed's origins would mean traveling thousands of years. The ancestors of the present-day Lipizzaner include the chariot horses of the Hittites, the stamping steeds of Homer's Iliad, the horses portrayed among the equestrian groups in the frieze on the Parthenon at Athens, relief sculptures of the School of Phidias, the stallions of Aquileia and the Quadriga horses of the Romans. But that is not all. Even the horses of the Muslim conquerors, the Arabs and Berbers, have a part in the Lipizzaner ancestry, as do the Iberian horses, the noble Castilians and Andalusians, Genettes and Villanos; and

to a skilled painter or serve a king as his favorite steed. Neither as light as the Berber nor as heavy as the Neapolitan, they possess the best qualities of both breeds. The Genettes have a fine and energetic pace, a high trot, a most remarkable gallop and are extraordinarily fast at speed. They are not very large generally, yet you will find hardly a more noble nor courageous horse."

Where Europe and Africa are divided only by the Straits of Gibraltar, the Berber developed as the native breed of the African continent. Springing from the Numidian horse descended from the original African breed, brought eastwards in the seventh century as the charger of the descendants of

THE LIPIZZANERS

Descended from breeds already gone, the Andalusians and the Neapolitans, toughened by the blood of the local Karst horse and lent grace and strength by the noble Arab, the Lipizzaners are the result of 400 years' breeding for purity.

the full-blooded fiery Neapolitans and the undemanding, tough horses of the Karst. The pairing of strength and grace, agility and endurance, courage and gentleness led to the ideal — the imperial horse, the horse of kings and emperors, the horse of the gods. So even in ancient times the seeds had been sown of this horse which still commands our admiration today.

In prehistoric times, Spain possessed outstanding white horses, famous beyond its frontiers for their speed and special gait. Since the Phoenicians landed there about 1500 B.C., oriental blood has run in the veins of these horses. "Made fecund by the wind," is how the Roman historian Justinus described the Iberian breed. These forebears of the Andalusians were highly esteemed at the games and races of Greece and Rome. Jacques de Solleysel, chief stable master of the French Court wrote in 1664, "They are extremely fine horses, the most suited of all breeds to stand as models

the Prophet Muhammad, and then refined by the Arabs, the Berber strongly influenced the development of the Iberian horse. In its original form, its large head, Roman nose, long ears, short thick neck, coarse mane and tail, thick-set croup and ungainly dock — features which distinguished it clearly from the related Arab — the Berber has died out. Yet, through the Andalusian, it has left the Lipizzaner one of the most marked features of the breed — a pronounced Roman nose. Over the centuries the classic Lipizzaner, with the exception of the Arabic Siglavy strain, has clearly carried this feature of its African ancestor. Perhaps it was through the famous horse market at Calpe, Gibraltar, through which a constant flow of oriental blood reached the Spanish peninsula, that in the eighth century the conquering Moors introduced more Arab blood into the Iberian breeds. The Muslim conquerors sought to endow their light, oriental horses with the endurance necessary to withstand attacks by

Colors of the baroque,
the classic Roman nose
noble shapes and gracious gaits:
the portrait of a Lipizzaner herd.

Mares at Lipizza. Painting by Julius, Baron Blaas, 1898. Spanish Riding School, Vienna.

proud show horse of its time. With its pliant limbs and delicate movements, the Andalusian combined a lively, fiery temperament with a great docility, obedience and good will, all properties which its descendants have inherited in abundance.

While the Genette, with its high proportion of oriental blood, was regarded as the lighter, finer Spanish steed, the Villanos, more common in the north, were the type of horse to carry a knight rather than pull a plough. Large and strong, it was more suited for war service and heavy duty. The beauty and agility of the southern horse were united with the strength and patience of the northern. These properties, together with their naturally high action, the Spanish Step, can be clearly traced today in the Lipizzaner.

Right: A group of modern Andalusians near Seville, the former breeding ground of the old Spanish horse. Today's Andalusian shows little resemblance to his ancestors. He is, after all, not a direct descendant; his ancestor was of the same breed as the Lipizzaner. The black Friesian, on the other hand, is beyond doubt descended from the old Spanish horse, as the neck arched in the Spanish step clearly testifies.

The old Spanish horse, the Andalusian, no longer exists in its original form. The breeding of Andalusians reached its peak in the fifteenth and sixteenth centuries, and the royal studs of the period left their mark on the development of many European breeds. However the breeding of Andalusians gradually declined. We have the Carthusian

Above: A typical Villano, with an Andalusian knight. The influence of Nordic blood is unmistakable among the heavy knightly horses. The difference from the prancing Genette is similarly obvious. The Villano is stronger and more muscular, better suited to war service and tournaments.

the heavier horses of the Christian knights. On the other hand, paladins of the north desired to impart to their cumbersome horses some of the agility and dash of the oriental horse. That was the origin of the Andalusian − the tall build, the neck majestically curved, the head noble and proud, the limbs strong and sinewy, the movements gracious and showy and the vitality and courage inexhaustible. Its elastic gait, in which the front leg is raised with the knee bent at a right angle, distinguished it as the

Above, an Andalusian mare with dark mane and her foal graze in Coto de Donana, the nature conservancy area in the Guadalquivir Estuary. Here too, the foals are born dark, developing their white hide in the course of time. Head and neck clearly show how far removed the present Andalusian is from the image of its forefathers.

monks, who opposed all crosses to strengthen the breed, to thank for the fact that the pure-blooded strains remained intact. The vestiges of this once important breed remain in the neighborhood of the old monastery in the province of Cordoba and in a few other private studs around Seville and Cadiz — all of them centers of present-day breeding of Andalusians. They are called "Cartujanos," i.e. "Carthusians." Along with the modern Andalusian, they have gained acceptance as true, full-blooded near cousins of this oldest breed in the stud book, the "Pura raza espanola."

Their aura of nobility, good breeding and

King Philip III of Spain seated on an Andalusian horse. The horse is commencing a Levade: the haunches are bent, forearms lifted. Compared with the Lipizzaner, this shape is lighter and less encumbered, recalling the "Dance of the Andalusian Horses" of which countless poets sang.

beauty, as well as their high action have been imparted to the present-day Andalusian and its Portuguese cousin, the Lusitanian. These properties endow the horse with a unique elegance and act as a reminder that the Andalusian of the twentieth century and the Lipizzaner are still closely related.

The Arab

The Arab has had its influence on the origins of the Lipizzaner breed through the Andalusian and the Neapolitan. However, an even more direct crossing took place at a later period. There is hardly a domesticated breed of horse that has escaped this method of enriching the native population. All of them were in need of the "salt of horse breeding" which the Arab could offer them. Even today the Arab is regarded as the natural source for enrichment of the equine race.

The Koran states, "When the Creator wished to create the horse, he said to the Wind, I shall have thee bear a being who shall carry my worshippers. This being shall be loved and regarded by all my slaves. It shall be feared by all who fail to heed my commandments. And he created the horse and said to it, I have made thee without equal. All the treasures of the earth lie between thine eyes. Thou shalt cast mine enemies beneath thy hooves, but my friends thou shalt bear on thy back. This shall be the seat from which prayers ascend to me. Over the whole earth thou shalt be fortunate and preferred before all other creatures. In thee shall be the love of the Lord of the Earth. Thou shalt fly without wings and conquer without a sword."

The Traditions go on to say, "I have created thee and named thee ‹Faras.› I have given thee my favor before all other beasts of burden and made thee their lord. Success and good fortune are woven into thy forelock; prosperity rests on thy back and riches accompany thee wherever thou goest. Without wings I command thee to fly, thou art created for persecution and flight. And thou shalt bear men who make my name great, and thou shalt make my name great through them."

As generation tells generation in the tents of the Bedouin, the son of Abraham, their ancestor Ishmael was the first to ride a horse. According to legend the angel Gabriel said to them, "This noble creature with the dark skin and flashing eyes is a gift from the living God who shall be to thee a companion in the wilderness and reward thee as you have not turned to heathen gods but remained true to the faith of thy Father Abraham." The mare was pregnant and gave birth to a colt. These two are the origin of the most famous of the Arab horses.

That the Muslim armies succeeded in spreading Islam was due primarily to the horses, these wind-born "drinkers of the air." Tradition tells us that on accepting

Above: The Holy Ferdinand, King of Castille and Leon, in the gold-encrusted armor of the sixteenth century, receives the key to the City of Seville as a symbol of power. Ferdinand had reconquered Cordoba in 1236 and Seville, with its important port, in 1248. This is a 16th century miniature.

five magnificent mares given to him by Yemenite tribes when receiving his doctrines, the Prophet Muhammad was so overcome by the beauty of the horses that he said, "Be thou blessed, oh daughter of the wind." The wind was regarded as breath from the soul of Allah and that is why Arab horses are known as the "Daughters of the wind" and "Drinkers of the air." They were a gift from God, true companions of man in the desert, and it is not surprising that Muhammad established the breeding of noble horses as a religious duty in numerous *suras* of the Koran. He issued precise instructions on breeding and promised heavenly rewards to the faithful, "As many grains of barley as thy givest thy horse, so many sins wilst thou be forgiven. Should Allah let thee enter Paradise, thou shalt find a horse of rubies with wings and it shall fly with thee wherever thou wishest to go. Every night an angel descends to every horse, kisses his forelock, and wishes the owner happiness."

Muhammad's wish that the new doctrine be brought to all the world by fire and sword could be fulfilled only with the aid of the horse. Without it, the Muslim armies could never have ridden from victory to victory. On the backs of countless thousands of horses, the sons of the desert rode into a kingdom which stretched across Egypt and North Africa as far as Spain and Southern France.

With their horses and their swords they gained an empire whose expansion was brought to a halt only in 732 A.D. at the battles of Tours and Poitiers in the heart of Europe.

The Muslim conquerors made the great leap from the northwestern tip of Africa into Europe in July 711. Their commander Tariq ordered his 25,000 men to make the crossing. Together with their horses they gathered on a mountain which they named Djebel al Tariq. An Arab name took possession of a Spanish rock. Later, it was to become Gibraltar.

From the earliest times Arabs horses were famed as the fastest, most fiery and noblest of their race. While breeding was originally restricted to the fertile crescent of Mesopotamia, Syria and the Valley of the Euphrates, in the first centuries of the present era it spread over the entire Arab peninsula. The noblest, most perfect Arabs were bred to the east of Mecca, in the highlands of the Nedjd, at an altitude of six thousand feet.

The Arab is unequalled in the nobility of its appearance and the imposing harmony of its parts, an exemplar of beauty and perfection. Its light, trim head displays the depression between forehead and nose-bone typical of the breed so that its wide nostrils appear yet bigger. The protruding eye has an enlarged, expressive and fiery effect; the fine curved neck is ribbed like a palm twig, set tall and high, merging well into the withers. The shoulders are sloped, long and neat, the withers well pronounced. The horse's overall appearance is square, with its short back and long limbs. Its fine hair gleams like silk and its movements are imbued with elasticity and elegance. The Arab's appearance is one of nobility, charm and temperament. Affection, courage, integrity, gentleness, loyalty and high performance its inner qualities which have been praised for centuries. Its characteristics are endurance, docility, fertility, longevity, good health and good spirit. The Arab has proved its extraordinary performing ability in competition with the English thoroughbred, covering nearly ninety miles from Cairo to Suez and back in barely eight hours. The Arab was still fresh on its return to Suez, while its opponent had collapsed on the way.

Today the Arab is still raised using the criteria of blood, speed and endurance. The ideals of the breeders vary. Performance and blood are regarded as the supreme criterion, beauty as a gift by the grace of Allah. Pure breeding is, and always has been, a matter of course to the Bedouin; noble blood is imperative.

THE NEAPOLITAN

Not only the Spanish but also the old Italian horse, and especially the Neapolitan, had a decisive influence on the development of the Lipizzaner breed. Many authors praised the Italian horse even before Roman times. In later centuries the Medici and other ennobled merchants imported the finest Arab horses from Syria in order to improve the local breed. These were followed by Andalusian horses which were particularly popular for breeding in the

tury, gaining a reputation for its elevated but very slow and compact stride. The high bend of the knee, the Spanish Step, secured it a place as an ideal horse for the haute école and for drawing the state coaches of princes and cardinals. Continuous wars and errors in breeding methods – crossing with Nordic rather than oriental horses – led to a steady decline in the Italian breeds. The purebred Neapolitan has now died out.

While Andalusians, Neapolitans and Arabs

northern end of the Adriatic in the ancient region known as Thrace. They were the finest and fastest horses of the time.

The Thracian horses, though like all Greek breeds inferior to those of the ancient East in stamina, were renowned for their courage and beauty. Thrace is where the piebald and spotted horses originally came from; Homer tells of speckled horses and Virgil mentions the dappled horses of Thrace. The Greeks, particularly concerned

Below: A Neapolitan, also after a print by Johann Elias Ridinger. Again, the graceful head is exaggerated, as is the swan neck. This old breed of horse was used for School riding and pulling the fine carriages of emperors and princes.

Spanisch Genett.   Genett.   Equus Hispanicus.

Opposite: A desert Arab, after a painting by Eerelman-Schoenbeck. Noble in appearance, it possesses a conspicuously fine head, expressive eyes and wide nostrils, fine mane and tail, a gracious body and clear-cut limbs.

neighborhood around Naples. In those days the Neapolitan horses were considered the best in Italy. Standing high yet gracefully, they combined docility with a fiery spirit and possessed properties which indicated their use for carriage and the riding ring. They were stronger than the Spanish Genette, maturing later, and were preferred for school riding. The Neapolitan achieved the peak of its fame in the seventeenth cen-

each contributed substantially towards shaping the Lipizzaner, the basis of the breed was still the native Karst horse. Horses had been bred on the Karst, in the area around Trieste, in antiquity and were sought-after for their dexterity, strength and endurance. The horses which formed the Quadrigas for the chariot races in ancient Rome were largely drawn from Aquileia, the flourishing Roman city at the

with maintaining the purity of their breed, paid special attention to the horse for their sacred games and for war. This included the careful keeping of a breed register. Thigh-brands helped to distinguish between the individual families. White had special significance from the earliest times; white horses were dedicated to the gods; they pulled the chariots of kings as symbolic representatives of peace and justice.

Right: This table shows the descent of the Andalusian from the Arab, Iberian and Berber breeds. The Lipizzaner breed developed from the Andalusian horse through the Karst and Neapolitan lines.

Because of their stamina, toughness, docility and sure-footedness, Karst horses were preferred for sumptering, transporting goods from the coast into the mountainous hinterland. Baron von Valvasor wrote in *The Honor of the Duchy of Carniola* published in 1689, "... and they were in high regard throughout Europe especially for their sterling quality, as they live long and endure both work and the rider at great length because they are used to it from a young age, being left to pasture on barren stone and rocks."

The principles of Roman horse-breeding, valid still in the present, were, according to Virgil: effective selection of the dam, choice of sire from the most spirited and courageous stallions, outstanding features

in the parents, accurately and scientifically recorded family trees, careful attention to the location of the stud and a continuing strengthening of the breed by the best types. There can be no doubt that discovering that excellent horses prospered on the hard Karstland, the Romans applied themselves to systematic breeding by mixing noble breeds from all parts of their empire which stretched over wide areas of Europe and as far as Asia and Africa. Hence the basis of the Karst breed, whose stallions were still being admired in the Middle Ages as horses for tournament and for war. Strength, courage, toughness and stamina, the characteristic features of the breed.

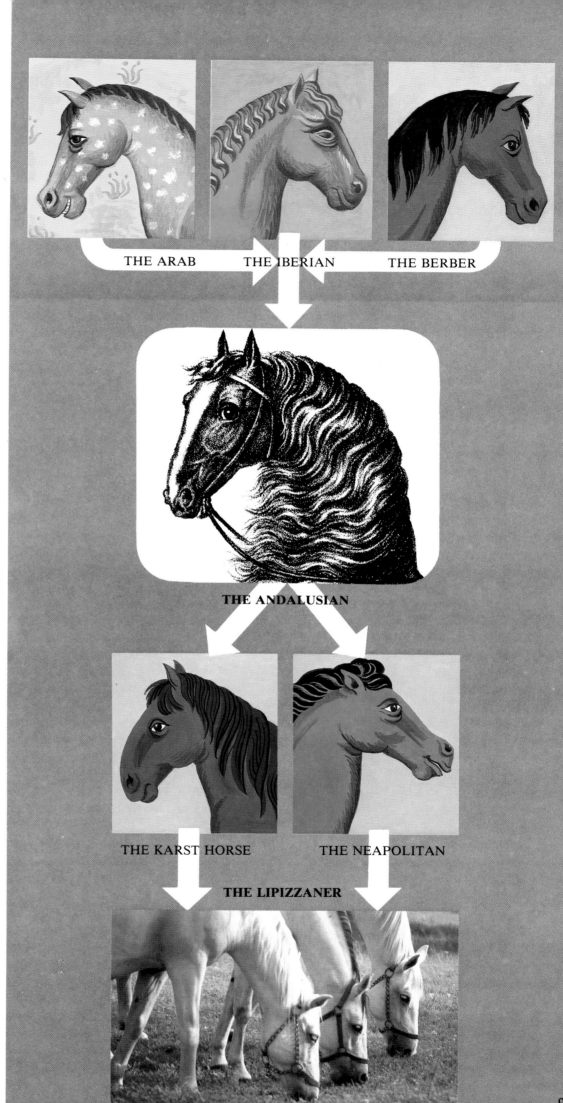

THE ARAB   THE IBERIAN   THE BERBER

THE ANDALUSIAN

THE KARST HORSE   THE NEAPOLITAN

THE LIPIZZANER

NINE HISPANIC STALLIONS AND THEIR SUCCESSORS

As we know, Baron Khevenhüller purchased nine stallions and twenty four brood mares of the old Andalusian breed in 1580 for the Court at Vienna. These Spanish horses were already important for ceremonial use at the princely courts of Europe, both as well-formed mounts and as elegant coach horses with high action. They gave their name to the Spanish Riding School,

"The Spanish horse is proud at the gallop and at the canter it is much faster than other horses ...", wrote the Duke of Newcastle. This copperplate engraving, "Horses at Pasture," is by Valentin Trichter.

first mentioned as early as 1565 as the "Horse tumbling ground" at the Hofburg Palace. Here, Spanish horses were used exclusively. Throughout Europe, every prince aimed to have his own small stud and to set up his own small royal stable, and generally invested a great deal of money and time in an attempt to accomplish this. That this costly luxury could also play a practical role is clear from the case of Count Oldenburg, who was able to persuade the commanders of approaching armies to leave his territory alone during the Thirty Years War by making discreet gifts of horses from his famous stud — some indication of how valuable these horses were at the time.

When the Viennese Court eventually decided that a new source for horses had to be found, because imports from Spain were becoming too risky, casualty-prone and expensive, the Emperor instructed his brother, the Archduke Charles II, to set up a stud which would in future supply the Court with horses of its own breeding. It shows the Archduke's percipience as a breeder that the Slovene Karst with its equestrian traditions should be selected as the location. In purchasing the "Villa of the Bishopric of Trieste" high on the Karst plateau near Sezana, which had been destroyed by the Turks, the Archduke took the first steps which were to lead the Lipizza Stud to world-wide fame. The place gave its name to the new breed that was created here, combining all the outstanding features of its ancestors. Pure-bred for more than four centuries, the horses from Lipizza were to conquer the world.

Much had to be done before the arid, dry landscape was could become the Karst Oasis of Lipizza. It was fortunate that the first Stud Master, Franz Jurko, was a horse expert of local origin. He began breeding Lipizzaners, which were then still known as "Horses of the Lipizzaner strain of the Karst breed," and was able to send the first home-bred horses to Vienna only five years after the Stud was founded. Ten years later, as many as thirty horses a year were being delivered to the Royal Stables in Graz. This

was equal to the numbers which were now being supplied to the Viennese Court. The number of brood mares then available must have been sixty to seventy. These figures rose continuously and in its heyday around 1768 the Stud had a hundred and fifty mares.

The imported Spanish stallions covered not only the similarly imported mares but also local Karst mares. We may also assume that good stallions of the Karst breed were using as sires for the Andalusian mares. After all, every effort would be made to benefit from the good local stock and combine it with the pure-bred old Spanish horses. The first crosses were so promising that they continued in this direction, with strict selection, choosing the best animals and weeding out poor material. It is a known fact that breeding is more favorably and rapidly influenced by sires who cover a large number of mares in one breeding season. In breeding Lipizzaners, therefore, more significance was attached to acquiring stallions than to purchasing mares. A mare can influence the breed only through its own necessarily limited number of foals while a stallion, depending on the number of times he is used, may pass his characteristics on to countless descendants.

In addition to the Spanish horses, stallions from neighboring Polesina were also used for breeding. Spanish imports then followed continuously. Only later, during the 18th Century, were Italian stallions of the old Italian breed from the area around Naples increasingly used. Stallions also came to Lipizza from other European studs that were similarly run with an old Spanish-old Italian base; for example the Court Stud at Kladrub in Bohemia, the Lippe-Bückeburg breeding center in Germany, and the Frederiksborg Stud in Denmark. One of these horses was the stallion Lipp, born in 1717; his descendants influenced the breed for more than a hundred years. Also important during this period was the Spanish stallion Cordova, imported in 1701. Many valuable brood mares can be traced back to him. The two service-

Ein Spanisches Pferd.   Cheval d'Espagne.   Equus Hispanicus.

stallions acquired in 1749, Montorodo and Toscanella, a dun and a piebald, passed on these fashionable colors of the time particularly effectively; they too, continued to have a decisive influence. Only at a much later date was Arab blood crossed in. That is how the Lipizzaner became the horse we know today – medium-sized, rather compact, with broad, deep chest, high shoulders, standing fourteen and three quarters to fifteen and a quarter hands, and with a high-set, strongly muscular, finely borne neck and unprominent withers passing over into a long, powerful back with muscular croup. The expressive head with the occasional Roman nose has an air of nobility. Trim, relatively short limbs show well-formed joints. The hoofs are hard and well-shaped, as one would expect from the rocky Karst soil. A lively temperament and high gait round off this picture of a horse of noble character.

THE BREEDING RULE BOOK OF 1658
AND FURTHER DEVELOPMENT

The Lipizzaner breed may be likened to a blood bank in which departed breeds such as the Andalusian, Neapolitan and Danish Frederiksborger continue to exist. The Breeding Rule Book (issued as far back as 1658) and a set of stud rules with twenty-three clauses, even today regarded as authoritative, and subsequent strict adherence to the breeding line, ensured that Europe's oldest man-bred horse has remained pure for four hundred years. As the old Spanish horse also carries a trace of the heavy Pyrenean horse, and the old Karst breed tends towards solidity and heaviness, there was always the risk, when breeding constantly to type without the admixture of ennobling blood, that the horses might become coarser and heavier like their ancestors. In the eighteenth century the names of oriental stallions appeared in the stud books only very rarely, but an extensive and methodical use of Arab blood was embarked upon in the nineteenth century. There were two particular reasons for the increased resort to Arab stallions and brood mares at Lipizza. First, there was a desire to improve the shape of the Lipizzaner; second, it was felt that since the Lipizzaner was bred from closely related horses there was an urgent need to extend its breeding base. In view of the large proportion of Arab blood in both the Andalusian and the Neapolitan, the subsequent addition of pure Arab blood to strengthen the breed was entirely in line with the principles of breeding thoroughbreds. When in the nineteenth century the old Spanish-Italian horses were no longer available, breeders turned to the Arab.

After the Imperial Stud at Koptschau was closed down in 1826, its predominantly oriental breeding material was transferred to Lipizza. An attempt to breed pure Arabs in Lipizza remained unsuccessful, yet the beneficial influence of the Arab on the Lipizzaner breed could not be denied. This was intensified in subsequent years. Of a major consignment of Arab horses from the East, unloaded at Trieste in 1875, two white stallions and sixteen brood mares

"Thirdly, the Stud Master shall diligently, in the early morning, noon and evening of each day, examine at random whether the stud and stable lads have industriously and assiduously discharged the tasks entrusted to them."

"Leopold I, Roman Emperor by God's Grace, at all times Defender of the Empire" signed a 23-point "Instruction for our Stud-Masters at Lipizza in the Karst" on December 7, 1658. This is one of the rules he laid down.

went to the nearby Lipizzaner Stud. So the period of strongest admixture of Arab blood with the Karst breed began. Names which appear in the old service register, such as Soliman, born in 1760; Sultan, 1768, Gazlan, 1840; Zaydan, 1843; Samson, 1849; Hadudi, 1850; and Kohailan, 1875, point not only to the founder of the Siglavy strain but also to the influence of Arab blood. By 1882, as many as four out of seven service stallions were pure Arabs. Barely three years later the last of the original Arabs, the sixteen-year-old Ben Azet, was retired from the stud. From then on, the scions of the Siglavy strain were chiefly used as a source of crossing in the Arab inheritance.

Breeding follows the classic stallion lines and has always done so. Up to the present day, six strains have been maintained at Lipizza as representatives of the breed; their origins can be traced back to the eighteenth century, to the ancestral stallion then introduced to the stud. As the stud books are almost complete from 1701 onwards, the ascendancy can still be traced without a break.

The ancestor of the Pluto line originated in the Danish Stud of Frederiksborg, formed in 1562. It produced a noble horse of the old Spanish-Italian type which flourished during the eighteenth century. Its most successful descendant was the white stallion Pluto, born in 1765. The brood mare Deflorata, also of Danish origin, was added to the breeding herd about the same period. She left such a positive mark on the Lipizzaner line that she became the founder of a family of mares that still exists today.

The two representatives of the old Italian blood were the black stallion Conversano, born in 1767 and the bay Neapolitano, born in 1790. Both are Neapolitans in origin and founders of lines at Lipizza.

The stallions Maestoso and Favory were obtained from the Imperial Stud at Kladrub in Bohemia, where old Spanish horses had been bred since the sixteenth century and where stallions imported from Italy were used in later years. Favory, a dun, was born in 1779 and sired the Lipizzaner strain of the same name. The white stallion Maestoso, born in 1773, is the ancestor of the Maestosos. When this line died out at Lipizza in 1837, a Maestoso X, born in 1819, was purchased the same year from Mezöhegyes in Hungary. The continued existence of this noble Lipizzaner strain was thereby secured. The founder of the sixth male line in Lipizza is Siglavy, an original white Arab born in 1810 and imported in 1816. Of the numerous Arab stallions used for servicing, only his progeny could assert themselves in the breed.

To these six classic stallion lines from Lipizza may be added the Croat Tulipan line and the Transylvanian Incitato strain. These noble horses of Spanish-Neapolitan origin had long been bred at Terešovac-Suhopolje, the country seat of the dukes of Jankovic on the River Draw, not far from the Hungarian border. In the Sixties of the previous century, the first stallions from Lipizza arrived here. The objective at the time was to produce faster and more efficient coach horses. Here in Croatia's first Lipizzaner stud the Tulipan line began, soon to achieve fame well beyond the national frontiers and still existing in Hungary

Emperor Leopold I (1657–1705) had such a high personal regard for the Lipizza Stud that in 1658 he issued an Instruction which remained the basis of many of the Stud's rules until the end of the Hapsburg monarchy. The print shows the Emperor on a Lipizzaner.

two from the East and one from Denmark. The best known of the brood mare families are named after the Karst mare Sardinia, born in 1770, and her descendants Canissa (1803), Betalka (1857) and Bravissima (1914). There were also Spadiglia, 1770 (descendents Monteauru 1852 and Montenegra 1915); and Argentina, 1750 (descendents Austria 1843, Adria 1863 and Slava 1921). Both brood mares were representatives of the Karst breed.

The five original brood mares from Kaldrub were: Africa, 1740 (Benvenuta 1781, Batosta 1887 and Barbana 1904); Almerina, 1769 (Albania 1826, Slavina 1834 and Slavonia 1915); Presciana, 1782 (Bona 1838, Bovania 1889 and Bonavista 1913); Englanderia 1773 (Andalusia 1840, Aleppa 1855 and Allegra 1868); and Europa, 1774 (Trompeta 1779, Troja 1859 and Traga 1865). The mare Deflorata, 1767 (Capriola 1834 and Canissa 1859), came from Denmark. The only original brood mare with oriental blood was Gidrana, 1841 (Gaeta 1873 and Gaetana 1887).
Djebrin, 1814 (Dubovina 1893 and Darinka 1903); Mercuri, 1826 (Gratia 1883 and Gratiosa 1889) and Theodorosta, 1865 (Wanda and Wera 1886) all came from Radautz.
The brood mares Africa and Almerina also founded female lines at the Imperial Stud at Kaldrub, formed in 1759 — a clear indication of how closely the two breeds are related. The Kladrubers are also horses of old Spanish-Italian origin with centuries of breeding behind them. Unlike the Lipizzaners, light chaise and riding horses, they are of a larger, heavier type, powerful dray horses with high knee action and ability to pull heavy coaches.

It was decided in the late 1860s to transfer the breeding of the semi-heavy old Italian dray horses to Kladrub; Lipizza would continue to supply horses of a lighter build, for use in riding. This is how Rudolf Motloch, former director of the Imperial Stud at Kladrub, explained the decision: "From then on, the two studs formed independent families, to be known as the Kladruber and

and Rumania today. It originated in a cross of the pure Lipizzaner breed with the ancient Terešovacer.
The ancestor and founder of the Incitato strain, born in Mezöhegyes in 1802, had a Transylvanian stallion sire and a dam of Spanish origin. His descendants are still to be found in Hungary and Czechoslovakia.
In addition to the male lines, well-known families of brood mares were also formed at Lipizza, numbered one to eighteen according to their origin. However three have died out, namely Rosza, Khal il Massaid and Mersucha. Of the remaining fifteen original brood mares, five came frome the sister stud of Kladrub, three from the Karst, three from the old stud at Radautz,

Lipizzaner breeds. They were permitted to do so only insofar as there was a clear differentiation in size and weight, despite their common origin."

At the turn of the present century, a distinction was still made between the two types of Lipizzaner, the "pure" and the "mixed." In the case of the former, the father and grandfather were held to be members of the pure Karst breed; the mixed horse clearly showed the influence of Arab blood. The pure Karst horse, standing fifteen hands at the withers, is characterised by its heavy but by no means coarse head, an unmistakable Roman nose, a fairly strong but graceful ewe neck, a long, powerful back and muscular croup, depth of body, short, sturdy crisp limbs and a high gait. The infusion of Arab blood is noticeable in the mixed horse, which is lighter and smaller and its gait lower. The less compact, more elongated neck bears a smaller, nobler head, with a barely recognizable tendency towards the aquiline nose. These horses are clearly shorter, the shoulder being more angled, the withers set forward and a more favorable saddle position. The loins are shorter and firmer and the relatively flat croup has a high dock. Nowadays we speak of the classic or baroque type of Lipizzaner, which is still the most closely related to the old Karst horse. However, the lighter, more Arab type is better suited to the present aim of breeding for riding and for sporting purposes.

Attempts to achieve crosses were certainly made in the past. The originally Spanish stallion Veridico, born at Aranjuez in 1860, was used as a servicer at Lipizza from 1870. He had much in common with the Lipizzaner breed, both in body shape and in natural gait. He worked at the stud for two years but as his progeny did not meet expectations, he was no longer used for breeding.

When the English thoroughbred entered its heyday, English thorough-bred stallions were repeatedly used for pairing. The object of these crosses was to give the Lipizzaner height and at the same time to improve the low withers and deep back. So,

Northern Light, a white stallion born in Britain in 1852, with well-shaped withers and standing sixteen-and-a-half hands, serviced sixty mares from 1865 to 1870. His progeny were larger than the pure Karst breed, with great stamina and performance. However, the improvements, the purpose of the cross, were not obtained. In fact, gait became flatter and the finer lines of the bone structure and hindquarters was regarded as detrimental, so none of this thoroughbred stallion's progeny was included in the official herd.

The transformation of the Lipizzaner from the type of old Andalusian and Neapolitan via the baroque show-horse of old Lipizza and the Spanish Riding School into a sporting and workaday horse was completed only in the last quarter of the stud's four hundred year history.

"There are no high-legged Lipizzaners, there are no flat-ribbed Lipizzaners, there

are no bad-tempered Lipizzaners. These facts reveal the outstanding qualities of the breed which made it so widely distributed. The easy feeding habits and performance are due to the build of these horses. Their fine temper is what every animal breeder looks for. They are always patient, adaptable, tractable, energetic, create no difficulties in harness and repond well to the bit, so even a poor driver can get by with them. The broad chest, the barrel rib cage and the muscular neck fit them well as dray horses which will not tire easily." That was the judgment of the connoisseur Gustav Rau forty years ago and it still applies today.

As a breed thoroughly bred, Lipizzaners have for centuries been regarded as reliable, fast "correctives" in breeding for agriculture. They have had an ennobling effect on agricultural breeds. Even today agricultural service stallions of this breed are used in

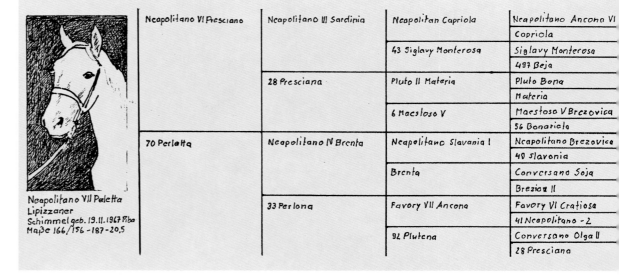

Neapolitano VII Paletta
Lipizzaner
Schimmel geb. 19.11.1967 Riba
Maße 166/156 -187-20,5

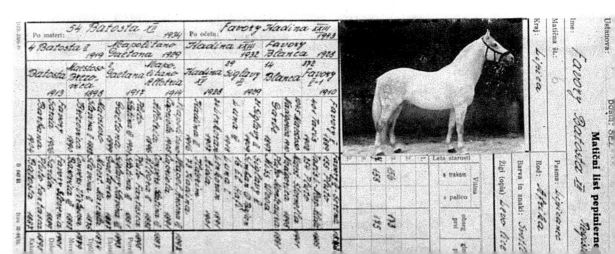

THE BRANDS

Overleaf: The family trees of the six Lipizzaner lines Pluto (P), Conversano (C), Neapolitano (N), Maestoso (M), Favory (F), and Siglavy (S). The abbreviations used in the family trees are L for Lipizza, K for Kladrub, M for Mezöhegyes, Te for Terešovac, P for Piber, Sz for Szilvásvárad, To for Topolčianky, Fa for Fágáras, B for Babolna and Dak for Djakovo.

areas without a Lipizzaner tradition in order to give the local breeds something of the desirable properties which make the Lipizzaner so coveted — contentedness and resistance, stamina and longevity, docility and beauty. Heavy breeds, in particular, are rendered lighter, more nimble and more useful after crossing with a Lipizzaner.

In the future, too, the Lipizzaner will be the ideal horse for improving other breeds, although its potential should not be over-estimated. In the United States several insemination centers have offered sperm from imported Lipizzaner stallions. It is hoped, among other things, that the Lipizzaner strain can be used to improve the local Quarter Horse — the "cowboy horse" which is employed to manage large herds of cattle — by transmitting more docility, stamina, powers of resistance and greater attraction.

The pedigrees on the following pages show the descent of the stallions at the Szilvásvárad Stud. They start with the founder of the line; then the best of his sons, those used most often for breeding, follow in a straight line for the first years of the breed. The pedigree then branches out. A number of a stallion's offspring were used for breeding, creating side-branches. Some of these have since disappeared, some have developed further at other studs. The formation of these side-branches, sometimes with very specific properties, offers a breeder potential for variation within what is naturally a narrow biological base.

Left, above: Pedigree of the stallion Neapolitano Perletta. The word "pedigree" a family tree, is derived from the French pied de grue, literally a crane's foot, referring to the symbols on the tables of descent of noble families, and transferred to the family trees of "noble" horses.
Equine pedigrees also contain information about the characteristic shape of the animals. 166 – 187 – 20.5 indicates the height and the chest and shank dimensions in centimeters. From these measurements, the expert can obtain a first impression of the horse's physical characteristics.

Left: Pedigree of Favory Batosta XII, born on April 20, 1948 in Lipizza.

A characteristic feature of Lipizzaner breeding at all studs is to mark the horses with family brands, which does more than merely identify the breed and stud. The fact that it is based in practical terms on only a few families of stallions makes this form of writing the pedigree on the horse easier. Without having to examine the family tree, the expert will immediately recognize the origin of the horse by its brand.

Brands are not an invention of recent times. The Greeks sought to maintain the purity of their horses' breed and took steps not only to keep registers of descent but also to distinguish the individual families from each other by marking them with thigh-brands. The most customary signs were the bull's head or the letters Tau, Sigma and Kappa. Equine figures from Egyptian-Persian times bear a stamp on the thigh showing the Nile. The Romans marked exceptional horses with a perfect circle on the lower jaw. Even today the Lipizza Stud brand is placed on the left side of the jaw. There is a specific brand for all male and female horses descended from a specific stallion. Each foal carries his brand of origin on the left side of its jaw — above the sire's, beneath or next to the dam's.

Accurate marking of horses is of particular importance in breeding. Originating with the marks of ownership and selection, the descent and family brands were added. Here, the symbolic language of olden times plays a major role. The sign embodies both tradition and pride in the breeder's achievement. Although the imagination is given free play in selecting the symbols, a businesslike approach has always been preferred in horse-breeding.

A distinction is made between stud brands, descent brands and foal brands, which may all be found on the same horse. Among breeding mares, the number on the breeding register is usually added as a neck-brand.

The differences between the various studs in the design of individual brands are slight. The reasons for this are the letters available, slight divergencies in applying the

brand, and the position of the iron during branding. Only the Rumanian stud of Sîmbăta de Jos shows substantial differences in the sign of the Siglavy line. Instead of the S, the marking is SC for Siglavy Capriola I — all descendants of this line have the brood mare Capriola I as ancestor. The brand was also used in the Czech stud of Topolčianky between the two World Wars. This practice

Continue on page 102

Bona
1881
Favory Sesana,
Bona, haister
1875
Neapolitano Mahonia,
Bona, haister
1856
Garlan, Orig Arab
Bona, haister
1838
Siglavy Africa, haister
Primavera, haister
Forester Arab.
Bellasiglia, hopschumer
1822
Lippi, hopschumer
Bellasiglia, hopschumer
1808
Maestoso Verluna, haister

Romana II
1882
Ben Azet, Arab.
Romana, haister
1871
Samson, Orig Arab
Romana, haister
1854
Garlan, Orig Arab
Romana, haister
1833
Kwfejl Hollibeck, Angl Arab.
Sardinia, haister
1827
Maestoso Swerum, haister
Plutona, haister
1813
Vezu, Arab.

Plutona, hopschumer
1801
Pluto, haister
Amorosa, Kladruber.
1792
Sanspareil
Presciana
1782
Kladrubern.

Family tree of a classic mare family from old Lipizza. This pedigree of the mare family Presciana shows that, unlike the stallion lines, the original dam's name is not retained. Similar names are adopted instead. For example, Bona is followed by her female offspring Bonavia, Bonavoja, Bonavista and Bonadea — some of which names we still find in the studs today. Studs which only breed stallion lines and leave the mare families out of account miss out on a very important aid to planned pairing.

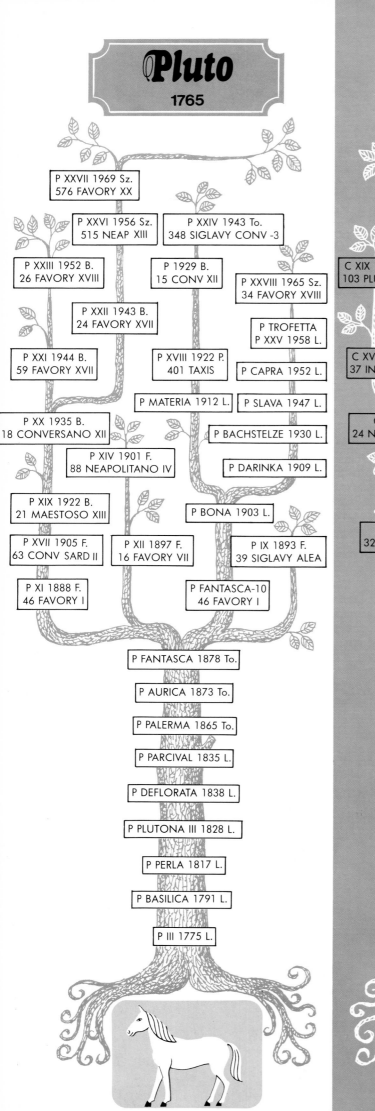
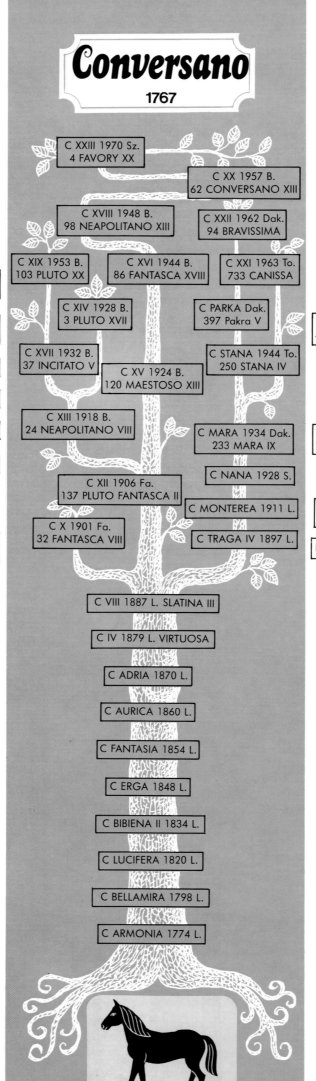

Pluto
1765

- P XXVII 1969 Sz. 576 FAVORY XX
- P XXVI 1956 Sz. 515 NEAP XIII
- P XXIV 1943 To. 348 SIGLAVY CONV -3
- P XXIII 1952 B. 26 FAVORY XVIII
- P 1929 B. 15 CONV XII
- P XXVIII 1965 Sz. 34 FAVORY XVIII
- P XXII 1943 B. 24 FAVORY XVII
- P TROFETTA P XXV 1958 L.
- P XXI 1944 B. 59 FAVORY XVII
- P XVIII 1922 P. 401 TAXIS
- P CAPRA 1952 L.
- P MATERIA 1912 L.
- P SLAVA 1947 L.
- P XX 1935 B. 18 CONVERSANO XII
- P BACHSTELZE 1930 L.
- P XIV 1901 F. 88 NEAPOLITANO IV
- P DARINKA 1909 L.
- P XIX 1922 B. 21 MAESTOSO XIII
- P BONA 1903 L.
- P XVII 1905 F. 63 CONV SARD II
- P XII 1897 F. 16 FAVORY VII
- P IX 1893 F. 39 SIGLAVY ALEA
- P XI 1888 F. 46 FAVORY I
- P FANTASCA-10 46 FAVORY I
- P FANTASCA 1878 To.
- P AURICA 1873 To.
- P PALERMA 1865 To.
- P PARCIVAL 1835 L.
- P DEFLORATA 1838 L.
- P PLUTONA III 1828 L.
- P PERLA 1817 L.
- P BASILICA 1791 L.
- P III 1775 L.

Conversano
1767

- C XXIII 1970 Sz. 4 FAVORY XX
- C XX 1957 B. 62 CONVERSANO XIII
- C XVIII 1948 B. 98 NEAPOLITANO XIII
- C XXII 1962 Dak. 94 BRAVISSIMA
- C XIX 1953 B. 103 PLUTO XX
- C XVI 1944 B. 86 FANTASCA XVIII
- C XXI 1963 To. 733 CANISSA
- C XIV 1928 B. 3 PLUTO XVII
- C PARKA Dak. 397 Pakra V
- C XVII 1932 B. 37 INCITATO V
- C STANA 1944 To. 250 STANA IV
- C XV 1924 B. 120 MAESTOSO XIII
- C XIII 1918 B. 24 NEAPOLITANO VIII
- C MARA 1934 Dak. 233 MARA IX
- C NANA 1928 S.
- C XII 1906 Fa. 137 PLUTO FANTASCA II
- C MONTEREA 1911 L.
- C X 1901 Fa. 32 FANTASCA VIII
- C TRAGA IV 1897 L.
- C VIII 1887 L. SLATINA III
- C IV 1879 L. VIRTUOSA
- C ADRIA 1870 L.
- C AURICA 1860 L.
- C FANTASIA 1854 L.
- C ERGA 1848 L.
- C BIBIENA II 1834 L.
- C LUCIFERA 1820 L.
- C BELLAMIRA 1798 L.
- C ARMONIA 1774 L.

Neapolitano
1790

- N XXII 1970 P. 50 PRIMAVERA
- N XX 1964 Sz. 568 CONVERSANO XVIII
- N VI P. 28 PRESCIANA
- N XXI 1963 Sz. 532 FAVORY POLA
- N III P. 45 SIGLAVY MONTEROSA
- N XVIII 1943 B. 57 CONV XIII
- N XVII 1949 B. 91 CONV XIV
- N XVI 1949 B. 69 INCITATO VI
- N XV 1948 B. 22 CONVERSANO XIII
- N XIX 1957 Sz. 523 CONV
- N XIV 1933 To. 217 N I – 3
- N XIII 1925 B. 18 CONVERSANO XII
- N GRATIA I 1922 To. 30 RIGOLETTA
- N XI MONTENEGRA 1912 L.
- N XII BONA 1911 L.
- N CAPRIOLA 1905 L.
- N GRATIA 1904 L.
- N ANCONA VI 1897 L.
- N TROMPETA 1875 L.
- N MAHONIA 1868 L.
- N CALDAS 1851 L.
- N VALDAMORA 1839 L.
- N GROCZANA II 1829 L.
- N AQUILEJA 1820 L.
- N BELLAMATA 1807 L.

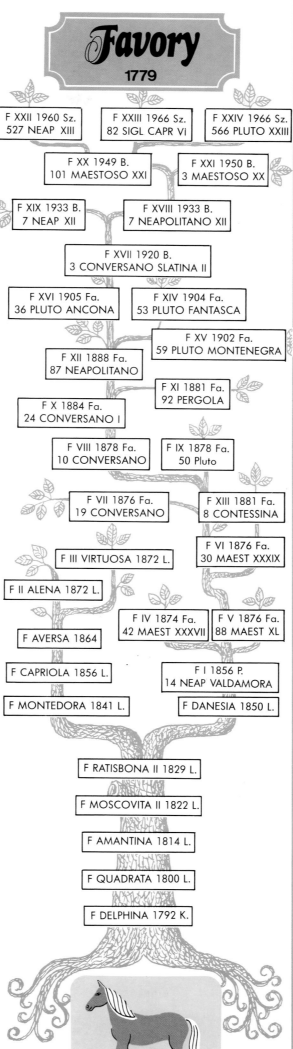
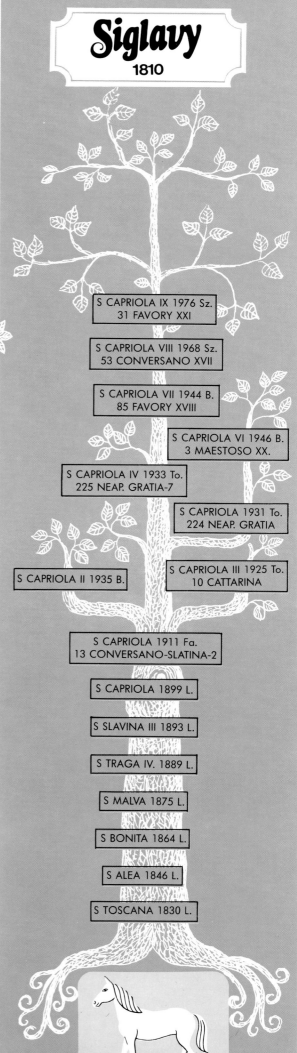

Maestoso
1773

- M XXVI 1945 B. 22 CONV XIII
- M XXIV 1942 B. 36 FAVORY XVII
- M XXIII 1942 B. 28 CONV XIII
- M XXII 1939 B. 25 CONV XIII
- M XXIX 1973 Sz. 580 CONV XVIII
- M XXI 1922 B. 27 INCITATO IV
- M XXVIII 1959 B. 15 FAVORY XVIII
- M XVII 1905 F. 41 PLUTO FANTASCA
- M XXV. 1935 B. 22 CONV XIII
- M XVIII 1903 F. 69 CONV VIRTUOSA
- M XXVII 1944 To. 231 M XIII
- M XI 1901 F. 76 PLUTO FANTASCA
- M XX 1926 B. 27 INCITATO IV
- M I 1928 To. 225 NEAP GRATIA
- M IX 1899 F. 27 PLUTO FANTASCA
- M XIX 1914 B. 52 M ERGA
- M TAXIS 1911 F.
- M X 1900 F. 30 FAVORY VII
- M XVI 1908 Te.
- M VIII 1898 F. 7 FAVORY VII
- M XV 1904 F. 92 BETALKA
- M SERVOLA 1892 L.
- M BAZOVICA II 1883 L.
- M VII 1881 Te. ERGA
- M MASCULA 1874 L.
- M DIDO 1876 Te.
- M PERLETTA 1854 L.
- M ERGA 1838 M.
- M II ESURIENCA 1813 M.
- M I VENTURINO 1798 L.
- M CREMONA 1786 K.

Favory
1779

- F XXII 1960 Sz. 527 NEAP XIII
- F XXIII 1966 Sz. 82 SIGL CAPR VI
- F XXIV 1966 Sz. 566 PLUTO XXIII
- F XX 1949 B. 101 MAESTOSO XXI
- F XXI 1950 B. 3 MAESTOSO XX
- F XIX 1933 B. 7 NEAP XII
- F XVIII 1933 B. 7 NEAPOLITANO XII
- F XVII 1920 B. 3 CONVERSANO SLATINA II
- F XVI 1905 Fa. 36 PLUTO ANCONA
- F XIV 1904 Fa. 53 PLUTO FANTASCA
- F XV 1902 Fa. 59 PLUTO MONTENEGRA
- F XII 1888 Fa. 87 NEAPOLITANO
- F XI 1881 Fa. 92 PERGOLA
- F X 1884 Fa. 24 CONVERSANO I
- F VIII 1878 Fa. 10 CONVERSANO
- F IX 1878 Fa. 50 Pluto
- F VII 1876 Fa. 19 CONVERSANO
- F XIII 1881 Fa. 8 CONTESSINA
- F VI 1876 Fa. 30 MAEST XXXIX
- F III VIRTUOSA 1872 L.
- F II ALENA 1872 L.
- F IV 1874 Fa. 42 MAEST XXXVII
- F V 1876 Fa. 88 MAEST XL
- F AVERSA 1864
- F CAPRIOLA 1856 L.
- F I 1856 P. 14 NEAP VALDAMORA
- F MONTEDORA 1841 L.
- F DANESIA 1850 L.
- F RATISBONA II 1829 L.
- F MOSCOVITA II 1822 L.
- F AMANTINA 1814 L.
- F QUADRATA 1800 L.
- F DELPHINA 1792 K.

Siglavy
1810

- S CAPRIOLA IX 1976 Sz. 31 FAVORY XXI
- S CAPRIOLA VIII 1968 Sz. 53 CONVERSANO XVII
- S CAPRIOLA VII 1944 B. 85 FAVORY XVIII
- S CAPRIOLA VI 1946 B. 3 MAESTOSO XX.
- S CAPRIOLA IV 1933 To. 225 NEAP. GRATIA-7
- S CAPRIOLA 1931 To. 224 NEAP. GRATIA
- S CAPRIOLA II 1935 B.
- S CAPRIOLA III 1925 To. 10 CATTARINA
- S CAPRIOLA 1911 Fa. 13 CONVERSANO-SLATINA-2
- S CAPRIOLA 1899 L.
- S SLAVINA III 1893 L.
- S TRAGA IV. 1889 L.
- S MALVA 1875 L.
- S BONITA 1864 L.
- S ALEA 1846 L.
- S TOSCANA 1830 L.

was discontinued after 1945, but Sîmbăta de Jos has continued to use the double-brand SC up to the present day. The female Siglavy brand, a circle with an arrow, is probably a combination of the Conversano and the Siglavy brands, but the reason for this is unknown.

The female Maestoso brand, with and without crown, undoubtedly of artistic appeal, has given the persons producing the brand irons at the individual studs room for

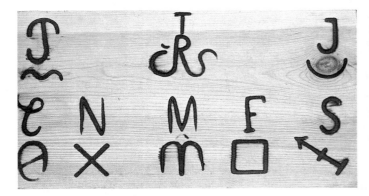

The brands still in use at the Topolčianky Stud today, burned on wood.

fancy. Even so, the similarity is great and the brands are unmistakable as Maestoso symbols. The crown brand is derived from the name "Maestoso" which in Italian means "majestic" or "worthy." The Rumanians believe there is also a link with the monastic sign, that is, the miter or bishop's cap. This indicates that Lipizzaners were for many years bred only for the courts of temporal rulers and the princes of the church.

The Favory brand is a square, except at Piber where, as opposed to the other studs, a rectangle is used. This had been used as a breed brand for the female of the Favory line in the old Imperial Stud of Radautz, which may explain why the female breed brands for the Lipizzaner differ according to the line to which the dam belongs.

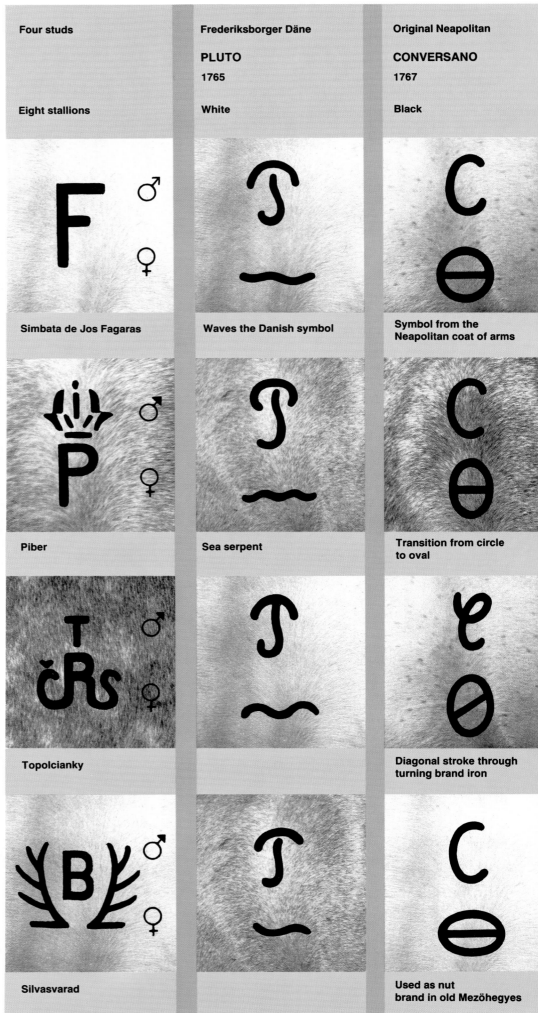

Four studs	Frederiksborger Däne	Original Neapolitan
	PLUTO	**CONVERSANO**
	1765	1767
Eight stallions	White	Black
Simbata de Jos Fagaras	Waves the Danish symbol	Symbol from the Neapolitan coat of arms
Piber	Sea serpent	Transition from circle to oval
Topolcianky		Diagonal stroke through turning brand iron
Silvasvarad		Used as nut brand in old Mezöhegyes

102

Original Neapolitan	Kladrub	Kladrub	Arab
NEAPOLITANO	**MAESTOSO**	**FAVORY**	**SIGLAVY**
1790	1773	1779	1910
Brown	White	Dun	White

Siglavy: SC = Siglavy-Capriola, i.e. all descendants of this line have the mare Capriola as dam. The brand was used at the Topolčianky Stud between the two world wars. This continued after 1945, with the Rumanian stud Sîmbáta de Jos adopting the double-brand SC together with Sigalvy-Capriola I, purchased in 1938, and have kept it to the present day.

The female Siglavy brand, a circle with an arrow, is evidently a combination of the Conversano and Siglavy brand. The reasons for it are unknown.

Crossed swords	Monastic sign or miter	Square, symbol of old Radautz	Arrow symbol

Extended shank, symbol of sword in greeting	Crown brand	Modified rectangle	Twin-barbed arrow, the old Siglavy Arab brand

	Symbol of majesty		Newly adopted at Babolna 1938 to distinguish from Arab brand

Renowned for its majestic bearing, its intelligence and its elegant movement, the Lipizzaner is famous for its many features which never cease to excite admiration. Centuries ago it was distinguished from other horses by its stately, measured step which suited it so ideally for court ceremonial — this it has retained to the present day. The Lipizzaner was predestined for the paces Spanish Trot, the Piaffe on the Spot and the Passage on the Light Trot, and it excels in these over all other breeds without Andalusian forebears. True, the paces and airs have to be continuously re-acquired through diligence and daily training but the Lipizzaner learns them easily. The Passage,

on a easy rein, to bear its head high and to arch it from the neck, what we have achieved is something that the horse itself takes pleasure in doing." And there is no denying that the Lipizzaner takes pleasure in demonstrating the Spanish step of its ancestors, whether under its rider or on the long rein.

The question remains whether the Lipizzaner, this ideal representative of the classic art of riding, is also suited as a dressage horse for the show ring. Its critics have pointed out that the Lipizzaner is too small and its neck too compact, so it loses flexibility at the crest. Furthermore, it has a tendency to tense up, as for centuries it has

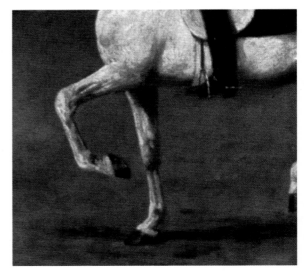

FEATURES OF THE BREED

Lipizzaners, the aristocrats among horses, still bear witness to their Andalusian and Neapolitan heritage, preserving the gait and head carriage that were their ancestors' most notable features. Their proud, compact pace, the Spanish Step to perfection, refines and echoes the beauty, perfection and harmony of movement of their ancestors.

Both horses, in the painting on this page and in the photograph opposite, show the inimitable perfection of the Piaffe. It is clear that the horse is delaying the action, having absolute command of the movement. The step — not learned but inherited from its sires — is full of grace and harmony.

practiced many times in its youth as a form of play indulged in by an excited young stallion, is slowly transformed to the suspended trot in the arena. The horse energetically lifts alternate front and back legs off the ground at the same time, flexing its foreleg into the right-angled "knee-bend" and freezing in this position for a fraction of a second. The return of the foreleg is briefly delayed. When the hoof touches the ground, the opposite set of legs does the same step in the same rhythm. The Piaffe on the Spot and the Passage on the Light Trot make an unforgettable picture for every lover of classic dressage. And how easily, how playfully, how effortlessly it is all done. As Xenophon wrote four centuries ago: "A horse will not master what it does under compulsion, nor will it look fine. If, however, the horse is taught to go

been bred for the specific effects of the haute école, for which a certain tenseness is necessary. All the Stepping on Air Schools require it.

Moreover, compared with other breeds the Lipizzaner has a differently modified, consciously inbred gait. Nonetheless, individual representatives of the breed have shown that the Lipizzaner is very capable of holding its own against strong competition in competitive dressage. Pluto Theodorosta under its rider Colonel Podhajsky, Conversano Caprice under its rider Joan Hall and the brood mare Thais under Alfons Pecovniak are just a few among a great number of Lipizzaners to prove their worth in international dressage.

The descendants of the six line stallions at Lipizza have continued to inherit the Li-

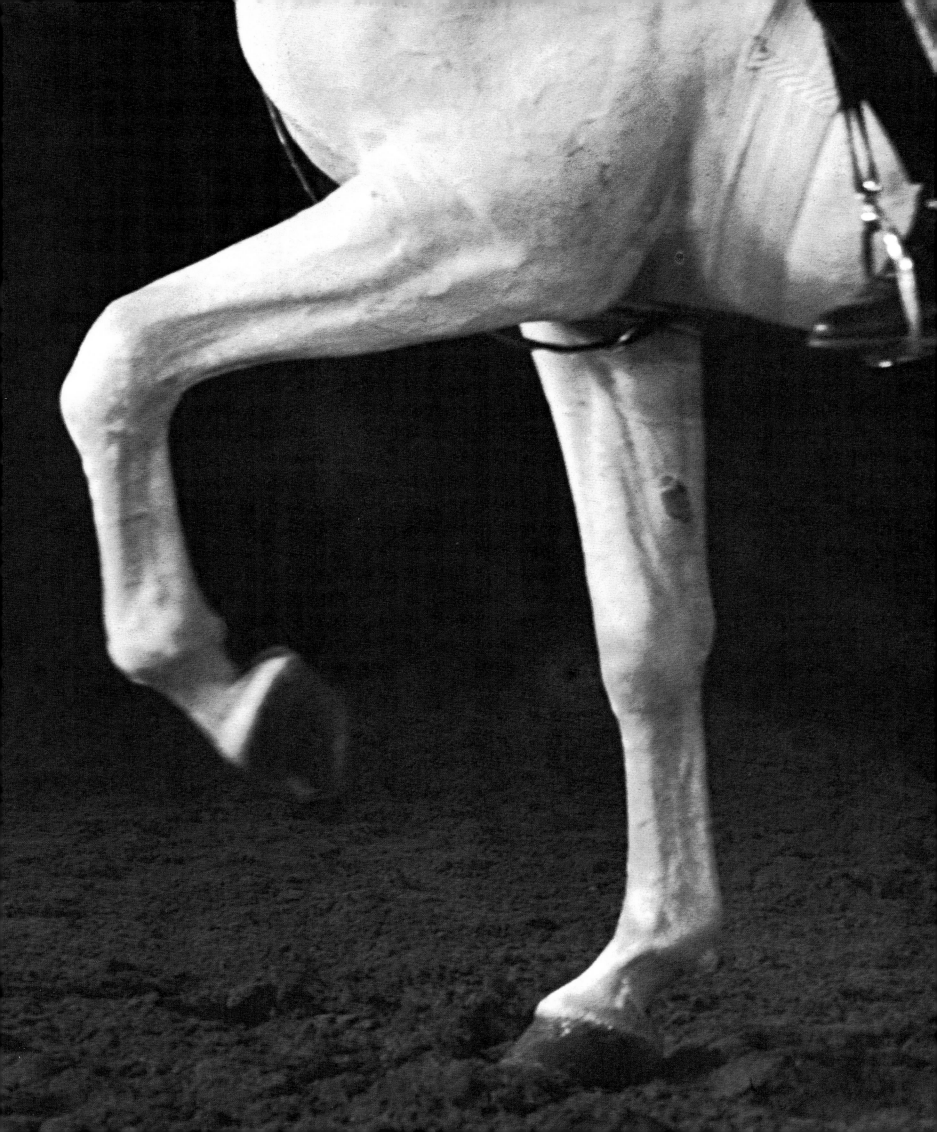

pizzaner's highly characteristic features and properties. Though membership of the line may not always be in evidence in every proud stallion after so many generations – since, after all, through the dams of all the ascendants other lines have given their share of blood to the progeny – there are still a number of characteristics that may be ascribed to the six breeding lines.

The Plutos are powerful, large-bodied, square-built horses with long backs. Particularly strong, they have a highly set neck and a slightly broken nose. Their movements are energetic.

The descendants of the Conversano line are distinguished by their strong Roman nose, their less highly set neck, their short back, broad haunches and particularly noble movements.

The Neapolitans, with their large heads and strong ribs in profile, are horses of a powerful appearance and high "knee-bend."

Below left: Neapolitano XX. Main service stallion at Szilvásvárad. With broad, deep chest, compact neck and rather heavy head, he closely resembles the classic baroque type of the old Karst Lipizzaner. At right, Coversano I Ravata, pepinière stallion at Topolčianky, an elegant stallion of the modern riding type. As at Lipizza and Piber, the stallions here have double names — that of the sire and of the dam. To which stallion line the horse belongs and to which mare family his dam is therefore immediately evident.

Representatives of the Favory line are finer and lighter in build. Their gently curved noses are a reminder of their ancestor from Kladrub. Their tendency to albinism is the reason for the frequent appearance of large sections of pink-flecked skin around the eyes, mouth and genitals.

The Maestosos are powerful horses with a long back, a strong muscular croup, and a strongly pronounced gait. Their heavy heads display only a mild "break" in the nose line.

The Siglavy line incorporates the Arab type of Lipizzaner. Their heads are straight and noble, their necks slender; they present a more extended, slightly curved line. The withers are higher, the back shorter, the general effect finer and lighter than the other stallion lines, the old rectangular ap-

...rn of the century a half-grown foal ...owed its family clearly from the shape ...d attitude of its head. Since then, how-...er, the shape of the individual lines' ...ads has been more or less standardized.

Selection for beauty, and the wish to breed out the Roman nose have led to the typical head shape of the original animal being lost. Another change arises from the attempt to replace the compact neck

of the baroque type with one that is lighter and more comfortable to ride.

The strong influence of the Arab on the head of the Siglavy line and the specially powerful head and neck of the Pluto line is clear from the horse-head sketches by Emil Kotbra.

Left: The outlines show both the classic, baroque type of Lipizzaner and the more easily ridden Arabized type compared with the noble horse of our equestrian breeds. As we can see, the Lipizzaner's shoulder height is substantially lower than that of the normal riding horse. The outline of the two types also clearly shows the significant differences. The elevated, clearly curved, compact neck, the rather heavy head and powerful back, with muscular, lightly raised croup are the characteristic features of the baroque type. The modern Arabized type, with good saddle position, less elevated, longer neck and lighter head better meets the requirements made of the modern hacking horse.

Left above: The very model of a fine traditional stallion's head. Considering the expression, nobility, brilliance and spirit of the mares of the home herd at Piber it is hardly surprising that this horse Neapolitano Perletta, was born at that Stud. At right, young stallion with the typical broken nose in the foaling stall at Csipkeskút. At Szilvásvárad this feature is considered desirable, as appropriate to the Lipizzaner. The curved "sheep's head" nose, a remnant of the old baroque, has however been regarded by many breeders over the past decades as a blemish. It is nevertheless proving hard to eliminate entirely.

107

The gait of the Spanish step, seen here from the front, never fails to impress. The delayed down-step at the canter is typical of the Lipizzaner, more inborn than learned.

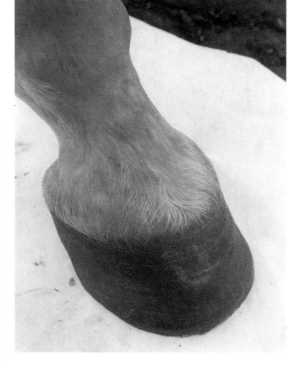

A well-shaped hoof left, fitting the ankle position, is a required for smooth movement. Generally speaking, Lipizzaners are not shod. The horn is hard and firm, and not brittle – a legacy of the hard Karst soil. Only when Lipizzaners are used daily on paved surfaces, as cab horses in Vienna, for example, is shoeing unavoidable. In the Spanish Riding School the stallions are shod only if special circumstances require it, and then only temporarily. A "pair of shoes" is kept for each stallion, numbered and named.

The relatively muscular croup (below) answers the horse's thrust. It is also beneficial in exercises of the Haute Ecole, when the animal has to bear its full weight on the hind legs.

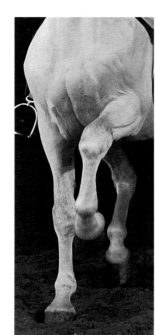

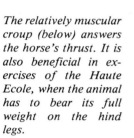

Below: The Spanish step in dressage and extended pace as a natural movement at pasture above and above right. It is the task of the rider or driver to use the appropriate aids to bring the horse into the correct gait.

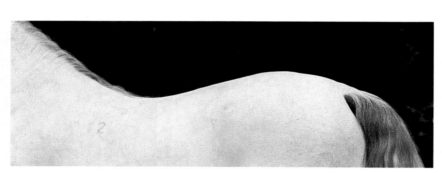

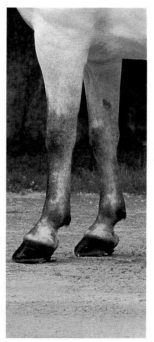

Left: stable rump is a requisite of both a good jumping horse and a coach horse. Horses standing correctly generally also have a regular gait. Faultlessly dimensioned members, with both pairs of legs parallel to each other, well shaped, clearly marked, tight joints, and firm ligaments guarantee a correct gait, good kinetic mechanism and uniform loading of all bones, joints, thews and sinews.

pearance being lost. The sharply pronounced gait is also missing.

These characteristics apply without reservation to the traditional Lipizzaners up to the First World War. The individual lines have since changed in type to a greater or lesser extent, partly in line with the differences in breeding conditions and policies at the individual studs.

The Lipizzaner makes up for its relatively short height at the withers its good shape, fine movements and well-set neck. As a result the horse seems larger than it really is. This is particularly so with the stallions, owing to their heavy heads on powerful necks.

Two faults are often ascribed to the Lipizzaner – a sloping back and an excessive croup. The greater height of the croup and the less pronounced withers give the

The tensed muscles at the bent haunches (below) show the load borne by the hind legs in the Levade.

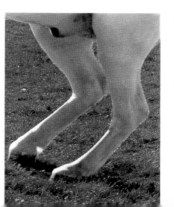

ments of all kinds. When the center of gravity moves forward in the direction of movement, maintaining a natural balance is a precondition for the harmonious combination of all horses. The horse must be fully balanced at every phase of movement and be capable of absorbing the impetus imparted at the hock. As it steps off on its rear leg, where the thrust of its force originates, the croup is the base from which it develops and the forward movement commences. The forearm takes up the impetus, and the center of gravity moves forward, the two other limbs following suit. In this way, the

Above: The brilliance of the gaits and the symphony of movement is outstanding in this championship team driven by the Hungarian György Bardos. He reckons on a preparatory period of about a year for a new four-in-hand. Up to ten horses must be tested, longed, ridden and driven before the truly intensive training starts. A fifth, substitute, horse is always trained as well.

The breast harness, double-ring bridoon and stockwhip is adapted to the flatness of the country. Broad roads permit a wide span. The picture at right shows the stylish movement of the Hungarian team in the fast trot, meeting a time-limit with expansive, extended paces.

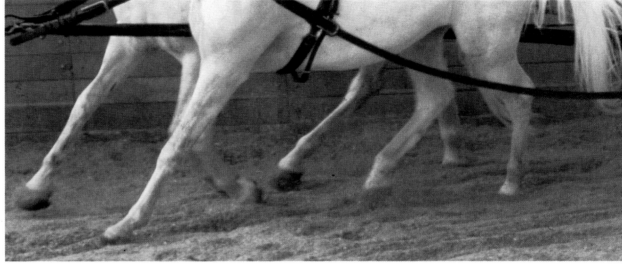

impression of a sagging back-line. The cause is a high rump and a massive, muscular croup. However both these features are highly advantageous in a good dray horse (for pushing and pulling forwards) and in a schooling horse (for exercises in haute école, in which the horse has to bear its full weight on the rear of its body). The low withers (the result of a very short neural spin), the steep rise of the shoulder blade and the high-set neck are not faults in a draft horse, though they would be in a riding horse, who must bear the main weight of the rider on the central part of its back. The more Arab blood added to the old Karst breed, the more the withers have developed in the direction of the riding type. The prerequisites for smoothness of movement are a correct gait, a well-proportioned body, and a natural propensity for move-

Double Lipizzaner team in Kummet harness below. This driving style with curb bits and bow-whip originated in Britain and allows a heavy carriage to be driven through narrow streets and city traffic.

kinetic movement proceeds continuously in the rhythm of the rise and fall of the hoofs.

The strength and stamina of the gait and the length of the pace are, on one hand, a natural propensity resulting from the horse's anatomy. They are also, however, the result of man influencing the animal through dressage, whether in riding or driving, and the sequence and length of the pace, the gait and the overall impression of the horse. What the spectator observes at the dressage stage is the complete utilization of every skill and natural feature.

Hungary is the country of the driver. It gains this reputation from its Lipizzaners. In the previous century, journeys of a hundred and fifty miles or more testify to the Lipizzaners' powers of endurance in so-called Jucker harness. Light hunting carriages, light coach harness and the light Jucker coach horse of extraordinary endurance were characteristic of Hungarian driving style. The present-day, stronger Lipizzaner from Szilvásvárad shines in dressage through its stylish gait and high action; in a marathon it is indestructable and on obstacle courses fast and elegant.

The main four-in-hand versatility test consists of team control, also known as "presentation," dressage, a marathon stretch and an obstacle course. When checking and assessing the team, the judges look at the

With flowing mane and bushy tail, the stallion trots into the paddock with a long, free stride. Next to it, a stallion with rider in dressage. Here, we observe a natural response, there the result of long training. As a matter of principle, in dressage exercises a horse should never be asked to do something which is not suited to its natural temperament. Watch the foals play, or the first trials of strength by the colts, and you will see the early stages of the dressage work to come. What the young stallion spontaneously displays in its first years at grass, from the Swaying Trot, through the Levade, to the Capriole, he will learn again under his rider.

The accusation that due to its short stride in a strong trot the Lipizzaner does badly in sporting dressage is refuted by these pictures. Of course, because of its conformation, the Piaffe, Passage and Pirouette will always be the high points of its performance. In these the Lipizzaner is superior to horses of all other breeds. However it need not come second to them in the fast walk or trot, as it crosses the dressage box in a wide, rhythmic and free-shouldered canter.

110

Below: A young stallion in the paddock piaffes with finely arched neck, lifting its forearm at right-angles as if led by the reins. The Spanish step of its ancestors is in its blood.

The attitude of this young stallion is fully and completely that of the trained riding horse standing collected at the rein. It again demonstrates that dressage at its best is simply the refinement of features originally instilled by nature.

Head of an old School stallion at the Spanish Riding School, in a detail from a painting. While experienced riders train the young stallion in the Spanish Riding School, an older stallion like this one also contributes to the education of the beginner.

driver and co-driver, the correct exertion, the gear, coordination between the horses and the overall impression. In the dressage test, they look for correct execution of the exercises set, command of the reins, driving style, driving in the bend, attitude and angle in turns, the change of pace, reversing, the volte and the stance of the horses.

The endurance test in the rough, the marathon circuit, measures the condition, perseverance and obedience of the horses. Stretches at the canter alternate with those at the trot. The high point of this test is an obstacle course with sandy tracks, declivities, sharp bends, water-splashes and narrow passages. The cone markers, each of which contains a control ball, allow for a margin of eight inches to the wheels of the carriage. Scraping the cone and causing the ball to drop counts as a fault. On the obstacle course and the agility test the Lipizzaners time and again prove their extraordinary capacity as a driving horse as they clear the hazards light-footedly at an astonishing speed.

A knowledge of the natural forms of behavior is of particular importance in dressage.

In the Spanish step an old service-stallion trots quietly and relaxed across a meadow, his neck curved, his tail blowing with the wind. Performing this, without bridle or halter, the stallion makes an extraordinary impression.

Piaffe beneath a rider. After years of dressage training, the forearm swings freely and almost horizontally through the air. The opposite hind leg follows suit. The horse, restrained by the bridle, responds to the rider's rein, the neck finely curved.

Young foals in a meadow attempt the Capriole. Unfettered play soon becomes a serious business when a stallion fights its rivals for the position of leader. When fighting for standing in the herd, a rearing horse lifts its forearm without bending the rear leg, in a display of strength and bellicosity.

Even the youngest above and right energetically play at jumping, and the beginnings of the Capriole are obvious. The movement is similar to the aerial jump of a deer in flight; as "deer" is **capriola** *in Italian, it is easy to understand how this School jump of the classic Haute Ecole gets its name. It is natural and an expression of pleasure in freedom, a "jump for joy".*

Three brown Lipizzaner stallions in the Busch Circus (below) perform the Levade. Almost two years of basic training are necessary to teach the horse balance for an ideal Levade. Twelve of these stallions performing free dressage in the circus tent always attracts storms of applause. The classic school of riding has developed the Levade from the movements of the rearing horse. The animal lifts its forearms off the ground and angles the front legs, the hind legs bearing the full load of the body balanced on bent haunches left. The stallion freezes in this position for a moment, until the forearms are again slowly lowered.

The horse's natural attitudes must be recognized and aggressive and defensive responses be developed further as natural forms of movement. This is how the well-known dressage positions originated — the Levade was originally a fighting attitude; the Pirouette, a fast turn on the axis of the rear foot to escape a bite or kick; and the Compliment, an aggressive stance in which one or both front legs are stretched forwards. In nature, the stallion tries to overcome his opponent by biting it in the front leg, as that is the leg with which an attack is usually made. The opponent attempts a feint by bending low. In dressage, this is the Gratitude position for accepting applause.

If we look at the brown Lipizzaners from Djakovo the threatening aspect in the three Levades is unmistakeable. The ears are laid back, often so strongly that they are barely visible. Eyelids and nostrils are squeezed, the corners of the mouth turned down. Often the whites of the eyes appear. This is the stance the stallion adopts in nature when he rises on his hind legs to strike his

113

rivals with his front hooves. The attitude of the Levade in the riding ring is therefore a clear reminder of its original function.

The further development of the Levade in the classic art of riding is the transition from the Schools on the ground to those in the air, the climax of which is the Capriole. Because of the qualities inherited from the Spanish-Italian horse, the Lipizzaner ranks both in its development and in its nature as an artist among horses. It is the representative of the classic art of riding, which refuses to demand anything of the horse which is not already inherent. These horses are not taught tricks, they are simply educated and achieve perfection through training. To be a master of the highest perfection, of the haute école, is the Lipizzaner's true goal.

Since ancient times the presentation of noble horses was the center point of the

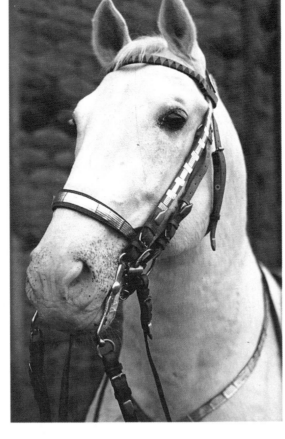

Proud and relaxed, a Lipizzaner eyes the visitor.

human contact and affection. How trustfully it approaches man is plain to see, often "sensing" him with its nostrils. It is a born family horse. Its great docility and good will, its even temper and its above-average talents both when saddled and in harness broaden its usefulness. Its extraordinary quality as a dressage horse for haute école is due to its keen intelligence and its fine temperament. The former head of the Spanish Riding School, Colonel Alois Podhajsky, has this to say about the Lipizzaner: "The high intelligence and extraordinary qualities of the Lipizzaner are already noticeable in its training. It is a pleasure to work with these astute stallions and it is therefore all the more understandable why the great masters of the Spanish Riding School championed it so passionately and were so taken with its fine

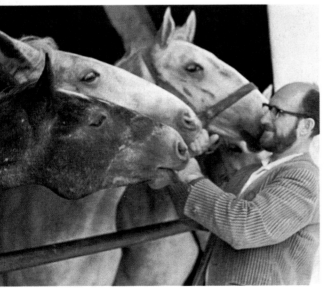

classic circus program. "Circus" and "horses" are inseparable terms. Both individually as a school horse and as a group in free dressage, the Lipizzaner is a special attraction in the ring. White circus horses never cease to captivate young and old.

When all is said and done, for the rider dressage means hard training, intuitive power, adaptation to natural attitudes, patience and love of animals.

The Lipizzaner appears to have a special affinity for man. It is a horse which enjoys

Above left: Trustingly, young stallions approach, formally greet a stranger by sniffing and nuzzling. Their trust in man is virtually without limit, even from an early age.

Above: The Lipizzaner is the essential circus horse. "Generous, obedient, loyal, devoted, full of temperament and still quiet and relaxed, docile and intelligent", in the words of an experienced dresseur, "a better Character than the Lipizzaner's cannot be found."

A white whirlwind with a rider flashes past in a stylish gallop.

*Opposite: A csikós with the Lipizzaner herd at Bükk demonstrating his dressage achievements. The horse obediently kneels, lies flat on the ground, again raises itself up from the front — and does all this without bridle and saddle. The crack of the **karikas** (whip) does not disturb its composure; the horse trusts its master and takes no notice of its surroundings.*

Passing through the water-splash in an obstacle race during the Marathon. The driver has firm control of his horses, who trust him. Even so it takes courage to cross the water in a steep descent. At the Budapest Championships in 1975 a team drove so far into the Danube that the water came up to the horses' necks, but there was no panic.

points. There is hardly any other breed of horses in which individual qualities combine so well with eagerness to learn and obedience."

"One could hardly ask for a horse with a better character than the Lipizzaner", according to Anton Supka, who has decades of professional experience as a dressage horseman. He fully endorses the qualities attributed to the Lipizzaner, namely that it is good-natured and obedient, faithful and dependant, full-tempered but quiet and re- laxed, intelligent and ready to learn, per- severing and easily satisfied. Time and again, the Lipizzaner's quiet, relaxed dis- position has been praised, especially in situations such as accidents with horse transporters or during minor surgery. All it needs is the soothing, reassuring voice of its keeper to settle any agitation. Even when the Lipizzaners of the Czechoslovak State Circus were subjected to enormous stress during a six-day typhoon in the Sea of Japan, they remained placid and confident.

Water penetrated into the boxes and the grooms waded up to their waists in order to lead the bewildered animals to stalls at a higher level — and all this while the ship heaved and the hurricane roared! Incredibly, the animals showed no panic. Closely crowded together, they had to stand two to a box for four days on end. And even then, there was not a single incident of agitation. The horses remained quiet, and ate and behaved perfectly.

Decisions on breeding are based on tests of performance. The training of young stallions and brood mares begins at the age of three. The horse has its performance test after training for a year or so under the saddle and in harness. Only when it passes the test can it be classified for breeding. The emphasis in the eastern studs is on driving; at Lipizza on the horse's potential for riding and dressage.

Dark foals, white dams. This harmony between black and white is characteristic of the Lipizzaner breed. Within a few years dam and daughter will be indistinguishable in size and color.

THE COLOR

Like nearly all white horses, Lipizzaner foals are born dark. For the first weeks of life they are either brown, blackish − brown or mouse gray. With each molt − if they are kept in the open this occurs in the spring and all of each year − the young horses become lighter in color. The first molt commences at three to four months. The covering hair is lost; the new, often bristly pigmented coat that grows up beneath is frequently of a lighter shade. Grayish patches commonly appear on the skin, first around the eyes, then on the head. These patches of dark foal skin on the light background give it a dappled, or even a checkered appearance. Finally, they lose the dark hairs in the tail and the mane. Generally speaking, the Lipizzaner becomes white all over between the ages of four and ten, usually around seven. When the skin is pigmented dark, the white covering hair has a silvery gloss, which justifies the nickname "silver horse" for the Lipizzaner.

The influence of Arab blood on color may be clearly seen. The herds at Lipizza, formerly multi-colored − dun, black, brown, cream, dappled and piebald, as we can see on the painting "Herd of mares at Lipizza in 1727" by J.G. Hamilton, the English horse painter − have become predominantly white. Since then white has been the dominant color for Lipizzaners. Only in those countries where Lipizzaners continue to be used for agricultural tasks − as draft horses on the hill farm and as spirited coach horses − is the dark color preferred, as it requires less care. In 1890, the distribution of color at Făgăras was forty-seven whites, thirty-three browns, six blacks, three bays, and two duns.

Technological advances and the subsequent decline of the horse used for agricultural purposes is balanced by the increasing need for sporting horses. Selection for dark color will therefore necessarily keep equal pace with the white color. Nor does it seem likely that brown and black will disappear in the future. This inherited factor has be-

come too ingrained through, the centuries. We must therefore expect that when white horses are paired brown and black will recur as recessive inherited factors in their offspring.

In 1880, eight of the thirty-two stallions trained at the Spanish Riding School in
Continue on page 120

The dark chestnut Neapolitano XXI, pépinière stallion at Sîmbăta de Jos. The brands clearly indicate that the sire is Neapolitano XIX and the dam is of the Siglavy line. The only representative of the dark color out of eight stallions at the main stud, it is clear that the aim here, too, is to breed for pure white Lipizzaners in future.

Left: The mixed gray and white of this horse is a permanent variant among Lipizzaners.

Mare with chestnut foal. Chestnut is a rare color for Lipizzaners, and is found only in Rumania. The color variant is evident from birth. Blacks and browns may change their youthful dress, a chestnut never.

Overleaf: Herd of mares at Lipizza in 1727, in a painting by the well-known English horse artist George Hamilton. At that time the "baroque colors" still clearly predominated at the Stud. All decorative and eye-catching colorations and markings were represented, the dapples, bays, duns, piebalds and skewbalds each having a rarity and corresponding market value.

117

Vienna were brown. This indicates that the color was still a dominant genetic occurrance in the breeding of Lipizzaners. Despite decades of selection, brown could not be eliminated at either Lipizza or Piber. Even today it is traditional for at least one brown horse to appear among the schooling horses, though its parents are white.

The Austro-Hungarian Monarchy, a world power at the center of Europe, consisted in dual form only from the time of Compromise with Hungary in 1867. In fact, many nations and kingdoms belonged to the polyglot empire held together and symbolized by the Hapsburg Crown. While the bureaucracy responsible for administering it were centralized in Vienna — the War Office, for example, and the Ministry of

Foals at play in their first weeks of life. The color change begins in foals with spiky gray tones. Below, foals nibble each other. This is part of body and hair care, for which the peer group's aid is required. Such social grooming is frequently continued from the neck down the back, all the way to the dock.

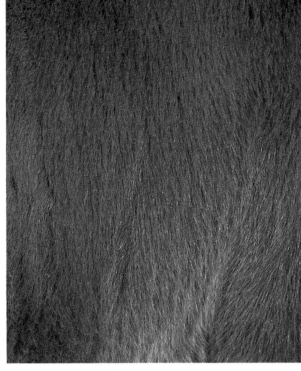

The individual transitional tones can be seen with particular clarity on these four close-ups of the hide. The dark brown, gray and salt-and-pepper tones merge into each other. The color thus changes quite gradually, the shift being specially noticeable during the spring and fall molts.

Above: the molt is most evident around the eyes and on the head. The foals are spotted and dappled on the first change from their dark coat to light gray and white.

Foreign Affairs — in many other respects it was federalistic and decentralized. The Imperial Studs were also distributed throughout the empire, from Bohemia to Galicia, from Hungary to the Italian border. A military stud was at one time situated within the bounds of Vienna itself.

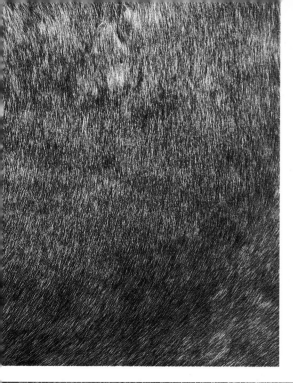

Below: Mares in the snow-white dress of the adult Lipizzaner. Sometimes seven to ten years are required before the change to "silvery white" is complete. A prerequisite is a dark-pigmented skin, which gives the white covering hair its silvery gloss.

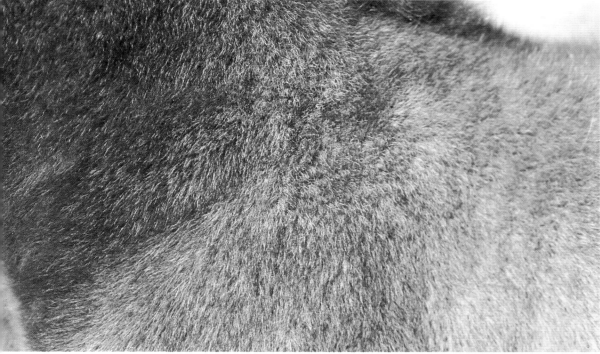

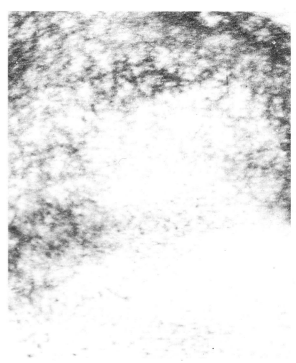

Above: Close-up of the hide of a dapple-gray horse. This is a common interim phase on the way to full white.

Left: Young stallions changing their color. The animals all the same age, showing how different the rate of color change can be. The middle colt will be completely white at the age of three. The mane of the colt on the left is still dark. The one at right will have to wait for several years before its dark juvenile coat has turned white.

Overleaf: The Lipizzaner is as resistant to the winter's cold as to the summer's heat. Rolling in the snow is an expression of contentment. Robust and hardened against the effects of weather, the horses have their daily round in the paddock and drink in the open no matter what the weather.

121

The former Imperial Karst Stud at Lipizza was the cradle of Lipizzaner breeding. From here, the development of new breeding centers for Lipizzaners was guided and the newly formed studs supplied with noble breeding material. The Lipizzaner studs subsequently formed have both peacetime planning and warlike events to thank for their origins. After the Treaty of Schönbrunn in 1809, Carinthia and Trieste were ceded to France. Six years of "exile" on the banks of the River Theiss was the consequence for Lipizza's horses. They were given shelter at Mezöhegyes in Hungary. Here they lacked the high meadows, the fresh mountain air, the crystal-clear, cold spring water, the stony soil, the spicy Karst

banks of the Theiss. The search for a breeding center for this mountain race indicated that the hilly pastures of Transylvania were the most suitable.

With a view to reviving the badly degenerated breed of Lipizzaners left at Mezöhegyes, the Hungarian State Stud of Făgăraş was formed in 1874 at the foot of the mountain of the same name. Here the descendants of the horses evacuated from the Karst more than sixty years previously found a new home. The "F" of Făgăraş and a crown was adopted as the brand. Ever since then Lipizzaners have been bred at Sîmbăta de Jos-Făgăraş. The re-formation of the present-day Rumanian Lipizzaner

FAR FROM LIPIZZA

Lipizza blood has now spread wide. With the original studs in the former Austrian Empire still breeding horses, Lipizzaners are being bred throughout Europe and even in America. The whole horse world now knows and admires the Lipizzaner.

Opposite: Typical Hùngarian six-in-hand in the Bükk Mountains.

fodder, the shady trees and the steep slopes so inviting to educative play. The mares aborted, foal mortality rose and the progeny lost its strength. The risk of a graudal degeneration of the Lipizzaner breed became acute. It was only halted when the horses eventually returned to their native "Karst oasis" after so many years in exile.

But not all returned. The Lipizzaners which continued to be bred at Mezöhegyes languished on the Hungarian plain. Even before the greater part of the herd returned to Lipizza serious consideration had been given to removing the horses to an environment more in keeping with the climatic conditions of the Karst. The plan was dropped when, after Napoleon was finally defeated, Lipizza and the surrounding countryside were handed back to Austria. It was decades later that events took a positive turn for the Lipizzaners left on the

Stud in 1920 followed the brief interregnum of the First World War.
The Hungarian stud management transferred the breeding of Lipizzaners from Făgăraş to the old, tradition-rich Arab stud of Bábolna in 1921. Here, halfway between Budapest and Bratislava, Hungary's Lipizzaners were bred until 1951 on the soil of the Bábolna-Pussta, which suited them well. Although they flourished wonderfully despite the flatness of the landscape, the Hungarian horse-breeders were well advised when, in 1951, they decided to transfer the Lipizzaner Stud to Szilvásvárad in the Bükk Mountains with its chalky soil and abundant wildlife. Since then Hungary's Lipizzaners from Bükk have used the old Bábolna "B" with a pair of antlers as their brand.

The Austrian Lipizzaners were withdrawn from their Karst home during the First World War. The Lipizza Stud was trans-

ferred to Laxenburg near Vienna in 1915, some of the foals going to Kladrub in Bohemia, fifty miles east of Prague.

The first breeding center for Lipizzaners in the then Czechoslovak Republic was formed at Topol'čianky near Nitra, Slovakia in 1921. Its breeding material came from Kladrub. The choice of brand was a "T" with the letters "RCS" (Republic of Czecho-Slovakia) underneath.

The stock from the Lipizza Stud which was brought to Laxenburg was divided after the war ended. Half went back to their old home, the rest to Piber near Graz in Styria in 1919-20. So another Lipizzaner stud was born. While the Lipizzaners bred in their Karst home continued to be marked with the traditional "L" brand on the jaw, those at Piber additionally carried the "P" brand with crown on their left upper jaw as the symbol of their new stud.

The colors on the map show the extent of the Austrian Monarchy.

■ *The existing Lipizzaner Studs*
● *The former Lipizzaner Studs*
○ *The capital cities (to aid orientation).*

POLAND

KIA

TOPOLČIANKY

SZILVÁSVÁRAD

BABOLNA   O BUDAPEST

HUNGARY

MEZÖHEGYES

F

FĂGĂRAS
SÎMBĂTA DE JOS

RUMANIA

K

KARADJORDJEVO

CABUNA

DJAKOVO

Đ

BELGRADE

OSLAVIA

BULGARIA

ALBANIA

GREECE

TOPOLČIANKY

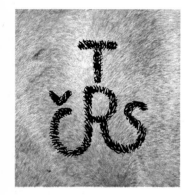

The Stud brand consists of the thigh brand ČRS, with a large T for Topol'čianky above. The sister Stud at Kladrub bears the same brand, but with a K instead of the T. The brand is placed on the left shank. The expert can thus immediately tell a horse's origin by the brands on the left flank.

Above right, Topol'čianky Castle, formerly the summer residence of the President of the Republic, used as a convalescent home. The façade of the building, in classical style, stands out clearly from the other three wings, which are built in the renaissance style.

Teams of nine and twelve white Lipizzaners, in full action under a firm hand, are part of the driving attractions. Such teams cannot be assembled every year. This photograph was taken at Topol'čianky in 1972.

Above, the Riding Hall and stables for sixty working and riding horses, at the entrance to the Topol'čianky Castle and park. They are used for training horses for export and for preparing the Stud's own stallions and mares for the breeding test. Riding and sporting horses are auctioned in the adjoining exercise yard in May each year. The Castle courtyard, right, forms an irregular quadrangle, arcaded on three sides. Valuable possessions such as furniture, tapestries, paintings, porcelain, wapons and the library are housed in the monumental front building, the guests residing in the wings. Dozens of trophies hang beneath the vaulting of the first-floor gallery, witnessing the wealth of wildlife in the neighborhood of Topol'čianky.

128

Topolčianky, the home stud of the Lipizzaners in Czechoslovakia, lies in the district of Nitra, in the foothills of the Slovak Tatra a good sixty miles east of Bratislava. Situated between the Inovec and Tribeč spurs of the Bohemian Massif, the chief stud of Topolčianky was formed in 1921, a mixed breeding center where Arab horses, sporting horses (English and Anglo-Arab half-bloods) and Huzuls are kept in addition to Lipizzaners.

As far as the plain of the Danube to the south, Slovakia is a thickly wooded, mountainous country in which agriculture has had a hard time producing sufficient quantities of food for livestock as well as for man. The Slovak farmer has therefore always valued the Lipizzaner as a horse which is sturdy, undemanding and easy to feed. Until the end of the First World War the stallions for the local stud farms were supplied by the studs at Radautz (the present-day Rădăuti) and Bábolna. Arab horses, too, were used for breeding in addition to the Lipizzaners, especially in the hill country. The Arab-Lipizzaner played a significant role in local breeding. After the collapse of the Hapsburg monarchy the young Czechoslovak state was faced with the need to set up its own breeding station to produce national studhorses. Thirty of the mares evacuated through Kladrub in 1915-16 from the former stud at Lipizza reached Topolčianky. Along with three older stallions from Făgăraş and Lipizza they comprised the basic stock for the newly formed Lipizzaner herd.

The herd of brood mares is located at Breziny, four miles from Topolčianky. The foaling stable with its roomy white-tiled boxes and the adjoining fodder room connect the individual stables. While the mares and their young occupy one stable those with larger suckling foals are housed in a stable opposite. The third section is reserved for brood mares which have been covered, some of them pregnant. From here they are moved shortly before the birth to the centrally located foaling stable, where they spend three to eight days in the box, until they are transferred to the stable with the young foals. In the running stable the mares can move freely.

The paddocks for the mares and foals are located in the immediate proximity of the stable. Ninety percent of the horses are

Plan of Breziny:
1 – Stallions' stable; 2 – Foaling stable; 3 – Mares' stable; 4 – Cowshed; 5 – Coach house; 6 – Breeding mares' stable; 7 – Farm building; 8 – Paddock, 9 – Meadow.

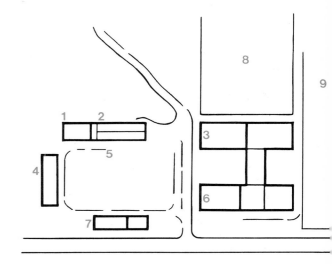

Below: Favory XXII from Szilvásvárad. Under the name of Favory IX, he is listed on the stud-books of the white Kladrubers as the chief stud-horse. The ancestor of this classic Lipizzaner line, born in 1797, came from old Kladrub. Now, his descendants return something of the genotype which he once contributed to benefit the breed. In this way, the narrow breeding base is widened and inbred defects are avoided.

white, the remainder are black or brown. They are powerful, relatively large animals. Measuring fifteen hands and over, among the tallest at the withers of this breed.

The main studhorses are also here. As at Lipizza and Piber, the stallions have double

names. Here are found the white stallions Neapolitano Perletta (imported from Piber) and Neapolitano Saragossa, and the blacks Conversano I Ravata and Conversano II Canissa. All are very elegant stallions, more the type of good riding horse than the classic baroque mount.

The young stallions are kept at the Hostie foal farm three miles away. Seventy colts, aged six months to three years, are housed in three stables; they are divided by year and not by breed. So the two-year-old Conversano rubs shoulders with the young Arab stallion Shagya in the same run and a small Huzul stallion pits his strength against a half-blood.

In Topol'čianky in September the three-year-olds enter the dressage stable immediately adjoining the riding shed. Horses not suitable for breeding are separated for use as work- and sporting horses.

In addition to reproducing the herd of brood mares, the stud also has the task of providing three or four new stallions each year for national breeding purposes. Eastern Slovakia, the area around Poprad, is the nucleus of the national breeding of Lipizzaners. Despite the high degree to which agriculture has been mechanized, the Lipizzaner is still popular as a reliable horse in Czechoslovakia. People are proud of their well driven-in, fast teams of Lipizzaners, which can replace the motor car when road conditions are bad, and are also always to be found in the leading teams in driving championships. The Lipizzaner is, in short, the ideal combination of work- and sporting horse for heavy duty as well as leisure activity.

The traditional stud at Kladruby and Labem, where the cousins of the Lipizzaners are kept in a small population of only thirty

Below: The Hungarian Post on five white Kladrubers in their home stud. The swift horses must be guided with a good feeling for balance and a firm hand. Here the postillion's boots rest in the saddle, while the Hungarian csikós stands more towards the croup.

An expansive park laid out in the English manner, replete with exotic deciduous trees and conifers, stretches from immediately behind the Castle to the thick woods nearby. There may be found some of the country's richest haunts of wildlife and finest hunting grounds.

brood mares, lies barely sixty miles from Prague between Kolin and Pardubice on the right bank of the Elbe. Here, too, we can find a white dam with her dark foal at grass and the chief studhorse in the stallions' stable.

But a Favory is also used here as a stud stallion. In this way, through this traditional line of Lipizzaner stallions originally from Kladrub, some of the old inheritance is being returned.

Like the Lipizzaner, the Kladruber matures late. However, it is larger, more powerful, and more solidly built than the Lipizzaner. On average, an adult mare weighs 1400 pounds and measures 16 hands at the withers. Stallions are slightly larger. The long, concave profile of the head, the often pronounced Roman nose and the high-set neck are typical. Steep shoulders, small depth of chest, a long, solidly bowed back and a short, sloping but broad croup characterize the build. With strong hindquarters, the Kladruber has a high action gait. As a sign of their breed, all white Kladrubers have a «K» branded on the left jaw.

The black Kladrubers are kept in a herd of much the same size at Slatiňany, ten miles south of Pardubice. Their breeding is supervised by the equine breeding research center at the Agricultural Academy, whose task it is to ensure the regeneration of the black Kladruber and the survival of the breed. After a successful attempt to build a new black herd from the sparse remains of the old Kladruber breed, an effort is now being made to extend the narrow base of the blood, as the recent use of the stallion Romke, a representative of the black Friesians, bears witness.

Below: Dressage quadrille at Kladrub, demonstrating the versatility of the Kladruber, which has other uses in addition to those of the strong, heavy, powerful coach horse of old. The similarity with the Lipizzaners is clear in their high action, attitude of the neck, and clearly evident extended step.

Generalissimus XXVIII, born 1960. This fine stallion is a good example of its type, with heavy bones, depth and breadth. On the left flank it bears the brand of its sire — the lazy G with number 23 and the dam's Favory sign beneath. The Generalissimus line has always been the most typical of the Kladruber lines.

Szilvásvárad

Opposite: Young stallions 2650 feet up on the high plateau of the Bükk Mountains left. In conditions similar to those of their former Karst home, the young Lipizzaners can grow into powerful, healthy horses here. A bracing climate, fresh mountain air, unprotected slopes, rocky terrain, spicy mountain herbs and crystal-clear, cold water are all requisites for a tough, disease-resistant animal.

The B in the Hungarian Lipizzaners' brand points both to their old home, the Babolna Stud, and to their new habitat, the Bükk Mountains.

Symbols of the Szilvásvárad Lipizzaner Stud. The Stud formerly belonged to the "Szilvásvárdi Allami-Gazdaság", the State Farm of Szilvásvárad. Today, it is managed by the State Forestry Authority. The wrought iron lamps hang in the stallions' stable. The horse's head, below right, decorates the gable of the Hotel Lipicai.

The road to Hungary's Lipizzaners in the Bükk Mountains runs in a north-easterly direction from Budapest, through Gödöllö, the former summer residence and hunting lodge of the Hungarian kings. It continues through Gyöngyös, with its famous herd of stallions, including forty to fifty Lipizzaners for national breeding, and on to Eger, a city as famous for its heroic struggle against the Turks as for its good wines. From here, it is a curving uphill route to Szilvásvárad, a town stretching for some distance along a pocket immediately at the foot of the Bükk. Only the stud's administrative center – surmounted with the stud's brand which is visible from a distance – and the bright dome of the church, a circular building in the classical style, stand out against the small peasant houses with their typical square plan, leafy arcades and red roofs.

Here in Bükk, at a height of 2,600–2,900 feet, is Hungary's largest single stretch of forest. It is famous well beyond the country's frontiers for its wealth of wildlife. In addition to deer and wild boar, there are wild sheep in abundance, as well as fox, wildcat, badger, marten, polecat and squirrel. The permanent population includes many rare birds such as the golden eagle. However, the last bear was shot at the end of the previous century.

Hungary's Lipizzaners were successfully bred for four centuries in Făgăraş, until

Rider in traditional Hungarian Hussar's uniform. Unlike driving, dressage is not especially popular in Hungary. This is one of the reasons why the Budapest Spanish Riding School, formed in the Thirties as an outgrowth of the Vienna school, was not reopened after World War II. The colorful uniforms of the former Hungarian Hussars are still worn today at Szilvásvárad on festive occasions.

Opposite: The Bükk Mountains. The green pastures are dotted with bushes and rocky outcrops. Juniper grows here in bush and pyramid shapes single and in clumps amid lush grass on the small slopes and in deep hollows.

they were moved in 1912 to the renowned Arab stud at Bábolna. Here, a start was made after the First World War on a gradual transition from the leisure horse to the workhorse. The relatively small horses from the foothills of the Făgăraş Massif became heavier, larger and more powerful on the more favorable soil of Bábolna-Pussta. Today, the Hungarian Lipizzaners are still among the strongest of their breed, standing the highest at 15 to 15½ hands at the withers.

The administrative block at the Szilvásvárad Lipizzaner Stud stands immediately at the roadside, the stallions' stable is a few hundred yards further along the drive to the home park. Here six main stud stallions

132

stand in their roomy stalls. The tall, lightly vaulted stable is whitewashed a snow white on the inside. A large wrought-iron lamp above the passageway gives the whole building a special atmosphere as a masterpiece of craftsmanship. By way of contrast, the artistically worked black wrought-iron frames of the pedigree tables stand out from the walls.

In most strains there is a representative of the old Lipizza's classic stallion — a Pluto, Conversano, Neapolitano, Maestoso, Favory or Siglavy Capriola — and also, since 1975, a stallion of the Croat Tulipan line recently built up here. A representative of the Transylvanian Incitato line from the agricultural breeding center is also

used at regular intervals. "Incitatus" was the name of a horse owned by the Roman emperor Caligula. A stable of marble, a manger of ivory and a purple robe and chain of pearls around his neck were the ornaments of the emperor's favorite horse. An Incitato from the Hungarian Lipizzaner line needs none of these. Without any trimmings it embodies the nobility of its breed. There are no doubts in Hungary that the line will continue.

Lipizzaners are also exchanged internationally to promote Hungarian breeding. For

Plan of Szilvásvád:
1 – Castle; 2 – Museum; 3 – Stallions' stable; 4 – Guesthouse; 5 – Hotel; 6 – Stud building; 7 – Riding Hall; 8 – Exercise yard; 9 – Workhorses; 10 – Coach house; 11 – Offices; 12 – Tack room; 13 – Paddock; 14 – Cottage; 15 – Smithy; 16 – Saddlery; 17 – Breeding mares' stables.

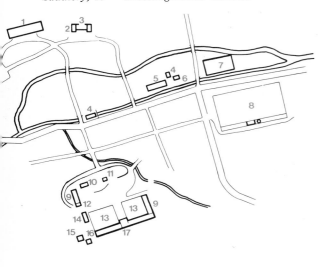

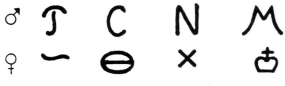

Not only the six classic stallion lines but also the Incitato and Tulipan lines are represented among the brands. The care and maintenance of the Incitato line in Hungary will alone decide whether this strain can continue to be retained in Lipizzaner breeding.

Right: Pluto XXVII and his keeper are firm friends. The horses are longed or ridden every day and kept under continuous observation at night.

example, the black stallion Conversano XXII from Yugoslavia stood at Szilvásvárad for two years as a proud representative of the black line which, while existing side by side with the whites on an equal footing, has always been pushed into the background by the silver-whites. The black horses have always been inferior to them in number, never amounting to more than ten to fifteen percent of the total herd. But who can say which is the more beautiful? The

play of muscles and sinews clearly visible, the hide smooth and gleaming in the sun, a well-formed, thoroughly trained black stallion can hold its own against any pure white.

The stalls for the seventy brood mares are located in the home farm's workyard, a little distance from the edge of the village. On the other side of the yard is the stable for the coach horses and young stallions. The yard is enclosed by various outbuildings. Here, too, the Lipizzaner brand appears on the gable – the old "B" of Bábolna with two antlers on either side of the Bükk Mountain. There are roomy paddocks in front of both sections of the stable for the brood mares and their foals. To one

Village views at Szilvásvárad. Farm houses below, church below center, and stallions' stable right form a rustic corner. The Stud management has set up a Lipizzaner Museum in three showrooms in the side wings of the stable. It contains a good record of the development of the breed and its significance to Hungarian horse breeding.

Below: The new Riding Hall at Szilvásvárad. Here exhibitions are held for tourists visiting the Stud. Lipizzaners under saddle and in harness, displays by csikós, and groups on horseback show off the versatility of the Lipizzaner.

side, there is another stable for forty coach horses and workhorses. The foaling boxes are also here, in which the mares play with their newborn for the first week of their lives. The foals then return to the main stable — this encourages the young animals' growth and resistance in the fresh air and less confined space.

old, traditional and only slightly modified lineage brands are burned on the left loin and the stud brand on the right.

Next to the smithy is the wheelwright's and coach-builder's workshop. The art of carriage-building has been highly developed in Hungary. Small coaches are still meticulously made by hand, even with some

hand-carving. Quite deceptively, a braided pattern is engraved into the wood; after the wood is lacquered it is barely distinguishable from a real braid. The wheels and axles, too, show that only quality work is done here. Hungary was famous throughout the world for fast hunting in secure carriages pulled by two, four or even

Above: The herd moves to new pasture.

Below: View of the foal farm at Csipkeskút, nestled at the bottom of a small valley 3,000 feet high in the Bükk Mountains. Only horse and nature lovers find their way to this foals' paradise.

In Szilvásvárad, the white mare predominates — only about fifteen percent are black. About a third of the whites are pure, the majority being toned slightly blue or gray. The herd is always accompanied by a "Csikós" (foal keeper), who must see to the welfare of his charges. Here, the young, dark or gray-tinged foals, still unsteady on their long legs, test their strength for the first time.

A short passageway from the yard leads to the smithy, where the show- and carriage horses are shoed. The hooves of the brood mares and young are merely trimmed every four to six weeks. Here the irons are kept for the foal and stud brands. When, at the age of six months the foals are weaned, the

more horses. The craftsmen engaged in carriage-building are traditionally known as harness makers and wainwrights. A particularly gifted representative of this trade lived in the middle of the fifteenth century in the small Hungarian village of Kosc, near Tata in the district of Komárom. It was here that the first comfortable travelling coach was built in 1457. Other vehicles were built to the same pattern and were known as Kosci, meaning "originating in Kosc." Because of their perfection, they conquered the roads of Europe. Their name was adopted in other languages, hence the German word "Kutsche" and the English "coach."

Hungarian bridles and coach harness are

The tradition of the old Hungarian harness has lasted to this day. The trappings of these teams on the Szilvásvárad exercise yard have been expertly crafted. The second team is harnessed in tandem, originally an English custom.

examples of the craftsman's art. Trappings, originally introduced as a protection against flies and gnats, developed into decorative leather straps, artistically worked in braided patterns, with gay ornaments of inlaid material. They are characteristic of Hungarian tack and give it its special quality.

The road to Csipkeskút, the foal farm built of bright blocks of mountain limestone, winds its way up the mountainside. After ten miles or so of uphill travel, the thickly wooded slopes, broken only here and there by outcrops of rock, open out. The valley widens into a high plateau of remarkable natural beauty. The road to the foal farm turns off halfway along the Bükk plateau. The visitor may encounter foals grazing in the side valley and may soon become surrounded by the trusting, curious animals in all shades of color — black, dark gray, light silver, even a few who are almost white.

After a short stretch of poor, uneven, stony track, the fenced-in paddocks and the first buildings of the farm can be discerned at the center of a hollow fringed with beechwood trees — two large stables with outbuildings of white sandstone and gray mortar. The gates and fences around the lush fields, which are divided for the various age groups, are painted white. In winter foals drink from the brick troughs alongside the spring; in the warm seasons the water wagons are filled here for the two-mile journey to the summer stable on the waterless high plateau of the Bükk Mountain.

Hungary is the citadel of horse-driving in Europe. The country owes its outstanding successes in international shows not least to

With the Hungarian six-in-hand, the two pole-horses are preceded by four horses abreast. This form of harness can be traced back to a ban by the Hapsburg Emperor who issued a decree forbidding driving in sixes — that is, harnessing horses in three sets of two — that privilege being reserved for the ruler. That was more than the Hungarian Duke Sándor Moritz, famous for his audacious driving and riding, could stomach. As a master of the Hungarian art of driving and a Hungarian patriot he evaded the Imperial order with this "protest harness".
Right: View from the coachman's box. The manes fall outwards. This leaves a clear field of vision for the driver to see the flexion of the necks and the carriage of the horses.

the Lipizzaners. Continuing the old traditions of driving is one of the tasks of the Hungarian Lipizzaner Stud. Teams from Szilvásvárad have gained laurels the world over. The coach-and-six in its original Hungarian harness is still a major attraction at international events. To emphasise the importance of the Stud to Hungarian driving, a new showground was created in 1976-77, tastefully designed from timber only, using beams, tree trunks, poles and shingles. A composition of natural wood, benches, the

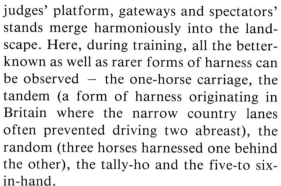

The trappings decorate the forehead on both sides of the bridle and also hang, as back trappings, from the harness. The brass buckles, stars and buttons show up clearly against the black leather and colorful fabric linings, known as **Pillango.** You can tell the team's origin from the traditional heraldic colors of these "butterflies". Szilvásvárad's colors are blue and red.

Shown here are loin trappings with metal decorations below, brow trappings with blinkers

far right, head trappings, originally intended to keep off flies and mosquitoes, now artistically braided bands of decorative leather right, and detail of harness bottom.

Above, original Hungarian **karikas** with intaglio pattern, Pussta motifs, year-date and name of the **csikós.** The six-and-a-half-foot plaited leather strap is fastened loosely with a belt to a wooden handle nearly sixteen inches long.

Below right, farming team in north Hungary, with the Bükk Mountains in the background. From the age of a few weeks the foals accompany their dams everywhere. The first signs of the incipient color change are already evident on the foals' head and limbs.

judges' platform, gateways and spectators' stands merge harmoniously into the landscape. Here, during training, all the better-known as well as rarer forms of harness can be observed — the one-horse carriage, the tandem (a form of harness originating in Britain where the narrow country lanes often prevented driving two abreast), the random (three horses harnessed one behind the other), the tally-ho and the five-to six-in-hand.

Every effort is made at Szilvásvárad to maintain the old breeding traditions of the Hungarian Lipizzaners and to promote them throughout the world. The revival of

a national sporting and training center has begun. In fact, a generously proportioned riding shed, 200 feet in length and 65 feet across, with a thousand seats for spectators, in already finished. The 1984 World Championships in four-in-hand driving was the fruit of hard work. International sales promotions ensure that the horses are sold throughout the world. The Hungarian Lipizzaner is in strong demand. Among national breeders too, it is regarded as a good, reliable coach horse and farm horse.

137

SÎMBĂTA DE JOS – FĂGĂRAŞ

The Stud's F brand comes either from the town of Făgăraş, six miles away, or from the mountain of the same name. The then Hungarian Stud was moved to Bábolna in 1912. The present Rumanian Stud of Sîmbăta de Jos was formed from the three stallions and twenty two mares left behind.

Above right: The two extensive stables for the herd of breeding mares, with typical gates at the entrance, each offer space for 60 mares with suckling foals. Foaling boxes provide protection for the newborn foals. Mangers and chains for tying the mares are fitted to the longer sides. The foal mangers with their first oats stand at the center of the stable.

The Rumanian Lipizzaner Stud of Sîmbăta de Jos lies about halfway between Sibiu and Brasov at the foot of the Făgăraş Mountain. With its one hundred and twenty brood mares and total of six hundred horses, it is the world's largest Lipizzaner stud. It is impressive not only for the size of its herd but for its large area and the sweep of the landscape.

The colorful peasant houses of the town with their ornamental plaster work and carvings on the wooden doors and window frames, and the covered passageways and gateways remind us of Slovakia and Hungary. A broad village street leads to the

The herd of breeding mares and their foals are put out to pasture each morning. At midday the herd seeks shady spots by the Sîmbăta stream. At right, the wells, of a kind typical in the Hungarian Pussta,

♂ 𝒯 C N M F SC 𝒯

♀ ~ ⊖ ✕ ⚘ □ ♂ Y

The sign at the entrance of the Stud, above. The Stud is controlled by the Central Authority for Horse-Breeding and Breed-Testing at the Ministry of Agriculture. An associated 7,900-acre farm makes the Stud self-sufficient. The wheat and hay harvests are the focus of farming work, some of which is still carried out with the aid of horses.

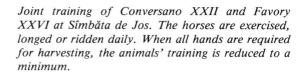

Joint training of Conversano XXII and Favory XXVI at Sîmbăta de Jos. The horses are exercised, longed or ridden daily. When all hands are required for harvesting, the animals' training is reduced to a minimum.

stud. Farmers in white linen shirts and dark hats return home from the fields for their midday meal with their teams of Lipizzaners. At the entrance to the stud, a portal with a wrought-iron gate flanked by two massive columns, a sign-board has been fixed – Herghelia, Sîmbăta de Jos Făgăraş. The administrative offices are housed in an old castle, the former palace of the governors of Transylvania, built at the time of Maria Theresa, who spent several days there. Spreading chestnuts and tall spruces frame the building. Past them runs the road to the stallion stable, a gleaming, whitewashed building nearly twenty yards long. The stud's eight chief service-stallions are

housed in roomy boxes in the first section. Here, all the classic stallion lines of old Lipizza are represented in addition to the Tulipan strain. Only a stallion of the original Transylvanian Incitato line is missing. This strain has died out at Făgăraş.

The young stallions are kept in another part of the stable, at stands with flanking beams. Outbuildings adjoin the stands, including a smithy, workshop, wheel shop, saddlery, bruising mill, a massive three-

A typical Lipizzaner farm team of mixed color, pulling a low, extended open-frame wagon. The farmer prefers the colored Lipizzaner as dray horse. Whites require too much grooming, though they are said to have a better quality hoof than the blacks and browns. Whites form barely ten per cent of the two hundred agricultural Stud-animals. Thirty per cent have dark coats. The blue roans predominate, forming more than half the stock.

Once again, the color white predominates at the Rumanian stud. Some seventy percent of all brood mares are light, the bluish sheen being common. About twenty percent are brown and ten percent are black. A few chestnuts complete the color mix of the herd. The main studhorses, with the exception of the dark chestnut Neapolitano XXI, are white.

As a stud brand, Sîmbăta de Jos continues to use the "F" (Făgăraş); however, the

are still used when storms cut the water supply. Drinking troughs stand both in the field and against the wall of the mares' stables. The horses are exercised in the yard after drenching.

storied hayloft, paddocks, riding and longeing rings, tack stores, coach sheds, dry rooms, and further stalls for the young stallions, young mares and workhorses.

Several wells, a few groups of trees, a drive of poplars and limes and whitewashed wooden fences complete the charming, harmonious picture of this generously proportioned establishment.

Two extensive stables for the herd of brood mares are on the other side of the Sîmbăta stream. They offer adequate space for a hundred and twenty mares and their foals. Immediately adjoining the stables are the meadows and paddocks, so that the young foals can run out into the open with their mothers from a very early age.

Plan of Făgăraş:
1 – Breeding mares' stable; 2 – Paddock; 3 – Cottage; 4 – Exercise yard; 5 – Kitchen; 6 – Guesthouse; 7 – Manor; 8 – Longeing yard; 9 – Stallions' stall; 10 – Garden; 11 – Hay store; 12 – Riding hall; 13 – Riding horses; 14 – Coach house; 15 – Smithy; 16 – Barn; 17 – Fillies stall; 18 – Farm building and saddlery; 19 – Cowshed.

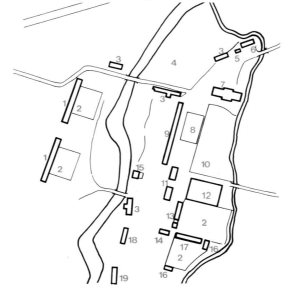

Building the ricks at Sîmbăta de Jos, with Lipizzaner teams bringing up the bales. Dray work at the Stud's large agricultural establishment is still partly carried out by horses.

crown of the old Hungarian brand is missing. The brand is placed on the right loin, together with the foaling serial number of the servicing stallion. The lineage brands on the left loin correspond with those of the old Lipizzaner brands, with only slight differences. The brands are applied when the foal is six weeks old, the sire's sign appearing on the left loin, with the dam's beneath it. The sire's brand is followed by the servicing stallion's number in Arabic figures, which marks its place in the "dynasty of the kings" in the House of Făgăraş, in chronological order.

The foal farm for the young stallions is six miles away, at Beclean, just beyond the town of Făgăraş. Two herds of about forty stallions each, divided into age groups, are accommodated here. The stallions return to the main stud at the age of three-and-a-half and are then trained for driving and riding for a whole year. After taking a performance test, they are graded and made available to the agricultural breeders as studhorses. The agricultural breeders need an additional thirty stud stallions every year. After proving their worth at a stud center, the horses may be used as *pepinniers* at the stud. Horses not suitable for breeding are separated from the herd and sold as work or sporting horses. The export of horses, especially for sporting purposes, ensures a good income to the stud.

The young mares are kept at Ucea de Jos, ten miles in the direction of Sibiu. The working buildings consist of a large complex of several sections – extended stables,

White stallion of the Siglavy line, of the Arabized type. The typical feature of the Lipizzaner, the Roman nose, is barely to be seen. The Stud is proud of having eliminated it almost entirely through fifteen years of selectivity.

Below: The horses leave their stables in the early morning and return only at sunset, guarded by two mounted herds at all times. The pastures stretch along the river Olt. In the fall the harvested wheat fields with their stubble are also available as pasture.

Bottom: Close attention. The foal looks fearlessly into the camera, in a meadow immediately adjoining the stable. Mount Făgăras is clearly visible in the background, rising to a height of 8,200 feet.

the oldest of which was built in 1748, wells, paddocks and fenced-in rings for exercising in winter. About a hundred horses aged one to three years are housed here in three groups according to age.

The horses leave the stalls early in the morning and are led back to them by their keepers at sunset. They are guarded at all times by two mounted herdsmen. The meadows stretch along the river Olt, the horses seeking shade from the noon sun beneath bushes and trees along the banks. The watering place is a flat, ford-like stretch further along the bank. The herd

approaches the river in a mass, enjoying the coolness of the water.

The foal's carefree existence ends after three years. Training takes place in the fourth year at Sîmbăta de Jos, followed by the performance test and allocation to the brood mare herd, depending on the results. The main task of Lipizzaner breeding in Rumania has always been to breed a good workhorse for agriculture. This still applies although there are certain limitations owing to the increasing mechanization of agriculture. However this is proceeding more slowly in the mountainous districts than in

The filly herd at Ucea de Jos is accommodated in various sections in extended stabling, the oldest parts of which go back to 1748. The herd is drenched in the yard entering and leaving; during the day, the horses slake their thirst in the nearby river. The one to three-year olds display color gradations all the way from dark to white.

Left: The herd of breeding mares go to drink and cool themselves several times a day. The water boils and foams under the movement of their hoofs and splashes on the neighboring horses.

Below: Horses follow a mounted keeper to drink. The Olt, a broad tributary of the Danube which borders the pastures to the north and here runs parallel to Mount Făgăras, subsequently turns in a southerly direction to cross through the Carpathian Massif.

the plains. The Lipizzaner usually excels in mountains up to a height of 2,300 feet. Only then is it surpassed by the Huzul. By careful breeding, success has been achieved through long years of selectivity in eradicating the drawback of the Rumanian Lipizzaner — its stocky build (its height under 14¾ hands at the withers) and low weight (under 1100 pounds) — and creating a more solid type. The broken nose, so typical a feature of the Lipizzaner, was also bred out; it is now scarcely found at all.

The stock of horses with a predominant proportion of Lipizzaner blood (not counting the foals) is estimated at eight thousand. More than two hundred service stallions of the Lipizzaner breed are used for agricultural breeding. Preference is given to dark Lipizzaners, as they require less grooming. Consequently, the percentage of pure whites among the stud stallions is small, there being numerous "blue roans" and examples of the *deres* color combination (white hair on a dark basic color), usually white with a chestnut or brown cast.

The Lipizzaner maintains its established position as a workhorse in the mountains, where machinery can be used only with difficulty, if at all. The horse is docile and resistant, not choosy about its food, hardworking and attractive. Breeding policy is aimed at "work and beauty," so the Rumanian Lipizzaner, too, combines nobility and beauty with resistance and performance. If, one day, the Lipizzaner work horse becomes superfluous in the wake of further mechanization, there will still be a place for the Lipizzaner as a well-formed, elegant coach and riding horse in its Rumanian homeland.

MONTEROTONDO

Lipizzaner mares in the Roman Campagna. The Stud Monterotondo lies close to Rome and is run by the Roman Institute for Experimental Zootechnology.

Below: Service stallion at Monterotondo – a representative of the Favory line on the longe.

During the period between the two World Wars, Lipizza was an Italian military stud. Breeding was aimed at producing the sturdy, large Lipizzaner of the riding type, suitable for army service. Stock of the former type (unremarkable withers, sloping back, small frame) was weeded out. Italian Lipizzaners quite frequently stood more than 15¾ hands, with a girth at the shank of 8 or 9 inches. These results were obtained by using such stock as Maestoso XVIII and Conversano Austria, two stallions with enormous proportions, and Favory Noblesse, who had fifty percent Kladrub blood, and six mares descended from Kladrub mothers. Unfortunately, little attention was

with the "Istituto Sperimentale per la Zootecnica." Lipizzaners are now bred here. Forty mares with their progeny and seven stallions of the six classic lines form the stock. The color gradations range from gray to white. The horses are at grass throughout the year, day and night. Traditional brands are no longer used; only the number is burned on to the front hoof.

The lines and nobility of the mares are particularly appealing at Monterotondo. Brood mare groups have been formed along the individual breeding lines. Individual stallions are assigned to them during the covering period so that a kind of "open stud" has been experimentally formed, the

paid at the time towards retaining the old type of Lipizzaner. The horses lacked extension and girth, their proportions were unharmonious and the general effect was coarse.

After the Second World War part of the herd was moved to Pinerolo in Piedmont, and from there to Montemaggiore near Monterotondo in the neighborhood of Rome, a state stud possessing the necessary financial base. The stud itself is associated

objective being to maintain the breed. Owing to the climatic conditions and the basic stock and breeding methods, some doubt may be justified as to whether Lipizzaners bred in Italy will be of the type of Lipizzaner in the former Austrian tradition. The fact that the young mares are covered at the age of three indicates that one characteristic trait of the Lipizzaner, late maturity, has been lost.

DJAKOVO

The Djakovo Stud brand is burned on the left hind shank. Apart from the shank brand, all Lipizzaners born at Djakovo bear the national symbol H (for Hrvatska, i.e. "Croatia") and the foal number beneath, on the left flank.

Above right: Croat farmer with Maestoso Bravissima, stud-stallion of the Lipizzaner Breeding Association in the village of Vuca. Every association is a member of the Savez Lipicanskih Udruga, the Lipizzaner Breeding Society. In twenty Udrugas, the selection center caters for some 600 registered Lipizzaner breeding mares, including 150 in the area around the neighboring stud of Karadjordjevo.

The Yugoslav studs of Djakovo, Vučijak and Karadjordjevo form the basis for agricultural breeding, as the Lipizzaner is used widely in Yugoslavia as a farm horse. Nearly one third of the total horse population carries some proportion of Lipizzaner

blood. The toughness of the Lipizzaner, its willingness to carry loads and its ease of feeding continues to ensure it an established place.

In addition to the pedigree mares kept at the studs and by the farming breeding cooperatives the stock of Lipizzaners in the country is estimated at some forty thousand. This number includes all the animals with at least seventy percent Lipizzaner blood. However, apart from the studs and cooperatives, the number of pure bred Lipizzaner mares with a proven pedigree used for agricultural breeding is small.

Breeding Lipizzaners are most widespread in Croatia; the center for breeding is the Djakovo Stud, standing about midway between the two tributaries of the Danube,

Above left: In the first weeks after giving birth, the white dams graze with their dark foals immediately in front of the mare stable. Only later do they move into the pastures adjoining the Stud with the herd.

Above: The interior of the stallions' stable in the yard of the administrative building above. The four-in-hand horses are accommodated here, in addition to colts undergoing training. Horses from Djakovo have participated successfully for years in many championships at home and abroad.

Left: The sign at the entrance to the "Horse Selection Center" in the town.

the Drau and the Sava, twenty-five miles to the south of Osijek. Formed in 1506, it is one of Europe's oldest studs. Originally, Arab-Oriental horses were bred here. The Lipizza Imperial Stud was housed at Djakovo for one year in 1806. When the Lipizzaners returned to their old Karst home, a few mares and stallions were left behind. Since then Lipizzaners have also been bred here. Djakovo became a pure Lipizzaner stud in 1854 when the famous

144

People still talk of the Queen of England's visit to Djakovo, which was arranged at her personal request during her state visit to Yugoslavia. A tally-ho brought her from the railway station. Thirty Lipizzaner farm teams with their fine horses and peasant costumes accompanied her to the Stud.

one trainer to every four stallions. The final test, on which inclusion in the breeding herd is decided, consists of a long-distance drive of six to seven-and-a-half miles, with minor obstacles on the terrain. Under the saddle, a basic knowledge of dressage is required. The best stallions enter the stud as chief service horses. However, they must first prove themselves for two or three years in agricultural breeding.

Of the seventy stud-stallions used for agricultural breeding, about two thirds are employed for crossing purposes. The combination of heavy mare and Lipizzaner stallion is very popular. Luka Stipič, the director, is justly proud of the broad basis of agricultural breeding, which is comparable to none. He is an enthusiastic Lipizzaner fan who coordinates all breeding in this area. In agricultural breeding the darker colors are more strongly represented, though in the stud itself the white color predominates. Sixty to seventy Lipizzaners are exported throughout the world each year.

Archbishop Strossmeyer, the "horse bishop" of Djakovo, purchased a large number of purebred Lipizzaner mares and stallions from Lipizza.

In the period between the two World Wars, the stud, with its eighty brood mares, was one of the largest in Yugoslavia. It lies three miles from the town, just off the road, surrounded by pasture and woodland. The red brick buildings, erected about one hundred and fifty years ago as the former episcopal farmstead of Ivandvor, boasts a mare stable over a hundred yards in length and three small stables for the young animals. The main stable also includes the foaling boxes and stands for the main service stallions. The young mares are accommodated here in addition to the forty brood mares.

As well as the shank brand, all Lipizzaners born in Djakovo carry the national symbol "H" (Hrvatska, i.e. Croatia) with the foal number beneath it on the left loin. If an oak leaf has been added beneath the "H", the horse has been bred elsewhere in the country and not at the Djakovo Stud. Not only the Croat Tulipan line is represented, but all the six other classic stallion lines of old Lipizza.

The young stallions enter the stud stallion stables at the age of three. Then the one-year training period commences. There is

Above: Siglavy Thoplica, 1979 Champion at the International Agricultural Exhibition in Novi Sad, a stallion of the modern type. He is shown in front of the breeding mares' stable at the former episcopal farm of Ivanfor and is one of four chief service stallions used at the Stud each year.

VUČIJAK

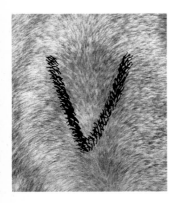

The Vučijak Stud brand is burned on the left flank.

The service-stallion Siglavy Sitnica, a nicely pointed black born in 1973, the pride of the Stud. He represented the breeding center at the International Breeding Show during the 400th Anniversary celebrations at Lipizza.

showing that until now a light mountain horse has been produced. The aim is to breed a taller, more powerful type of Lipizzaner in the future. In addition to the six classic stallion lines of Lipizza, the Tulipan line is also represented. Within a circumference of six miles, some fifty mares from farming establishments have been combined into the country's first Lipizzaner breeding cooperative.

The Serbian Lipizzaner Stud at Karadjordjevo is about sixty miles away from Djakovo, on the eastern bank of the Danube. It was formed in 1903, but has bred Lipizzan-

Brood mare herd close to the Vučijak Stud. A high proportion of dark colored horses is clearly visible, a sign of how closely the Stud is aligned with agricultural breeding. As a workaday horse preferred for mountain use, the Lipizzaner will not be supplanted by machinery in agriculture for many years yet.

The Lipizzaner Stud at Vučijak lies in northern Bosnia, a few miles from Prnajavor, itself thirty miles east of Banja Luka. It was formed in 1946 with the aim of producing studhorses for agricultural production. The basic herd consists of four brood mares and more than thirty percent the horses are in dark color. The frame is smaller than the average Lipizzaner in other Yugoslav studs. The mares stand 14½ hands, the stallions 15 hands at the withers,

ers only since 1946. The stock came from Djakovo and Lipizza. The brand is a "K". The brood mare herd consists of thirty horses with progeny; forty service stallions are available for agricultural breeding.

KARADJORDJEVO

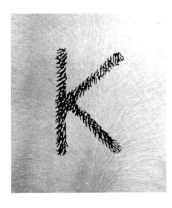

The K brand has been used since the Stud was formed in 1923.

Below: The Stud's pastures in and around Karadjordjevo offer the horses generous amounts of space. One of Karadjordjevo's aims is to breed the black Lipizzaner as well as the white. Today, more than ten percent of the two hundred horses kept are black Lipizzaners. The Stud hopes to increase this to fifty percent in the future.

The twelve-year-old stallion Conversano Wera, one of the chief stud-horses at Karadjordjevo.

The sixteen-year-old stallion Siglavy Vuka II standing by the stallion stable. Lipizzaners bred at Karadjordjevo are rather heavier and bigger than those at Lipizza, partly because of the soil in this part of Yugoslavia and the fact that they are largely used for agricultural purposes. The horses are also trained in dressage and for driving work.

TEMPEL FARMS

In the countryside north of Chicago is a Lipizzaner breeding and training center that is the largest and best established in North America. Tempel Farms is a rolling 7,000-acre farm where horse pastures are woven between wheat and cornfields and large pastures of wildlife preserve. Tempel Steel Company, the Farms' parent, was founded in 1945 by the same Tempel Smith who in 1958 acquired twenty Lipizzaner mares and stallions from the Austrian State Stud Farm. Mr. Smith and his wife were moved profoundly by what they saw at the Spanish Riding School in Vienna that year and they were drawn to visit the bloodstock at Piber. Inspired by the dream of bringing this breed and its tradition of classical dressage to the United States, Smith understood that

148

Tempel Farms, below, had to purchase additional stables and barns to house its growing Lipizzaner herd. Today it consists of some 175 animals. The Stud covers an area of 6,900 acres of lush pasture amid fields of wheat and corn north of Chicago.

Opposite bottom: Mares and foals at pasture. Tempel Farms' first twenty mares and stallions came from Piber. They were followed by stallions and mares from the Hungarian Bábolna Stud and Lipizza.

he would have to emulate the missions of both Vienna and Piber and so form the foundation of the Tempel Lipizzaner. A staff was sought to undertake these two interdependent but discrete disciplines — breeding and training.

This was an undertaking that was not without its false starts. One blessing that overcome many setbacks was the arrival in 1961 of Dr. Mikulas Ferjencik, a veterinarian who had been a Czechoslovakian Cavalry General in charge of his country's entire army stud before and during the war. Ferjencik's lifelong familiarity with the Lipizzaner and his vast practical experience were ideal attributes for the task of building a healthy and excellent herd at Tempel Farms. Aiming to breed Lipizzaners of the finest conformation and movement, in 1964 Ferjencik imported six more Lipizzaner mares from Babolna, Hungary and three stallions and three more mares from Lipizza. Five Hungarian stallions purchased in 1958 and 1959 and trained in Vienna arrived later. A celebrated addition to the herd in its beginnings was Pluto Ancona, grandson of Pluto XX, the stallion presented by Austria in gratitude to General George Patton. These and the original imports were the foundation bloodstock of the herd which reached, at its height in the

A five-day-old stallion foal with his dam. Some forty mares from the lines Almerina, Fantasca, Prima Donna, Slatina, Garafolina and Duba are used for breeding at Tempel Farms today.

late 1970s, over 500 horses and today numbers approximately 175. The six service stallions employed today represent the venerable lines of Neapolitano, Siglavy, Maestoso, Pluto, Conversano and Favory. Among the approximately forty active brood mares are these outstanding families: Almerina, Fantasca, Prima Donna, Slatina, Garafolina and Duba. Ferjencik built a staff and carried out his work for nearly a quarter of a century in a number of barns and stables which had been acquired by Tempel Farms to accommodate the burgeoning herd. Today the Tempel herd is directed by Alexander Cassatt assisted by veterinarian Gary Koehler. Cassatt, who joined the farm in early 1985, also has a keen interest in driving, as did Ferjencik, who developed several Lipizzaner pairs for show on the farm and gave initial prepara-

Tempel Lipizzaners have plenty of opportunity to demonstrate the artistic movements and paces of classic dressage in America. Above, a quadrille at a charity show for the Lincoln Park Zoo in Chicago.

Left: Tempel Lipizzaners at the Inauguration festivities in Washington for President Ronald Reagan in 1981.

Below left: The Pesade, executed by Favory Slatina under her rider Karl Bergmann. In the Pesade, the horse lifts its forearms as in the Levade, but by more than 45 degrees.

Below: The Piaffe, demonstrated by Neapolitano Prima Donna under First Rider Alf Athenstaedt. Athenstaedt introduced training in classical dressage at Tempel Farms in the Sixties.

tion to a number of pairs that have been sold. Some of these have had great success in national competition.

While Ferjencik was tending to the growing herd, dressage training was undertaken, but its soundest foundation was laid in the mid-1960s with the arrival of Alf Athenstaedt of Hamburg, Germany, a distinguished student of dressage mentor Willi Schultheis. Athenstaedt was assisted in the early years by the tutelage of Hans Irbinger, an Oberbereiter at the Spanish Riding School, who

150

The Capriole under the rider below and on the long rein bottom. This movement of the Haute Ecole is one of the most difficult of school jumps. It is practiced first at the hand, then on the long rein and subsequently under the rider. The jump requires a special predisposition and receptiveness from the horse. A team of riders and trainers works with the horses daily at the Tempel Farms training center. Hans Irbinger, a First Riding Master at the Spanish Riding School, did much to help with training in the early days. This is now the joint responsibility of Alf Athenstaedt and Karl Mikolka, also products of the Vienna School.

later spent summers in Illinois working with riders and horses. Another veteran of the Spanish Riding School who has become a prominent participant is Karl Mikolka who joined Tempel Farms in 1980. Athenstaedt and Mikolka co-direct the training operation today with a full-time staff of rider/trainers. There are now some fifty stallions in daily training at the Tempel Farms Training Center. In accordance with tradition, the education of the stallion begins at four years old on the longe line and continues for years in a systematic regimen which emulates the Viennese model. A few riders are encouraged to pursue initiatives in dressage competition. Included in the responsibility of the riding staff is the preparation of some horses for sale to the public.

Throughout the Farms' first two decades, the Tempel Lipizzaners have performed at many cultural events, charity benefits, business gatherings and special exhibitions at competitive horse shows including the World Championships of 1978 in Lexington, Kentucky. The Tempel Lipizzaner have also appeared at four presidential inaugurals and in performances at the White House and the U.S. Capitol. In the 1980s Tempel Farms began presenting regular twice-weekly public performances at the Training Center during the summer months, each of which are attended by over two thousand spectators. The proximity to the herd operations affords the opportunity to show the progression of the Lipizzaner from the early days of its schooling. The

program includes mares and foals, the carriage tradition, young stallions, all steps and movements of the Classical School, work in hand, work on the long rein, Airs Above the Ground and the Quadrille.

Tempel Farms continues to pursue the mission of its founder, Tempel Smith — preservation of the purity of the Lipizzaner breed and improvement by careful selection; continuation of the Lipizzaner tradition at the highest levels of classical dressage; and preparation and distribution of Lipizzaners to American horse enthusiasts for use in competition and pleasure.

151

THE EUROPEAN LIPIZZANER BREEDING SOCIETIES

In the last twenty years Lipizzaner breeding establishments have appeared in many countries. They cannot be compared with the large state-owned studs. Amateurs have begun to import Lipizzaners from the countries of origin for use as riding and driving horses. Universal interest in the breed is increasing continuously. Lipizzaners with their rhythmic gait and light colors attract attention; they are frequently put on show on festive occasions. Dressage performances of high quality have frequently formed the highlights of riding and driving trials. The early attempts at breeding have borne fruit. Small studs have resulted with up to four brood mares and their progeny.

These establishments had to be helped along and their successes recorded. Lipizzaner societies have therefore been formed whose task it is to draft appropriate guidelines for breeding, maintain contact with the original studs and forge new links with breeding societies in other countries.

The German Lipizzaner Breeding Society (the LZD) was formed in 1977 and is one of Western Europe's largest, with exemplary organization. Its efforts are aimed particularly at breeding pure-blooded Lipizzaners. With this in view, a new model Register has been introduced, based on the strict standards of the registers kept in the classic studs. For a horse be included in the main Register, it requires a good assessment of its appearance and gait as well as impeccable proof of descent.

With more than fifty mares registered, the LZD breeders can choose their service stallions according to the lines along which they wish to breed. They can call on Conversano Traga, for instance, who was bred in West Germany and exemplifies the traditional type of baroque Lipizzaner, or the stallion Favory Santa from Djakovo, a Lipizzaner of the modern type for riding. Genetically valuable material was added to the German breed by Favory Dubovina 4, a stallion on loan from the Spanish Riding School. This was the first time that a stallion from the school was lent to a Lipizzaner society for any length of time. Favory Dubovina 4 was kept at the well-known Lipizzaner establishment at Utten-

Western drivers are increasingly using Lipizzaners for international driving. Above is an example of a Lipizzaner team of the German Lipizzaner Breeding Association, with its driver Hans Ernst Reker on the obstacle course during the Danube-Alps Cup Championship at Kecel, Southern Hungary, in 1981.

Right: A Piber brood mare from the Lipizzaner Stud at Uttenstetten with her foal. This foal received an award as its year's best and boasts excellent lines. Its sire is Favory Dubovina IV from the Spanish Riding School in Vienna.

There has been a large Lipizzaner society in Sweden since 1974. At present two hundred horses are registered with the Svenska Lipizzaner Forening. The horses originally imported from Hungary were followed in due course by Lipizzaners from Piber, Lipizza and Sîmbăta de Jos. Conditions for breeding a pure strain were therefore favorable from the start. The declared aim is to breed only strictly purebred Lipizzaners, especially as viable coach horses. The successes achieved by Swedish breeders have been confirmed repeatedly by experts from Austria and Hungary who have attended exhibitions and breed shows. It is therefore hardly surprising that interest in Lipizzaners is rising steadily in Sweden and demand for the horse outstrips the supply. There is also a small Lipizzaner breeding society in Holland, the Werkgroep Lipizzaner Nederland (WPN), which is a member of the Dutch Pedigree Society. It draws its breeding material from all the established Lipizzaner studs in the main areas. There has also been an independent society in Belgium for some years. In France, there is an association of Friends of the Lipizzaners, "Les Amis Français du Lipizzan," to which all breeders and admires of the breed belong. The interests of British breeders are represented by The Lipizzaner Society of Great Britain. Breeding material imported from Austria, Italy and Hungary includes Siglavy Alda, a former stallion with the Spanish Riding School who spent two years servicing at Piber. He is now kept at Starrock in the south of England with five brood mares.

The possibility of combining all studs and breeding societies was first discussed at the breed's quater-centenary celebrations at Lipizza. The Lipizzan International Federation has now been formed, an international breeding association to promote and coordinate all breeding activities. As the Lipizzaner societies of a number of countries, including the United States, have agreed to cooperate, we may hope that all studs and breeding societies can eventually be persuaded to join. Only then will the conditions be right for successful breeding.

stetten-Fremdingen. Together with the Lipizzaner Stud at Sturnehof near Halver-Kierspe in north Germany, these farms are among the best known and largest within the LZD. Both farms use mares from Piber.

Members of the LZD play an active part in national and international driving events. Displays of the classic art of riding in the saddle and on the long rein appear in show programs and the Lipizzaners are introduced to a broad public with all their beauty and appeal.

The work of the Lipizzaner breeding society formed in Denmark in 1972 is based chiefly on imports from Hungary. However, Lipizzaners have also been introduced from Yugoslavia and Czechoslovakia. The hundred-or-so brood mares include some non-purebred Lipizzaners. Attempts have been made in recent years to breed a Lipizzaner corresponding in type and size to those of the home countries. Imports of breeding animals, stricter rules and careful selection of the sire will, it is hoped, promote a pure strain.

PIBER

The Stud brand – a P with Imperial Crown – shows the horse was born at Piber. Each Lipizzaner can be precisely identified by its descent brand on the left flank. It consists of the first letter of the sire's name, the symbol for the mother's line beneath, and, on the right flank, the foal's register number.

The Romanesque parish church at left dominates the small village of Piber. It is first mentioned in the Salzburg Proclamation of 1066, which elevated it to parish status. For centuries, Benedictine Monks from the Monastery of Saint Lambert worked here.

Below: The initial letters of the stallion lines Pluto, Conversano, Neapolitano, Maestoso, Favory and Siglavy. Symbols, some of whose origins are now obscure, are burned in beneath the initials of the stallion name. The Neapolitano symbol is a Neapolitan sword, Pluto's (whose ancestors are Danish) are the sea's waves, that of the Arab scion Siglavy an arrow.

The fairy tale life in an ideal world almost comes true in the countryside around Piber. What we find in this part of Western Styria is not just a sunny idyll. The smiling hills pose no threat, the meadows are lush and green, the pasture of a gentle roughness – landscape, quite simply, whose charm imposes itself by its congeniality.

In these surroundings symbiosis of horse, man and landscape has been proceeding

right environment for the breeding of noble horses.

Western Styria is steeped in history. Two thousand years ago the Celtic Taurisci lived near Piber. A mountain on which a Carmelite monastery now stands was revered by the heathen tribes of those times. Buried beneath the spoil of centuries, the Roman occupation has left sculptures which are still archaeologists' pride and joy. A thousand years later, the medieval barony of Eppenstein delegated a small, local fief to the Lords of Piber. Both the manor and the village are said to owe their name to the rodents which then inhabited the marshes in the low-lying parts of the neighborhood – the beavers (German *Biber*).

In 1066 Monte Cassino, the world's oldest Christian monastery, burned down by the Arabs, was rebuilt. Near the town of Hastings in southern England, William the Conqueror defeated Harold, the Anglo-Saxons and their army – and the Norman kingdom was born. It was also the year that

A view of the Renaissance castle of Piber, built by Domenico Sciassio towards the end of the Seventeenth Century, now the Stud's headquarters.

Right and opposite, Piber offers its horses plenty of space.

successfully for some two hundred years. The fact that the Austrian Lipizzaner herd, adrift after losing its Lipizza birthplace at the collapse of the Habsburg empire, found a new and permanent home here in 1920 is living proof that this region provides the

an exalted spiritual lord placed his name and seal on a document by virtue of which the village of Piber was granted parish status and all the privileges connected with it. The long arm of Salzburg's powerful archbishops had made its mark.

Right: The inner court of the splendid castle of Piber in Styria. The building also houses the Lipizzaner Stud's administrative offices.

However, secular force soon reached up from the south. In 1104 Henry, Duke of Carinthia, donated the parish and its lands to the Benedictine Monks at the newly formed foundation of Saint Lambert. The dispute between the Lambertians and the Salzburgers which dates from those times was finally settled three hundred years later. The ultimate victors were the persistent

Below: Brood mare and suckling foal amble across the paddock at Piber.

monks. The handsome residence which they then built for themselves was replaced towards the end of the seventeenth century by a new building in the Late Renaissance style, designed by Domenico Sciassio, Saint Lambert's monastic architect.

Emperor Joseph II, son of Maria Theresa and enlightened despot on the Hapsburg throne, looked askance at ecclesiastical possessions. Between 1782 and 1786 he dissolved 738 monasteries because "no Order can be pleasing in the sight of God but is care for the sick and educate the young." The Lambertine monastery and all its rich possessions were merged into the Religious Fund. Nowadays, we would call it nationalization. Eight years after Joseph's death in 1798 the monastery was converted to a mi-

litary stud farm. English thoroughbreds and Anglo-Arabs – the horses at the Styrian stud, whose fortunes soared and fell – soon enjoyed an excellent reputation. However, when this news reached Vienna, Court officialdom took over and every decision it made proved a wrong one. The stud management at Piber were simply astonished when, towards the middle of the

nineteenth century, they were instructed "on the highest orders" to transfer their best mares to Radautz, the Monarchy's largest stud. Again, between 1853 and 1869, the extremely successful breeding of service stallions producing Lipizzaners for agricultural use had to be suspended. Now the official policy was not to breed Lipizzaners but English shires and half-bloods. The result was a fiasco.

Piber and the Lipizzaner were not to be reunited until the Austro-Hungarian Monarchy had faded, at a time when people had other things to worry about than the fate of the imperial show horses. When after the First World War Austria was granted 91 horses from Lipizza, then Italian territory, in the opinion of many starving Austrians, this meant ninety-seven unnecessary hungry mouths to feed. But two years after the end of the war the spirited representatives of the world's oldest domesticated breed of horses found quarter in Piber. They settled in side by side with the established Arabs and Noricans, Haflingers and Anglo-Arabs. The Lipizzaners took to the mild mountain climate and the luxuriant fields. The era of sparse Karst provender was past. However, despite living in a land of plenty, they retained their slender build.

Their progeny also did well, to begin with. Every year more than twenty — sometimes as many as thirty — foals were born. A more than satisfactory fertility rate, which was to reach its peak in 1928 at one hundred percent! However the needs of the populace and the political confusion appear not to

The stables board at right bears the names of the sire (here Pluto) and dam (Alda), and the horse's year of birth.

Below: The Lipizzaners at Piber are housed in large partitioned stables where they can move freely about. They are tied only while eating, in order to make sure that the fodder is evenly divided.

Opposite: For the lover of noble horses there is no finer sight than the happy unity of animal and surroundings, as here in a rich Piber meadow.

Below: Leading the way to the exhibition ground near the castle.

The Austrian, Italian and Yugoslav Lipizzaners were grouped centrally in Hostau, formerly Bohemia and now part of the Third Reich. Piber became a military remounts center for the German Army's mountain pack animals.

The fate of the Lipizzaner in these dark days has already been described in detail elsewhere in this book. The Hostau interlude – despite the contrary times and even if for only a few years – proved beneficial to breeding. This had been put into the hands of first-class circumspect specialists and the effect on the horses was invigorating all around.

As from the start, the Lipizzaner breed has consisted of a very small population. If only because of the special requirements made of these horses, inbreeding could never be avoided. Therefore, problems have always existed. Between 1765 and 1810, for example, Lipizza changed tack and started breeding a lighter horse – perhaps for precisely that reason. The stud did so although it could have built on a base of some one hundred and fifty brood mares. The stock that was available at Piber in the post-war years was miserable by comparison.

Until then, every director of the stud had had his own philosophy. All of a sudden, catastrophe struck again in 1983 – within no time at all, equine rhinopneumonitis was to kill twenty-two Lipizzaner foals and

have left the condition of the white horses at Piper untouched. WHen civil war and dictatorship in 1934 put an end to Austrian democracy, only twelve Lipizzaner foals at the Lipizzaner Stud saw the light of day in a steadily darkening world.

In the opinion of Heinrich Lehrner, director of the stud from 1957 to 1983, "They were essentially sound, fine horses. Horses which did every credit to their forebears; however, despite all the care and conscientious management, there may have been a certain lack of style – in the atmosphere at the farm, in the way things

were developing, and also the basic approach to breeding policy itself."

Nor were matters improving. In March 1938 Hitler entered Austria and now that this small country had been completely robbed of its self-awareness, in Piber, too, events unfolded in equal measure. In 1942 Piber was dissolved as an independent stud.

Piber has been the home of the Lipizzaners only since 1920 but has been a military and remount stud for some 200 years. The rooms containing the various tack, some of it quite valuable, reflects this long history.
Far right: Plan of Piber; 1 – Castle, the administrative headquarters; 2 – Wheat store; 3 – Training department and Stallions' Stable; 4 – Coach house; 5 – Open Stable I; 6 – Riding Hall; 7 – Foaling Stable, open Stable III and Tack Room; 8 – Veterinary department and farmhouse; 9 – Open Stable II and Boxed Stable; 10 – Farm building; 11 – Smithy.

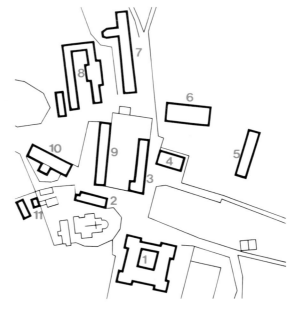

eight brood mares. Many experts expressed the view that the stud now needed fresh blood with all possible dispatch.

The new director of the stud, Dr. Jaromir Oulehla, was appointed in the fall of 1983, but already had a long connection with the riding school and the stud as a veterinarian. It is now left to him to search through the five hundred-or-so Lipizzaner breeding establishments the world over for suitable material. However, he says, "there's not much room for experimentation." The Lipizzaners are bred at the individual studs today for quite different purposes. In Hungary, they are bred chiefly as coach horses, in Rumania, as work horses. In

Below: Colts spend the summers of their first to third
years on the Stuba pasture above Piber, the fillies on
the Brentl.

neither case is the objective specific as that
set by the breeders in Piber — to produce
young stallions as the succession for the
Spanish Riding School in Vienna, with all
its traditional requirements.

The future for the Lipizzaners at Piber
is bright — new blood has been found.
Oulehla purchased fourteen horses from
Yugoslavia, Hungary and Czechoslovakia.
After a long quarantine and thorough exa-
mination, they were moved straight to the
stud and have settled down very well. A
happy announcement appeared in the Press
early in 1985: thirty of the Lipizzaner mares
at Piber are expecting! "On this basis, the
Lipizzaner stock is secure for decades to
come," was the director's optimistic comment.

The horse-lover on pilgrimage to Piber sees
little of the toil and trouble associated with

breeding Lipizzaners. The visitor no longer
needs to wonder how these aristocrats can
put up with floors of compacted clay, as
they did up to a few years ago. The stables,
too, have been brought up to present-day
standards, as have the hygienic conditions.
It is always a pleasant surprise for the
horse-lover strolling through Piber to come
unexpectedly upon an entire herd of Lipizzaners, some horses still with dark coats,
and to accompany them for a little way
along the fenced-off paths. It may well
raise a smile to see the horses, as they leave
their pasture, putting their Roman-nosed

160

In the hill meadows around Piber, Lipizzaners show their joie de vivre.
Lipizzaners at play, above and right, try out movements which will later be developed into paces of the Haute Ecole or airs for the schools above the ground. They are as it were born to the Passage, Piaffe, Levade and Courbette.

heads together or instantly taking the lead when banded with the half-bloods. After all, the half-bloods also have a noteworthy tradition – the horses for the Imperial Cavalry were bred at Piber.

The Lipizzaners have plenty of room in which to spread themselves. For example, at Wilhelm, one of the stud's outer farms, the young stallions have an extended romping ground. When we observe them, we might think that one was attempting a Passage and the other a Piaffe, or a particularly boisterous colt might seem to be raising itself in the Levade. The Lipizzaners

have an inherited biological tendency towards these movements. On reaching the age of three, the more gifted stallions will develop their inherited skills into a high art. While the farm at Wilhelm may offer the young stallions a constant supply of fodder, the "gentlemen Lipizzaners" will spend the

summer in the high pastures learning how to cope with the rougher side of life. The landscape here brings them back to the conditions their bred endured for centuries in the harsher realities of the Karst. Up here, the climate is more bracing than in the valley, and provender has to be sought between rocks and stones. It may well happen that the young stallions lose a little weight. However at the same time they acquire the condition which has made them the toughest horses in the world.

Miles away from the young stallions the mares are at pasture. They have grazing rights throughout the year at the Reinthaler Farm and they spend a relatively well-protected summer on the grassy slopes of the Brendl.

Back in the valley, we may be fortunate enough to meet a four-in-hand or even a six-in-hand composed of Lipizzaner mares. These too are a traditional and honored attraction.

Piber is, in short, a landscape that landscape which offers the Lipizzaners plenty of scope for development and deployment. This is a place where Lipizzaners can look forward to a future as promising and honorable as their four-hundred-year history.

Quiet reigns in the lofty white sun-bathed hall. Beams of golden light fall between the columns diagonally through the tall windows. The gigantic crystal chandeliers beneath the richly coffered roof glow softly, a symphony in white and gold over the dark-brown tones of the floor of the building. The only spot of color are the two red-white-red banners hanging at an angle from the tops of the light-gray pillars at the center of the arena. Just audible is the sound of blowing, a soft tinkle; the muffled sound of hoofs approaches. The silence of the tall enclosure seems heavy.

him are two flashes of color — a scarlet saddle-cloth on a striding white horse. A First Riding Master at the Spanish Riding School salutes the image of the builder of the Hall, the emperor Charles VI, the last of Austria's baroque rulers.

The visitor enters the Riding Hall as if it were a cathedral, its elevated, light solemnity demanding silent attention. The salute that each rider offers the Emperor's likeness whenever he enters the arena, no matter how often he may have changed horse during the morning's work, increases the impression of ceremony.

THE HAUTE ECOLE OF HORSEMANSHIP

Opposite: Brown top-coat, white buckskin breeches, black knee-boots with buckled spurs, and the traditional cocked hat — riders enter the arena. They first salute a portrait of the Emperor Charles VI.

Overleaf: The School Quadrille. In the center, two horses perform a demi-traverse to the right in an exhibition before the handsome façade of the Palace of Schönbrunn during the Spanish Riding School's 400th anniversary.

At a busy, measured pace a white horse appears through the left of the two small open doors at the corners of the shorter wall. Its head nodding lightly in time with the step, its mouth playing with the snaffle bit, it raises a light clatter. The rider in his long, buttoned-up brown tunic and black riding boots solemnly lifts his gloved right hand and raises the gold-edged bicorn. He glances to the right, towards the proscenium arch, backed by a life-size portrait. It shows a man clad in dark armor. Beneath

People come here from all over the world. Whether they are horsemen or not, this is the high point of their visit to the Austrian capital. The allure of the supreme art of riding in the baroque setting of the Winter Riding School at the Imperial Palace, the Hofburg in Vienna, escapes no one.

It is here, within the splendor of the Imperial Riding School, that unity was created between the architecture of the Baroque and the art of decorative riding. Here the horses of the Imperial Court and their rid-

ramp and the school used as an auditorium. Composers whose works were performed here included Handel and Mendelssohn. In 1835, a hundred years after it was completed, the Hall was even used for a trade fair, when Fischer von Erlach's masterpiece accommodated the first public industrial exhibition. Even stock exchange dealings were transacted beneath its fifty-six foot high plaster ceiling.

ful of being overtaken by Jakob Degen, publishing the first classic work of aviation literature and so founding the science of aerodynamics. However, Cayley's fears were aroused unnecessarily; a reporter in Vienna had, in order to enhance the sensation, omitted to mention that in setting off on his flight Degen had fitted a gas balloon above his wings in order to neutralize his body weight. The Riding Hall in this way

plans for the magnificent baroque buildings completed by his son Johann Emanuel. They include the Carolingean Church (1716 – 1739) and the Court Library, construction of which started in 1723, the year of his death. The initial plans for the Winter Riding School in the grounds of the court's pleasure-garden were also Johann Bernhard's but it was his son, who came to Vienna as his father's apprentice during the last year of the regency of Emperor Joseph I, who began to build it in 1729, finishing in 1735. Vienna had recently been freed of the Turkish threat and in the times of peace that followed the accession of Charles VI in 1711 erected many splendid buildings. The Chancellory Wing of the Hofburg Palace (1726 – 1730) was also built from the plans of Joseph Emanuel Fischer von Erlach.

Baroque architecture mirrored the spirit of its age. It was concerned with the shaping of space. In pompous and passionate gestures it conveyed a feeling of strength, of pleasure in gloss and richness; and the developments in music, painting and literature showed a delight in decoration. The younger Fischer von Erlach was working on the Winter Riding School at much the same time as Matthew Daniel Pöppelmann was building the Zwinger in Dresden and the Church of Our Lady in the same city, Balthasar Neumann's pilgrimage church of the Fourteen Saints in Oberfranken and Kno-

The height of the Hall proved particularly useful to an inventor early in the nineteenth century. An Austrian watchmaker of Swiss origin called Jakob Degen (1760 – 1848) had been experimenting since 1807 with a flapping-wing machine driven only by muscle power. In 1808 or 1809 (the year is not certain) he demonstrated his flying machine in Vienna and is said to have risen as far as the ceiling of the Hall. It is not so much the flight itself which gives historic importance to the event and the location, but rather the reports which appeared about it in the Press. Ultimately they led to the Englishman Sir George Cayley (1773 – 1857), fear-

became a place where aviation history was made.

The Riding Hall in the Winter Riding School has been the Lipizzaners' workshop for two hundred and fifty years, formerly before invited guests but now for paying spectators. It is a masterpiece by the Viennese Court architect Johann Emanuel Fischer von Erlach (1693 – 1742), son of the master mason Johann Bernhard Fischer von Erlach (1656 – 1723). The elder von Erlach was a native of Graz and regarded as the founder of the "Imperial Style", the German architecture of the Late Baroque which originated in Vienna. His were the

Overleaf: The last carousel in the Winter Riding School was held in 1894, the theme being "The Empress Elisabeth Christine brought home by her spouse the Emperor Charles VI." For the first time, low-born officers and staff of the Spanish School could participate. First Riding Master Franz

Gebhardt and Riding Master Johann Meixner, with two other riding masters formed a quadrille of one in the numerous scenes. The drawing by Moritz Ledeli shows the historic pageant which opened the proceedings. Charles VI is portrayed by the Duke of Schönborn.

Above: Archduke John (1782 – 1859), elected as titular head of the Empire by the National Assembly at Frankfurt in June 1848, had resigned his office by December 1849. Here, on 20 July 1848, he opens the first Parliament of the Hapsburg Monarchy in the Hall of the Spanish Riding School. The home of the school's Lipizzaner stallions for two hundred and fifty years, it has thus done equal justice not only to art and culture, but to politics.

Left: The historic pageant, horse ballet and equestrian carousel of 1853, mounted for a royal audience. King Frederick William IV of Prussia and King Leopold I of Belgium were guests of the Emperor Franz Josef I.

belsdorff's Palace of Sans-Souci in Potsdam.

Only this age was propitious for establishing the highest form of decorative riding. The Haute Ecole, with its paces and movements still practiced today, was the equestrian counterpart to the spirit of Baroque art and architecture. It was not by chance that the "Directives for the implementation of the Spanish Riding School" raised the work of a French riding master of the time into an authoritative work – the "École de Cavalerie" by François Robichon de la Guérinière.

For this art – stirring, decorative, flamboyant and yet so deeply rooted in the nature of the horse – Johann Emanuel Fischer von Erlach created a noble and festive frame in the world's finest riding hall, 180 feet long, 59 feet wide and 56 feet high. It had two galleries, the upper supported by forty-six Corinthian columns, all in white; the proscenium arch was at the narrow end, illuminated by a single colorful ornament – the painting of its builder, Emperor Charles VI.

In the periods between the great festivities – the carousels, balls and brilliantly-lit assemblies, with guests crowding on the

169

stands or on the pine boards which were laid on the arena — a deep stillness would reign in the Hall. The atmosphere was unique, one of gentle, patient, concentrated work with not a voice raised. The whispering of the few spectators in the galleries; some subdued murmuring, often from the enclosure beneath the proscenium or the

and to learn from them. They came to experience how the thoughts and teachings of the grand masters were put into practice in the saddle, how the art had to be relearned again and again, how the display took

lasted for centuries. The Riding Hall at the Hofburg in Vienna is both the showroom and the studio for the artist on horseback. Just as the sculptor uses his chisel and mallet, so the school rider has to approach his work as a craft. As with any craft in riding, too, there are apprentices, skilled workers, and artists.

Imperial Box; the clatter of bits; the creaking of leather; now and then a stirrup knocked against the wall; occasionally the dull rumble of a stallion's whinny as it greeted a stall-mate on the track. Much has been said and written about the public exhibitions, the luster and gleam of the lights on the gold trimmings of the white horses, of the impressions that the School's horses leave on their masters after having completed difficult exercises with apparent ease, when the last entrance of the Quadrille is no more than a fleeting, vibrating passage in the visitors' minds.

This is how it must have been when royalty and nobles attended the performances. It was, however, the finished picture of a consumate art, the goal of the patient work in the stillness which for centuries was the true characteristic of the Spanish Court Riding School. The morning's work was attended by the connoisseurs and the professionals who wished to study the riders' methods

shape over the course of time, much longer than an orchestra might take in rehearsing a master's work for a concert. The art lay in movement, the lively movement of a horse beneath its rider formed to his will, with training and exercise, all muscles steeled, obediently pursuing its invisible aim, a horse in full harmony with its rider. Together they perform movements, figures and jumps, merging centaur-like from two bodies into one will, guided by human intelligence, controlled by a common feeling, yet fully in tune with the nature of the animal, revealing its beauty, its ability, its expression.

This was the work of art which was to shine in the carousel, the pageant, the competition and the horse ballet, capturing people's hearts; a work of art closely akin to music in that, like music, it exists for the moment only, must continuously be recreated, and at its highest moments comes together like a chord.

The art of movement on horseback has

The art of conditioning a horse to high artistic expression while retaining all its natural propensities — to train it to the perfection of movement under its rider so that it can romp as if it were free yet stay obedient to the rider's will — is proof that the classic art of riding has its roots in Greek antiquity. As witness we have an ancient sculpture and two ancient books. The Greeks' advanced horsemanship is nowhere displayed more expressively than on the marble frieze which stretched along the cornice above the naos of the Parthenon, the Temple of the Virgin Goddess Athene Parthenos. It portrays the Panathenic Procession, the parade of young men on horseback under the gaze of the Olympian gods on the greatest of the religious-political occasions of the Athenians in honor of their city's patron goddess. These reliefs were brought to Britain between 1803 and 1812 by the Scottish noble Thomas Bruce, Earl of Elgin and Kincardine (1766–1841), together with a collection of precious items,

and by an Act of Parliament in 1816 purchased by the state for £ 35,000 for the British Museum. Today visitors still marvel at these masterworks, which demonstrate the high level of horsemanship attained by the ancient Greeks. See how easily the riders sit on their horses, with what perfect balance. The attitude of head and hand and the

his own experience, he emphasizes the proper handling of the horse, avoiding any compulsion that might jeopardize the horse's spirit. The finest quotation is his comparison with the dance: "A dancer who is forced to leap around with whip and goad is no more appealing than a horse treated in the same way."

young men's movements show their complete relaxation in the saddle, the first prerequisite for controlling the horse. The horses are shown with great realism, though for artistic reasons connected with their original placement on a temple façade high above viewers' heads, the proportions are slightly distorted. Completed around 432 B.C. by Iktinos and Kallikrates under the supervision of the sculptor Phidias, the reliefs could have been illustrations for two textbooks which appeared about ninety years later.

In the opinion of leading horsemen of our time, these are among the greatest treasures of equestrian literature. The books are known as the *Hipparchikos* ("The Leader of the Horsemen") and *Peri Hippikes* ("Concerning Horsemanship") and their author was the Greek writer and historian Xenophon (born c. 430 B.C., died after 355 B.C.).

Xenophon, a member of the gentry and a pupil of Socrates who wrote in the purest of

Attic Greek, is remembered for causing generations of schoolchildren to toil over his "Anabasis." In this work he describes the "March of the Ten Thousand," namely the campaign of Cyrus the Younger against his brother, the Persian king Artaxerxes II, with the support of Spartan auxiliaries who, under their leader Carrisophos, and under Xenophon, retreated from the Tigris to Trebezond after losing the battle of Kunaxa (401 B.C.). The humanity of his thought and his clarity of expression still mark him as one of the most important school authors. However, his works on horses have made him one of the most important writers in equine literature. In his two treatises on the art of riding and on the commander on horseback Xenophon examines the relationship between man and animal for the first time on a scientific basis. In training the horse, he builds especially on empathy with the animal and on complete comprehension between the rider and his mount. With a clear assessment of

There are many riders today who should take his chief principle of dressage to heart. "When we seek to exhibit our horse in such a way that it attracts attention beneath its rider through its fine apperance, let us first forget to tug at the bridle at its mouth, to treat it to the spurs, or to use the whip ... when we learn to lead the horse forwards with a light pull on the reins, with its head held high and arched from the neck, we shall then succeed in inspiring the horse to do what it has pleasure in doing and in which it takes pride ... when in bringing the horse to a stop we cause it to do so by itself, when it wishes to put on its finest appearance, we show ourselves in possession of a horse which is joyful and magnificent, proud and attractive."

Here we have our first and supreme principle of the classic art of riding in a nutshell. All subsequent great masters of the art have understood this and have always returned to it during further development despite many an error.

For a long time festivities and carousels at the Spanish Riding School looked back to the time of the Turkish invasions in the 16th Century. "Moorsticking" is an example. Wooden Turks' heads on poles had to be hit with the pistol or lance at the gallop. Such a display is shown here in a painting by Ignaz Duvivier dating from around 1780.

Through a series of great equestrian artists in Renaissance times who revived the principles of classic dressage according to Xenophon's doctrine, which had lain dormant for centuries, the art of riding can be traced directly to the masters whose works were quoted in the "Directives" for training at the Spanish Riding School – François Robichon de la Guérinière, Max Ritter von Weyrother, Louis Seeger and the Baron von Oeynhausen.

Today at a time when horsemanship is dominated with "fast dressage" on the bit rein, when a "bit check" has to be made before any major dressage event because after five hundred years restraining bits seem to be making a comeback, the Spanish Riding School is one of the few, if not the only, institutions in the world where the basic principles recorded by the Greek riding master Xenophon more than two thousand years ago are still observed.

With the rediscovery of antiquity during the Renaissance, institutions were set up at many of the Italian princely courts for young noblemen, equestrian academies which attracted the nobility from many European countries. Here, the Italian School of Riding began to take shape. In 1532, Federigo Grisone formed such a school in Naples which became famous under him, his pupil Cesare Fiaschi and Fiaschi's pupil Pignatelli. Grisone had carefully studied Xenophon's works and quoted him extensively in his book *Ordini di Cavalcare* ("Riding Instructions"), published in 1550. Cesare Fiaschi was the first to describe paces and figures on the track; the dressage of horses was slowly transformed into the Haute Ecole. The expansive action of the horses corresponded to the great gestures of the men of that age in nature and art. Pignatelli, a riding master of the Neapolitan School, had a pupil from France, Antoine de Pluvinel de la Baume (1550 – 1620), then only seventeen years old, who later made a name for himself in his home country. He became stable-master to the duke of Anjou, who subsequently mounted the French throne as Henri III. He also served Henri IV, under whom he

At a major festival in the Riding School, held in 1743 to celebrate the recapture of Prague during the War of Austrian Succession, Maria Theresa herself led the Ladies Carousel. Two riding quadrilles and a driving quadrille performed an artistic routine. This painting, by the Dutch master Martin van Meytens (1695 – 1770), hangs in the Schönbrunn Palace in Vienna.

formed an *académie d'équitation,* and taught the Dauphin, who later ruled as Louis XIII. In his book *Manège Royal* he postulated the treatment of the horse as an individual and rejected excessive compulsion in training. In doing so, he turned back to the writings of Xenophon, to the principles of the Greeks of classical antiquity. He is regarded as the inventor of the pillars and the cavesson.

It is hardly surprising that in that age when riding was being developed into pomp, circumstance and decoration, masters also appeared who led the art into a dead end. In 1658, a work appeared by an Englishman which, in equestrian literature at least, is distinguished by the longest title of any printed riding manual. It began, *Méthode et invention nouvelle de dresser les chevaux ...* and would take up at least twenty lines here. Its compiler, William Cavendish, Duke of Newcastle (1592 – 1676), was tutor to the Prince of Wales, who became Charles II. Cavendish fled with him from the Puritans under Cromwell during the Revolution and lived in France and the Netherlands; he built a manege at Antwerp and taught in the city. One of the most important properties of a good rider is missing from his work — humility. The more he praised himself, the more he put down his horses. His methods were disreputable — he was all for short paces and made sure that a training gallop covered no more than a hundred and fifty yards within fifteen minutes. He was also the inventor of the bit-rein, which has caused untold damage to so many horses when held in unskilled hands, and he drove his horses in the most complicated postures with spurs and whip. He must have ruined many horses. He also taught the "cleft seat" and insisted that the rider should not sit back on his buttocks. He believed that horses should be pulled around a turn with the inner rein instead of being ridden on the outer.

The teachings of the man who was the greatest master of the Baroque, which even now forms the basis of work in the Spanish Riding School, put an end to this foolishness. Under François Robichon de la Guéri-

nière (1688–1751), equestrian principle once again becomes entwined with developments in the art field. Just as colors and outlines begin to appear lighter and more lively in painting, as the rigid lines of buildings break down into fecund curves in architecture, so release, freedom, looseness and compliance emerge in riding.

Guérinière had his pupils sit easily and in a relaxed fashion, well back on the buttocks, as a precondition to the obedience of the horse, which is no longer forced to do his bidding. In the history of the art of riding Guérinière's name is linked for all time with the introduction of the concept of "shoulders first" which still plays a decisive role in training the dressage horse. His book

L'École de Cavalerie published in 1773 led to a turn-around in school riding. François Robichon de la Guérinière brought rider and horse into balance.

Among those who have preserved the traditions of the French riding masters from classical times to the present day many names survive. The Directives for Training helps keep them alive.

Max von Weyrother worked at the School from 1813 to 1833, the last eight years as First Riding Master. Three years after his death his friends published a volume of his writings, and in addition his teaching was forcefully propagated by his pupils.

Overleaf: A performance in the decorated Riding Hall, with the stand sold out as usual. More than 1,000 spectators witnessed this display of the riding art. No circus for the paying public, such an exhibition is in fact a rare authentic example of a living cultural tradition.

The Berlin Stablemaster Louis Seeger, founder of the City's first private riding establishment, studied with Max von Weyrother and defended the classic principles in the face of many fashionable eccentricities encouraged at the time. His horses were not merely trained circus performers; they could perform ordinary horse work in the rough just as well. His book, *System of the Art of Riding* (Berlin, 1844) was awarded with the Prussian Gold Medal for Merit.

We must also mention a man whose methods did a great deal of damage to equestrianism, the French schooler François Baucher (1796 – 1873). A gifted horseman, he was instrumental in introducing the most

contrived kinds of artificial gaits to the ring, while having nothing to do with galloping or even jumping. He had no success in promoting his techniques with the officers of the French cavalry school at Saumur. The French were delighted by his tricks, but could see no place for them in military horsemanship. The newspapers took Baucher's side, giving him far more publicity than he deserved. He had more success in Prussia. A cavalry colonel translated his *Méthode d'Équitation basée sur des nouveaux principes* of 1842 into German and a squadron of heavy cavalry was formed on the lines he advocated.

However, when parading at the gallop before General Wrangel during a cavalry exercise, the display went seriously wrong, turning into such a catastrophe that trials by Baucher's method were banned forthwith. Baucher's circus tricks were attacked by Stablemaster Seeger in a widely circulated pamphlet, "Mr. Baucher and His Arts: a Word in the Ears of Germany's Riders". In it, he defended the classic principles which he had learned in Vienna and exposed the gimmickry. In one passage he hit upon a basic truth — "Never forget that forward movement is the soul of the art of riding and that it springs from the hind leg!" In this case, as in so many others, riding had

for the first time precisely described the natural and equestrian gaits of the horse. Here again we see the influence of the riding masters at the Vienna School, as we do to our own day, far beyond Austria's frontiers. Even Britain, the home of racing and hunting, shows examples of this. One

British preserve the memory of their first riding master. When King George III founded the Royal Artillery's first riding school at Woolwich in south-east London in 1802, he brought the Hanoverian Captain C.A. Quist to England the first instructor. Quist had been a pupil at the Spanish Riding School. He used to ride a famous white stallion called "Wonder," which lived to the age of 41 and was to all appearances a Lipizzaner. Quist was responsible for raising the standard of riding among British officers to a high level, and the coat of arms with its horse and pillars reminds us of his connection with the Spanish Riding School.

to be protected from eccentrics and charlatans.

The third name which deserves mention is that of Baron Oeynhausen. A scion of a north German equestrian family, he studied with Y.H. Ayre, the riding master at the Georgia Augusta University in Göttingen who, like his father, a pupil of Max von Weyrother at the Spanish Riding School, had the status of professor. In his work *Gait and Seat* (1869), Baron Oeynhausen

of the most remarkable is the coat of arms of the King's Troop Royal Horse Artillery, the saluting battery of the British Monarchs in London. This is a battery of six guns, the last mounted unit of the British artillery, greatly admired for their outstanding riding. The shield over their guardroom in St. John's Wood shows a horse in the Pesade, between two pillars, the columns still to be seen today at the center of the arena in Vienna. In this way, the tradition-conscious

This story points to yet another function of the Spanish Riding School that is still important today — to exert a positive influence on the art of riding in other countries, to keep it pure through practical tradition, and to train gifted pupils and instructors who will pass on the doctrine, as did Baron Oeynhausen and Captain Quist. Equestrian art is an element of human culture which can be kept alive only by riding — nurtured and refined day by day accord-

from well-ridden horses who would not dream of acting upon on a false aid. The seat – the rider's weight which must at all times be fully balanced with the horse that bears it – is of fundamental importance because an incorrect seat will cause the rider's weight to distort every movement of the horse.

The last word on this, the true basis of all riding, comes from the Director of the Spanish Riding School, Kurt Albrecht, in his book *Dogmas of the Art of Riding* (1981). It sounds almost too simple: "The rider must seek to distribute his own center of gravity over the horse and maintain it there throughout every movement, whatever the

ing to the old principles. This is obviously possible only at an institution which is free of the compulsion to excel in competitive sports, where riders and tutors can devote themselves entirely to educating the horse and the pupil by proven methods, with the help of time, patience and perseverance.

Today, the School's Riders and First Riding Masters, who have served a long apprenticeship in their profession, are such

guardians of tradition. They started as pupils in the stables wearing a simple gray uniform. They then learned their trade, and a good seat in particular, on the so-called "Professors", the old, tried stallions of the School, because learning to sit comes before learning to ride, and only from a secure, pliant, well-balanced seat comes a feeling for the correct aids. Those fine, invisible signs by which the rider communicates with a horse were in fact learned

gait he may require of the animal..." However, it is no easy thing when the horse canters, gallops, turns, bends, and rises on its hind legs, or even makes a frightened sideways jump. In all circumstances, however, Albrecht says, "... security of the seat is not a matter of keeping a grip with the legs or holding the reins, but entirely of maintaining balance in the saddle."

The balance is disturbed as soon as the rider stretches his head forward, an error often

The horse should be a dancer, a dancer at the hand of man. It should pose light-footed under its rider, as it would before its peers in nature. This requires long, patient schooling, training, gymnastics and exercise. Whoever rides and teaches the horse must learn to wait until the wonder is made manifest, until nature returns in astonishing facility in the unnatural pairing of man and horse, inwardly and outwardly. The wonder is achieved without ultimately distorting nature only through man's self-effacement.

A moment in the Pas de Deux, above, an important number which is generally the third item in a complete program. Two School stallions demonstrate exercises in exact mirror image. It demands the strictest precision in riding. The spectators' attention is, after all, concentrated on two horses only. They must show their best, excelling in all airs and paces. And yet the point of contact must be accurate to the nearest inch. Here, the leading stallion is just reducing his pace, which was started fairly energetically, so as to encounter its partner precisely at the predetermined spot. In doing so, for a second its nose line drops below the vertical, its neck becomes too cramped and it loses forward impetus, errors no doubt corrected in the subsequent paces.

Opposite: The School Quadrille performs the Herringbone maneuver, separating left and right after passing through the Pillars.

seen in dressage trials. It moves the rider's center of gravity forward, so that equilibrium — the correct relationship between the horse's center of gravity and the rider's — is lost. Once the horse has found its center of gravity under a properly balanced rider's weight, it should not be disturbed by unnecessary, voluntary or involuntary changes in weight. Changing position of the weight in itself is an aid, an instruction to the horse to change its carriage, its gait, or the placing of its hoofs. And these "weight aids" can in no way be replaced by commands with the leg or rein.

Summarizing, Albrecht says, "In past centuries the seat had a decisive influence on the quality of riding in whole nations and judgments on this quality always contain a judgment on the seat. In future, too, the quality of riding skills must be measured by the seat and the rider's influence, unless we accept responsibility for deterioration by omitting an essential point."

Only through long study of the inner properties of the horse and through lengthy, patient physical exercise can rider and horse reach a harmony which gives them the appearance of a unity, and which also gives the rider in the saddle a feeling of this unity. At first, these moments are few but highly rewarding. Then this a kind of centaur-like being emerges, man melds with animal in movement and in sense, and a work of art for which mankind has striven since the beginnings of horsemanship in classical antiquity comes into existence. The essence of this does not lie in difficult exercises and movements; it does not prove itself in terms of the Piaffe, Pirouette and airs at the gallop, but rather in the degree to which the harmony sought between man and horse is achieved. This is one of the dogmas of equestrian art. "It is not measured by the degree of difficulty of certain exercises but simply by that of coordination between rider and horse, and its outward expression," says Albrecht.

This is not the place for discussing equestrian doctrine, but a glance at the task that the Spanish Riding School has set itself clearly shows how lengthy the road is which a young rider must cover before he acquires the skill of training a horse. The comments on seating on horseback shows this clearly. How detrimental to riding "short cuts" can be, which may be taken through sloth or ambition and impatience. How often in modern riding we neglect even the basic

equine gymnastics which create the necessary physical condition for the horse to move under the rider's weight. How many trainers are required to produce quick successes in horse trials! The art of riding is quickly lost in a profit-oriented stable, unless those basic principles, nourished day in, day out at the Spanish Riding School, are steadfastly applied. The long school of self-knowledge and patience through which the pupils and apprentice riders have to pass is the only one which leads to lasting success in riding. To demonstrate this, to make it apparent and to teach it, is the Spanish Riding School's first and most important mission.

The young rider's education proceeds according to schedule. He learns from the experienced School stallion, as the young stallion learns from the experienced rider. The pictures on these pages show fully trained School stallions in exhibitions for which the tickets have been sold out weeks, even months, in advance. It is here that the art of riding is displayed in all its glory, the final achievement made real. Displays in historic costume, with ladies riding sidesaddle, remind us of the times of the grand baroque horse ballets and take us back to Maria Theresa's era. The magic of this public entertainment is of course without equal. But even the ceremony of the simple morning's work, the calculated quiet, the incredible discipline, the uniform of the riders — this alone leaves its effect on the spectator. Many of them, of course are not riding enthusiasts or experts, but purely tourists. Yet even for them, unaware of the great efforts, the endless patience which lie behind it, of the dearly won mastery and the important cultural implications, the beauty and historic drama is evident. If this book serves to suggest some of the meaning behind the spectacle it will have performed a large part of its duty, since to reduce the Spanish Riding School to a circus attraction would mean irreparable loss to the world of civilized culture.

The spectator should not therefore be taken in by the fine costumes. This external form

The School Quadrille. Festive entry in common step to the music of Georges Bizet's *L'Arlesienne;* eight riders at the salute.

Right: Traverse to the right, the last of the threefold sideways movements at the start of the trot exercises, in which eight horses shift precisely in unison.

Crossing in between the pillars in the Passage: highest precision, exact spacing and perfect timing of the School stallions, whose trotting length in the Passage must be coordinated.

Far right: Meeting at the Pillars at the center of the arena in two squares before leading into the gallop Pirouettes. This is tight formation riding with the ultimate expressiveness of horses at the gallop.

Below: Further in the Passage after the crossing. None of the élan may be lost, but positioning within the group must be precisely one horse's length.

of homage to a bygone era of great riding masters merely underlines the real task, the inner relationship between a rider on horseback and the art of riding. True enough, only with the work at the School, and with the commitment of the riders, the pupils

and the stable lads is the magnificent frame filled in and given its real content, a content for more important than the gleaming spectacle. The horses' training follows a pattern strictly laid down which, however, must allow for adjustment to the individual strengths and weaknesses of the animal. So there is a simple reason for the apparently solemn stillness that prevails in the large Riding Hall at all times, forcing visitors to drop their voices to a whisper. Throughout the process of training a Lipizzaner stallion, from the colt that is allowed for the first time to run freely in the Hall with its contemporaries, to the Caprioleur that so effortlessly masters the difficult School jump under its rider, everything must be avoided that might excite the horse. Fear and anxiety are learning's worst enemies; an excited horse learns nothing. One loud, angry word can double the sensitive horse's

usually takes four to five years before the School stallion is fully ready and trained, prepared for all tasks. The "Schools over the ground", the School jumps on the hand or under the rider, are a chapter in themselves. Not all stallions are suited to this; they are specially selected for the task after their abilities have been carefully observed. Even so, the young stallions already on public display after the first year. The young horses under the saddle, some of them still in their dark mottled gray coats, demonstrate that they already willingly accept the rider's aids and even under the mental pressure of an audience, applause and music, maintain their trust in the rider and obey his commands. They show what a year's careful training has achieved — regular, natural, well-timed gaits and, already, extended paces and jumps at the trot and gallop, the link between the rider's hand

heart rate. Thus the need for silence. All this, and much more, is instinctive to a rider who has reached the level of skill sufficient to educate and train a horse.

At the Spanish Riding School, such training starts when a stallion is four years old. Depending on its physical and mental abilities, it takes eight to twelve weeks at the longe before it proceeds peacefully in a straight line under its rider. On this basis, the importance of which cannot be too highly stressed as it will substantially determine the horse's subsequent mental attitude, it

and the horse's muzzle remaining light and even at all times. As an important prerequisite, the horses have already gained some of the strength they will need for their later tasks.

The intensive gymnastic training for the Customary or Campaign School begins in the horse's second year. It is the basis of everything that follows. Without it, the Haute Ecole would be inconceivable. However, the School horse must also remain serviceable for normal riding at all times.

Detail from the painting "Morning Work" by Julius von Blaas (1845 – 1922) (see also overleaf). It shows a Courbette, an exercise of the Haute Ecole, as in the photograph on the opposite page. The horse raises itself on its hind legs and jumps forward several times without touching the ground with its front legs.

The aim of the Spanish Riding School is not to produce trick horses capble only of performing specialist exercises, but riding horses with particular skills in addition to all the normal attainments of a fine saddle horse.

In the Campaign School, performance standards are slowly raised. Ease and relaxation are now followed by tensing those groups of muscles whose special strength must be developed for certain exercises. Joints become more supple and pliant as the first "assembly" is introduced. The horse is encouraged to use its powerful hind legs or under its own and the rider's weight, and to carry rather than to push these legs. This leaves the movement of the front legs more free, more elevated, and extendable at any time at the rider's command. Now, the first sideways paces come in, exercises on two hoof beats, the "shoulders inwards", "travers" and "renvers", which lead towards improving the horse's strength, enabling it to move more elegantly and light-footedly. Similarly, comprehension between rider and horse is improved, so that the "aids" — signs given by the rider with his weight, leg and rein — become increasingly easier and less visible. At the same time, the strengthening of obedience leads to a kind of voluntary cooperation by the horse.

In the third year of training this is supplemented with work on the hand. It is intended to improve the horse's bending of its hind legs without the rider's weight, and to strengthen its muscles, sinews and tendons, which the shift of weight towards the hindlegs permits. Work on the hand is the quadruped athlete's "keep fit" training. In it, the individual stallion shows its propensities for the various kinds of School jumps, for the "Schools over the ground" for which preparation is so carefully made. The horse will be ready for dressage trials in the light to medium classes in its second to third year of training.
However, the training program is not so precisely broken down and timetabled that

the same provision can be made for each horse. Every transition from one stage to the next is flexible. Not all horses learn equally fast nor do they all have the same physical attributes. Each pupil under the saddle must be treated as an individual. The training program lays down the goals on an approximate basis but achieving them does not depend on the horse alone but also on the rider. Everything dovetails. The younger, inexperienced rider learns from the experienced School stallion and attempts to transfer the "feel" he has obtained to the animal being trained. With such sensitive creatures as horses, it may happen that the one rider is less successful in this process than another. Consequently, ways must also be found to ensure that the two individuals who work with each other are really compatible. In most cases this has less to do with skills or ability than with personality. The artist's lively sensitivity needs reciprocation and a strained atmosphere may be the result as easily as harmonious cooperation. Only responsive partners will do for the Haute Ecole.

After three years of exercising and training, the final refinement now begins, proceed-

ing to the most difficult lessons of the Haute Ecole. There are, in fact, no rules for keeping to a particular teaching program. The horse's propensities are utilized; the stallions have much to offer which can be accepted and perfected, if only to maintain the animal's pleasure in working. After all, all work is governed by feeling and good sense. In many cases the first lesson of the Haute Ecole will be the Piaffe, the cadenced, elevated trot on the spot or with only slight forwards progress, with the hind leg bent low, as it bears the bulk of the weight in the well-sprung joints and allows the front legs to trot freely and elegantly. Here, the riders must help each other. Particularly when developing the first exercises of Haute Ecole, two riders will almost always be seen attending a stallion, either with work on the hand or with one in the saddle and the other standing next to him. Gradually, the difficult exercises of the dressage are learned, practiced and brought to ultimate perfection in this way, working well into the fifth year of training. Finally the level reached is of the Grand Prix, the Olympic Dressage prize.

This long road is never covered without problems and the idea of "absolute obedience" so often heard in connection with dressage riding is in no way compatible with the principles of classic dressage. A horse which always obeys implicitly without showing its own will from time to time or suddenly "exploding" for one or other reason would be the object of much suspicion. It would seem that in this case violence had been done to the animal's personality during training and that its desire to cooperate has not been strengthened but broken. Such a situation would spell the end of progress.

However, even when everything seems to have been achieved with the eager, lively cooperation of the horse — Piaffe, Passage, flying change of gallop, the Pirouette, the entire program of the "Schools above the ground" — the stallion's training is not yet at an end.

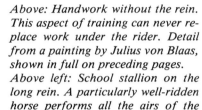

The extreme of obedience, docility, discipline and strength of nerve requires the most difficult exercises to be performed in the group, with other horses together at the precisely determined spot — namely in the Grand School Quadrille. Such playful ease should have been gained in mastering all the exercises individually that the spectator has

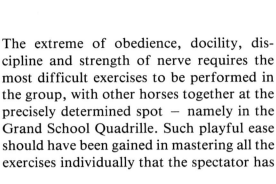

Above: Handwork without the rein. This aspect of training can never replace work under the rider. Detail from a painting by Julius von Blaas, shown in full on preceding pages.
Above left: School stallion on the long rein. A particularly well-ridden horse performs all the airs of the Haute Ecole solely with the aid of the light rein and crop.
Left: Morning work, still performed today as it was as painted by von Blaas a century ago. The Piaffe between the pillars is a training exercise designed to prepare the horse for executing the movement under the rider.

the impression only of smooth, effortless action. Unless this impression is achieved, there is no "art" in the riding. This, too, is the way the appreciative layman can assess the quality of an equestrian display. Its perfection is the consummation of the rider-trainer as artist, having created something with a living being — if only for the moment — which may claim to be a work of art.

In the Quadrille, where the sensitive individual must bend to an exacting choreography, demands reach their peak. The School Quadrille is therefore the last test, the seal of mastery for horse and rider. It would be no exaggeration to say that anyone who has trained a horse for the School Quadrille, bringing it to the level of excellence where it can show off its beauty and splendor within the exact order of the group, without a loss of personality or a dimunition of its nature, has achieved more than is required of an Olympic dressage rider.

We must remember that School riding reached its peak under the great masters of the Royal Courts of Europe at a time when

Above and left: The Piaffe correctly performed under the rider. Here the nobility of the educated horse achieves its highest expression.

cavalry could still decide a battle and the training of horses as a fighting arm was very important. It is here the "Schools over the ground", the School jumps, originate. They were used in battle. Levade, Pesade, Courbette and Capriole were exercises by means of which the horse was made into a weapon or protection for the rider. Behind a horse rearing in the Levade, the rider

could shelter from a enemy attack. Few infantrymen could stand their ground before a horse jumping forwards on its hindlegs in the Courbette. And the rider could use the Capriole, with the horse kicking high in the air, to disengage himself from attacking foot soldiers.

While the origins of the "School over the ground" may be found in military riding, a

The expression of visibly restrained force,
where the restraint in no way detracts from the nobility,
is the goal of true equestrian art.
The instrument that creates this art, as the cutting does to the diamond,
is the horse.

Above: Capriole beneath the rider: an explosive release of power that remains severely controlled. This jump makes the highest demands both on the horse's strength and agility and on the rider's seat.

Right: The jump at the pillars, a preliminary to the Capriole beneath the rider. Detail from a painting by Julius von Blaas, 1890.

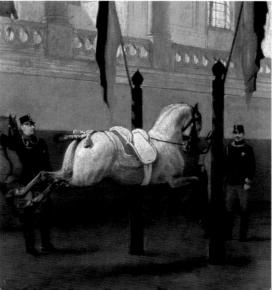

correctly executed Levade would rarely be seen in the heat of battle. More commonplace were the Caprioles, which many horses probably performed of their own accord when shouting, weapon-wielding opponents came too close for comfort. The School jumps were then cultivated in the riding ring by the masters of the Haute Ecole.

193

School jumps are something quite different from steeplechase jumping with a horse galloping forwards over obstacles. When jumping during the hunt the horse uses the speed granted it by nature; it is in line with its essence as an animal built for fleeing an enemy. The School jumps, the beginnings of which may already be observed among horses at pasture, result from the stallion's

Above: The Renaissance Court in the Imperial Stables. They first became a home for the Imperial horses in 1565 and the three-tiered arcades comprise one of Vienna's oldest and finest inner courtyards. The stable lads live above the stables, close to their charges. But art has also found a home in this building; the New Gallery of the Museum of Art occupies the second floor. The Lipizzaners of the Spanish Riding School live on the ground floor next to the Court Pharmacy. The passage across the court is their daily path to work — their road to school.

typical response to disputes within the herd. They are a fighting attitude.

Three kinds of School jumps are displayed today in exhibitions at the Spanish Riding School — the Levade or Pesade, the Courbette and the Capriole, each in two aspects, at the hand and under the rider. The training of stallions particularly suited for these executed also begins on the hand. For this, the horses require special intelligence and enormous strength, which must be developed initially by work on the hand. After all, the entire weight of horse and rider must be borne on the hind leg, balanced, and thrust up into the air on the spot.

All School jumps are developed from the Piaffe. As the hind leg is lowered deeply on bended joints beneath the weight, so much weight is eventually taken off the front leg that it can be raised. And so we have the Levade, in which the horse can remain on its hind legs for a brief time, depending on its strength and agility. If the hind legs are not so deeply angled, but stand somewhat more stiffly, the exercise is called the Pesade. This lesson has nothing to do with the rearing of the horse objecting to its rider or taking fright. It is, rather, the logical conclusion of a long education which through schooling, training and gymnastics allows the horse to take ever more weight on its powerful hind legs until everything can be borne, balanced and even projected into the jump.

When this is done, and the stallion tends to jump down from a Pesade at the hand, and the jump is not taken diagonally forwards, but with a brief upwards raising of the feet, we have dicovered a gift for the Courbette. This is a rare event. Often, years go by without talent for the Courbette appearing. This jump requires extraordinary strenghth and the finest feeling for balance. The stallion raises itself in the Pesade and then will jump once, twice, three times, even up to ten times forward on the hind legs without touching the ground with its forelegs.

The Capriole, perhaps the most spectacular of the School jumps, may in fact be ob-

to the freedom of the Piber Stud, where they are used as service-stallions. Each year, towards the end of October, eight to ten playful, excited young stallions arrive to begin their training, the first step of which is to accustom themselves to boarding in the big city after a youth spent at grass.

served among young horses playing in a field. It name comes from the Latin *Capra,* goat, because a playful kid will also often jump into the air with all four feet lifted, kicking its legs. This is precisely the movement required for the Capriole, jump, but on command, on the rein, at the rider's signal, at his request and on a particular point. This jump, too, is developed from the Piaffe, which often translates into several successive Levades shortly before the take-off. Here, the front legs are briefly elevated, are again lowered, with the hind legs following at the jump. The old masters also knew this exercise under the name of "Mezair". From this position the stallion takes a mighty jump into the air and "stretches," kicking out with both hind legs while suspended horizontally in the air. He then again lands in the same spot from which he took off.

A firm seat and skillful adaptation to the horse's movements are of course an important requisite for the rider if he is not to be thrown from the saddle. Concentration and a feeling for the right moment are also necessary before the aids for the take-off can be given. At the Spanish Riding School the "Schools over the ground" are generally ridden without the stirrup. Stallions appear for their exhibition with a black bridle and dark-green saddle-cloth, the red saddle-cloth accompanying the gold-encrusted gala bridle being reserved for festive displays.

A complete exhibition at the Spanish Riding School nowadays includes, in seven sections, the whole of the training program and a display of everything that can be achieved in the Haute Ecole with a Lipizzaner School stallion.

The School Quadrille
is the culmination of years of training.
Nothing can be seen here of the long,
arduous road that led to it.
But let the spectator never forget!

It begins with the young stallions who, bridled on the snaffle and under the English saddle, display the basic training of every young riding horse. Running straight, rhythmically and in the simple sequence of basic gaits, they demonstrate how they have learned to accept the rider's aids, illustrating to any perceptive person in the audience how young horses should be taught obedience and carriage before starting specialized training.

The second number "All Airs and Paces of the Haute Ecole" is presented, as a contrast

to the juniors, by fully trained School stallions in a display of dressage by the riders in a loose form. It covers the lessons of Olympic dressage with Piaffes, Passages, à-tempo flying changes of gallop and Pirouettes. Each rider will have chosen a display program suitable to his particular stallion.

Each of these lessons is repeated in the third numer, "the Pas de Deux," but now with the highest precision and in strict form. The choreography aims at reflecting in movement the grace and elegance of the music — Mozart's Symphony in G Minor.

Then, "Work at the Hand-rein" harks back to the training program but also shows the perfection achieved. It is consists of the short trot at the hand-rein, in preparation for the Piaffe, and finally in a graceful, rhythmic Piaffe at the pillars under the rider. This is followed by School jumps at the hand — Levades, Courbettes and Caprioles.

Then a single stallion appears on the track on the long rein, with a red bridoon rein and red saddle cloth embroidered with the double eagle in gold. The rider paces behind him on foot. This star among the Li-

pizzaners then executes the entire dressage program, doing so in such a way that his guide can follow him on foot without having to run. It is a demonstration of the finest physical and mental coordination between man and horse.

As the next to last item on the program, the Lipizzaner stallions enter the arena on the black rein and with dark green saddle

cloths, the riders all seated on their horses without stirrups. The strongest, most intelligent and most gifted in jumping, the elite of the School horses, display the "Schools over the Ground."

The crowning finale is the School Quadrille, the "Ballet of the White Stallions." Eight horses are united in the most difficult of exercises, executed with consummate ease and unsurpassed pomp within the strict figures of the dance. The theory of dressage is quite lost here, in the aesthetic enjoyment of a work of art.

The dialogue between man and horse begins here in the stall and is continued in the arena. It never ends. The two key places in the Lipizzaner's life, the Stables and the Winter Riding School, become indivisibly one. The merger with the humans who handle them, which forms a basis for learning as a School horse, and the horse's trust in teacher and keeper, arise from the conviction held by the animal that the most careful attention is paid to it at all times.

Horses cannot just be put away and forgotten after work, switched off like machines. Here too, as with training for dressage, the Spanish Riding School practice is an example to be emulated.

The riding horse, of course, spends most of its life in the stable. Here, to the company of its contemporaries, which gives it a certain sense of security, is added the continuous company of man. The hours in the stable are not spent in idle boredom. There is constant diversion in the repetitive rhythm of such daily chores as cleaning, feeding, mucking-out, a nudge with neighbors and exchange of endearments with the

man it knows – all these serve to keep the horse's spirit alert and awake.

There is thus good reason why future riders should serve as stable lads during their time as pupils. Here, meeting the horses in private, they develop an understanding and feeling for the animals. The rider must know more about his partner than its behavior under the saddle. The art of riding which builds depends on a keen study of the horse's character and mental propensities. Without friendship, without mutual regard, the partnership which is the goal of all riding could not be achieved. The first step towards such a partnership is taken in the stable. At this point, the horse has already progressed far from its home in the open plains. And although the Lipizzaner, in particular, bears in itself the inheritance of trust in man through many generations, the willingness of each individual stallion to cooperate can never be assumed. It must be won, by learning to know the horse's essence, and by instilling in the creature not only the necessary respect for man but also the self-assurance necessary for any achievement. It is a form of dialogue which allows the horse to maintain its nobility and personality despite man's demands on it. It is the stable were this dialogue begins.

While the exhibition and its crowning glory, the School Quadrille, may be a magnificent display, sold out months in advance and an attraction for both tourists and guests of State, it should never be regarded simply as a show purchased for the price of a ticket. It is the end of the road to perfection. No short-cuts are allowed, nor should they be. If it were ever decided that the Lipizzaners might as well be trained to do a few hops at a saving of time and energy, to be displayed to packed galleries, an inestimable cultural heirloom would be lost. The art of riding itself would be jeopardized.

It is in fact the perfected art of riding which is demonstrated here and it is therefore worthwhile to remember a few lines which the School's Head, Kurt Albrecht, wrote in his *Dogmas of the Art of Riding:*

The art of riding is never measured by the difficulty of certain exercises but simply by the degree of coordination between rider and horse and its visible expression. In a word, the same beauty with which every foal strikes the eye of the observer at pasture should eventually also distinguish an equestrian performance, at whatever level.

The doctrines of the classic art of riding now also appear in the rule books of the International Equestrian Association, the highest authority for riding and the sport, for the World Championships and for the Olympic Games. How these rules ought to be observed is nowhere more effectively demonstrated than at the Spanish Riding School. Sporting success will always be tied to these classic doctrines. And this is the real success of the Spanish Riding School — the enchantment of the onlooker, whether expert or not, and the example of quality set for the world by the white horses and their riders in this baroque hall in Vienna.

THE SPANISH RIDING SCHOOL TODAY — AND THE CHALLENGE FOR TOMORROW

An institution whose roots stretch so far into the past is easily suspected of not sufficiently facing up to the demands of the present. Such thinking is due not least to a long-established stereotype, to expectations, while well-intentioned, that are perhaps misplaced — people forget that the festive displays of the Spanish Riding School are only the end-product of hard work.

In the four hundred years of the school's existence, one of the chief reasons for its survival has been the unswerving pursuit of the task for which it was originally created, namely to maintain the art of riding at the acme of perfection without departing either in spirit or in practice from the habits of ordinary riding. These principles have long continued to govern the period of training. The highest level had always to be preceded by those which enabled the horse to meet the increasing demands placed upon it without excessively straining its physical and mental capabilities. (This can be summarized in the principle that nature is conceivable without art but not art without nature!) Persistent adherence to principles of this kind has on one hand prevented deterioration to the level of the Roman games and, on the other, promoted the objective succinctly stated in the "Directives": "even a ready-trained school horse at a stage where through its agility and endurance it excels in brief and exalted school movements must also be capable of the faster paces and perform at any time as a fully serviceable campaign horse."

To meet this requirement unflinchingly through such a lengthy period of time must have been all the more difficult since apart from these Directives written in 1898, there were no working instructions at all.

In fact, each generation of riders received their knowledge and expertise from the previous generation and in turn passed them on to the next. How easily persons with above-average gifts can force Art into the mainstream of calamitous charlatanism, or how the desire to equal or better the "champion" ends by transforming valuable

disciplines into their opposites can be seen today from the many institutions which, originally starting with the same objectives, have long since ceased to exist.

However high the requirements of horse and rider in the Spanish Riding School, what was achieved had to serve practical, everyday riding and military riding in particular, the quality of which was often decisive when the horse played a major part in determining the human struggle for existence.

The institution which was to concern itself with the pursuit of the high art of riding was therefore in no way mere caprice on the part of a vain or ambitious monarch but had a very real background. From it, lead of military equestrian formations derived their knowledge and skills; and from it too came the impetus which riding in general needs like a medicine.

It has therefore always been a principle of the Spanish Riding School to strip the high school of the art of riding of all mystique and instead to pursue aesthetics and harmony as the motivation for its work.

The Lipizzaners had a very great share in this when, after a lengthy interval during which horsemen were concerned exclusively with functional riding serving military and everyday purposes, the forms and disciplines of an art of riding were suddenly re-discovered. These were in line with the analogous principles already adopted in classical times, and centers for pursuing the art were set up in many of the courts of Europe. In those times a horse had to be found which had the character and physical properties and the high intelligence which would be equal to the task. This proved to be the Spanish horse, with its Arab and Berber blood. With these qualities, the horse was soon to form its own breed, destined to meet the equine requirements of the Court in Vienna and which was to become one of the most important of domesticated breeds under the name of its breeding place.

From its very beginnings, the Spanish Riding School was called upon to test the suit-

ability of the breeding product for the high art of riding. Thanks to uninterrupted selection of the breed with the school's tasks in mind, the Lipizzaner has over the centuries retained its valuable properties and talents. However, just as in the past, it needed great equestrian skill to bring them into full flower. While many a rider may not succeed in doing the same, this is hardly the horse's fault; it merely testifies to the strong traits of the equine personality of the Lipizzaner.

The fascination which the image of equine strength restrained by the rider's ability exercises on the individual was discovered very early. It inspired a multitude of artists; indeed, the animal's nobility has never failed to impress the simplest human who has come into contact with this wonderful creature.

When the School began, after the First World War, to make this art of riding accessible to a wider public by holding exhibitions, the brilliant horseback ballets which had been the most highly regarded of festivities through the centuries were recreated in new shape.

These displays have since become the institution's best advertisement; each year they attract thousands of people. They have not only ushered in a new, completely changed phase of existence for the school, but have contributed significantly towards overcoming the dire crises at the end of the Second World War and the post-war period.

Attempts have been made to analyse the reasons for the fascination which this institution exercises on people at all levels. In doing so, factors have emerged which are no doubt valid, such as, for example, the need of many people to escape, if only for a moment, from an over-technical and mechanical world; or the need to mitigate the feverishness of everyday life by a moment spent in an atmosphere of harmonious relaxation. Perhaps there are many other good reasons but there are none which can truly explain the phenomenon. The inescapable conclusion is that deep down in many people there is a feeling to which small endearing weaknesses make a very special appeal. They enjoy perfection all the more if it is flawed. Thus, they willingly turn their backs on records and superlatives. The Lipizzaner as a creature possesses so much nobility and expresses such proud strength that, without its rider, no one is left unimpressed. However, this is lost as soon as the rider does not himself perform to equal measure or brings undue pressure to bear and, generally through a false assessment or through circumstances, makes requirements of the horse which it is no longer able to fulfil. The spectator often thinks more highly of an act of tolerance than of a command which is correctly carried out to the limits of perfection if the compulsion required to achieve the performance is evident.

The Spanish Riding School has therefore regarded as a chief criterion of its work the achievement of its training goals by requiring the greatest consistency and performance from both parties without degrading a horse to the level of a machine, as that would mean that all its movements its temperament and every other aspect of its behavior were subject to the rule of force.

Of the many truths that can be derived from the rules of the classic art of riding, one is that the value of a horse's achievement cannot be measured entirely, or even predominantly, by its physical performance. The most important criterion is the harmonious, clearly demonstrable cooperation of both horse and rider. Even the best performance will not be recognized if the charisma of a work of art is missing.

It has never been in character for the School to seek to impose its views on training. However, it has never failed anyone who has sought its advice. Its strength has always lain in the silent demonstration of the precious legacy to which many generations of riders have contributed. While for centuries it was predominantly the "pupils" who passed on the instruction they received here (providing of how carefully and strictly the inheritance is continuously

transformed into new achievements by riders and horses), this task is performed today by the displays and foreign tours.

Here the individual influenced by no expert prejudice can lend his approval solely on the basis of the feelings to which these moments of the art of riding give rise. It is from this devotion that the art thrives, devotion which should not be thrust into a corner with the shrugging of shoulders and mocking smile of the expert. The art of riding is far too fine to be turned into a straitjacket without leaving room to breathe. True, the principles which have traditionally applied to the Haute Ecole have been incorporated almost in their entirety into present-day rules, but people often forget to breathe into such rules the necessary pulsating life they need if they are to cast their spell on mankind.

Although the demands on the horse and rider at the highest level of training for dressage and the Haute Ecole are the same to the letter, the objectives and the approach adopted are different. Both require similar work on the basic levels. However, the paths begin to diverge when the purely functional rises into the region of art and creativity. For today's dressage rider, the book of rules is a straitjacket into which he and his horse have to crawl, even if the size is wrong. Things were different for the former Haute Ecole rider. For him, the achievement of top performance for both horse and rider was the desired goal. Even if the skills were not sufficient to reach the highest level, the self-assurance gained was sufficient reward. People knew that the greater reward was not that given by man but by the horse.

The concept of the Haute Ecole has always included the rider — and still does today — and demanded absolute equality. Never was the horse required to make good the rider's mistake; the opposite has always applied.

All the future activities of the Spanish Riding School will have to be subordinated to the requirement that the only rider to be highly regarded by the spectator must be one who succeeds in controlling the strength and the noble pride of the horse through the human spirit, creating a symbiosis which includes peak performance and artistic expression in equal measure.

The Spanish Riding School reserves the greatest splendor at its command for the School Quadrille, performed with the noble economy of movement that the horse elevates to true beauty. There is no change in the Riders' uniforms; they wear the same clothing as for the morning's work — high-necked brown top-coat with two rows of gold buttons, white buckskin riding breeches, black knee boots, cocked hat, and leather riding gloves, carrying a simple birch crop. The stallions for their part wear gold trimmings, bits garnished with polished brass, and white buck-skin saddles with gold bow-rolls and cantle-rolls. Yet nothing is pompous or gaudy. Nothing of it conceals the grace of the horse, the sheen of its hide, the play of its muscles. Everything is done in the best of equestrian taste. There is no conflict in emphasis, any more than in the riding itself. Yet the overall effect is festive and solemn. What is celebrated is a goal achieved since, logically, the School Quadrille is the highest point, the crown to all the work and patience. Promotion to the School Quadrille at the Spanish Riding School is the premier mark of achievement for rider, trainer and stallion.

GENERAL KURT ALBRECHT

Epilogue

When the young horse first approaches man, carefully, with ears pointed and eyes wide, when it stretches its neck and, sniffing lightly, seeks to grasp the scent of the human, he takes the first step towards the confidence that mankind must ever preserve. On what happens here, the art of riding is built – trust in man, so long as the horse shall live.

Let us end by leaning once more on the paddock fence at Piber, watching the dark-hued Lipizzaner foals and their dams so quietly that they forget humans are present. The horses show their character better here in the pastures. Their real nature emerges, that of animals free to roam wide open spaces. Through the two thousand years of its development, the aim of the art of riding has been to give back to the horse this same freedom, in spite of the weight of its rider. Every rider must hold in his mind the sight of the young horses like these at pasture, because what nature has created remains the horseman's guiding light and supreme commandment. Should the freedom of horses be offered up to the vanity of man, the light would go from a living work of art.

These foals will later enter a life in the service of man, a life which is foreign to their nature. But their masters, teachers and educators will never forget this image of their free unbridled beauty. From the first day the trainer knows that the horse's nature must be developed and ennobled but never distorted, suborned or broken. This is at the very heart of the teaching that the Spanish Riding School keeps safe and spreads through the world of horsemanship.

One of the great Masters of the Haute Ecole, Antoine de Pluvinel de la Baume, whose principles stand to this day, may well have had young horses at grass in mind when early in the fifteenth century he wrote in his book *L'Instruction du Roy:*

"Let us take great care lest we sadden the young horse and stifle its nature, as this is as the fragrance of fruit which once it departs will never return."